IMAGES
of America

FORT SMITH
AND SEBASTIAN COUNTY

IMAGES
of America

FORT SMITH
AND SEBASTIAN COUNTY

Lola Shropshire

ARCADIA
PUBLISHING

ISBN 978-0-7385-9704-1

Published by Arcadia Publishing
Charleston, South Carolina

Printed in the United States of America

Library of Congress Catalog Card Number: 98-88468

For all general information contact Arcadia Publishing at:
Telephone 843-853-2070
Fax 843-853-0044
E-mail sales@arcadiapublishing.com
For customer service and orders:
Toll-Free 1-888-313-2665

Visit us on the Internet at www.arcadiapublishing.com

To my mother, Edith Page Brewer Wright, and my granddaughter, Katelyn Elizabeth Shropshire

Contents

ACKNOWLEDGMENTS

For the cooperation of Fort Smith Historians, and others interested in making the photos in this book available to the public, a resounding thank you. With your help I've studied many interesting volumes of photos throughout the city. What you see in this book is the result of that search. I could never have completed the project in the time allotted without the total and complete generosity of Julie Galonska of the Fort Smith National Historic Site, and Patti Zabel and Sheila Brushes of the Fort Smith Public Library. Others at those facilities were wonderfully cooperative as well. Also very helpful were Cissy Walker of the Fort Smith Chamber of Commerce, Jeff Barrows of the Fort Smith Police Department, and Jerry and Wincie Hendricks, Ruby Yeakley, Wayne Bledsoe, and Lillian Golden Hissom of Fort Smith, and Cinda Bell of Greenwood—all of whom were very generous with their private collections.

There are other photos, some very interesting, that I did not have time to research. In all instances I used only photos that were readily available to me. The photographers of this city began many decades ago to record, for succeeding generations, the dramatic events which transpired here. They were professional photographers in studios, traveling photographers who developed their glass plates in wagons, and family non-professionals whose passion and artistic expression are unmistakable. There would be no visual record for descendants to gaze upon without their initiative. For their contributions I am grateful. I knew, when I began this pictorial book project with Arcadia Publishing, that I was in for a very challenging period in my life. I was not mistaken. It is a time I will never forget, due to lessons I've learned and the friends I've made.

Thanks to the following people: Lynn Riebow, Bedford Photo, Fred C. Kirkpatrick, Tena Coker, Mark Coker, Julie Lind Northrip, Polly Wood Crews, Sherry Toliver, Chester Cowen, Dusty Helbling, and others that I have probably forgotten. And most of all thanks to my family, who have endured my absence, of both mind and body, these last months.

INTRODUCTION

La Belle Pointe is a lovely French phrase given the beautiful sandstone bluffs, soaring 55 feet above the shoreline, at the confluence of the Poteau and Arkansas Rivers. A post, later to be known as Fort Smith, was established on that promontory in 1817. Its purpose was to protect white settlers and maintain peace among warring Osage and Cherokee Nations. Pioneers and trappers began to seriously explore and settle the area once the Louisiana Purchase was completed in 1803. Belle Point was known as a rendezvous point for trappers and traders who journeyed up the Arkansas to exchange jackknives, glass beads, and other trinkets for furs with the Indians. In 1822, Captain John Rogers, a veteran of the War of 1812, became the post sutler, in partnership with Colonel John Nicks, for the first Fort Smith. He vigorously promoted business in the little Belle Point village. The town today, through the efforts of a dynamic chamber of commerce, has the same enthusiasm for enterprise that it enjoyed more than 180 years ago.

The close of the Civil War spawned an era of terror and savagery in Indian Territory never before equaled in the annals of criminal history. Robbery, rape, and murder were the rule rather than the exception. Outlaws used Indian Territory as a safe haven after robbing banks, stagecoaches, and businesses in neighboring regions. The railroads, after 1870, brought additional problems. Overnight railheads were the source of brawling construction crews, tinhorn-gamblers, thieves, prostitutes, whisky-sellers, and others outside the law.

One might draw parallels between the outlawry and sin that defined the early-day settlement of Fort Smith and an era of remarkable church construction. The general population was disturbed by the characterizations given Judge Parker's Court—on the floor of Congress Parker's Court was referred to as a "slaughter-house." The citizenry realized that Parker's was a difficult and necessary job. They were at once supportive and revolted. The spiritual aspects of their lives may have given them the strength necessary to endure this difficult era. The more wretched and depraved the situation became down on the waterfront, and in the courtroom, the more spiritual and more aesthetically pleasing the churches became. The greater the sins, the higher the church-spires extended heavenward. The "daughters of joy," by the standards of Fort Smith's "decent society," spent their existence engaged in amoral activities. At the same time another group of young women of similar age called the "Sisters of Mercy" spent their hours instructing children, ministering to the sick, and generally helping others "live better lives." The last brothel in existence from those days is the old Commercial Hotel, or as it's known today, Miss Laura's Social Club and Visitor Information Center. It was renamed for

Laura Ziegler, the brothel's most colorful owner. Somehow Fort Smith has managed to strike an edgy, uneasy balance between the two histories. Volunteers, many of them church members, guide tourists through the old brothel, telling them the way things used to be down on "the row."

Belle Starr and her bunch at Younger's Bend—the Buck and Bill Cook Gangs, Cherokee Bill, and others of their ilk—"went on the scout" in Indian Territory. There was no enforcement of white law to protect the innocent Native American from the criminal, and the tribal courts could not punish white lawbreakers. The tribal law enforcement was ill-equipped to stem the tide of crime and violence. At the conclusion of the Civil War, Fort Smith's federal judge was William Story, whose office was involved in coercion, bribery, and extortion. Some Civil War reconstructionists believed that the Native American, as punishment for aligning with the Confederacy, deserved his fate. Native Americans who sided with the Federals were treated in a similar fashion. All Native American treaties entered into prior to the Civil War came under scrutiny. Into this dilemma walked a "knight in shining armor" and "Champion of Indian Rights" in Judge Isaac Charles Parker. He was a man of integrity and courage who was determined, with his army of marshals and deputies, to clean up Indian Territory. He was young for a federal judge (only 37 years old), but what he lacked in years he made up for in resolve. Fort Smith grew and flourished after the era of Judge Parker.

In continuing the tradition John Rogers established in early Fort Smith, its citizens have always welcomed constructive, new business into the community. It began with the river trade, and later the discovery of rich deposits of gas to fuel the large factory furnaces. They used the ancient forests to supply furniture manufacturers with needed hard and soft woods, and eventually built beautiful homes, shopping malls, grocery stores, and restaurants. They constructed beautiful churches and shared their bounty with institutions that assisted the needy, and then volunteered their time to run these organizations. They founded playgrounds for children with disabilities and established nature parks for everyone. They promoted the city and her events with parades, rodeos, the circus, and music in all forms. They acquired outstanding health care, the best lodging for visitors to the city, and allowed themselves to benefit financially from the great presence of the military at Fort Chaffee. The city of Fort Smith and her citizens have enjoyed a profitable and exciting existence.

The village of Belle Point, which grew into a beautiful city, has had its share of tragedy and controversy. From the untamed period, which took the form of tribe versus tribe and white man versus Indian, the tragedy of the Civil War, the era of crime and violence in Indian Territory which was addressed by the Federal Court in Fort Smith, to tornadoes, fires, floods, and the unique problem of housing immigrants at the military base until relocation could take place. The city has had its share of woes. The citizens have, however, overcome these misfortunes with a spirit of good humor and a dogged, optimistic view that things can and will improve. The celebration of that spirit is never more aptly summarized than in the phrase which Mayor Ray Baker often repeats, "life's worth living in Fort Smith."

One

LOOKING AT HISTORY

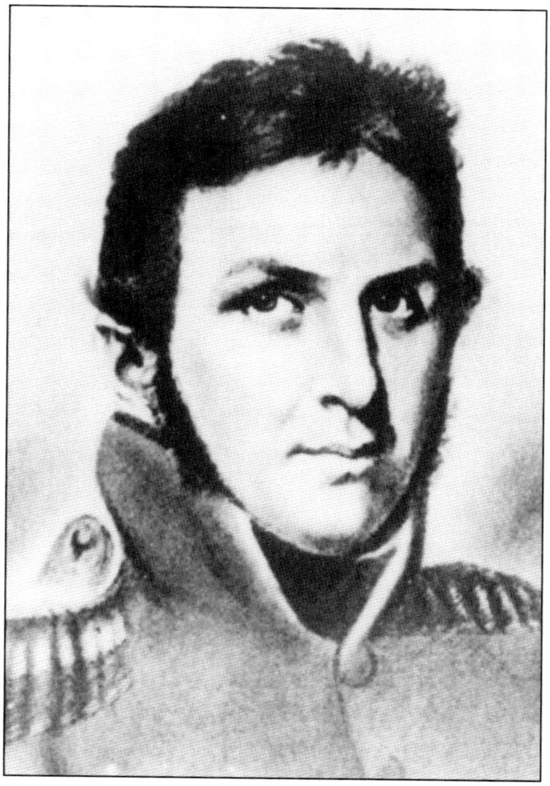

On September 15, 1817, General Thomas A. Smith, shown here in the early 1800s, announced that a new fort was to be built on the Arkansas River to halt the fighting between the Osage and Cherokee Indians. Army Engineer Major Stephen A. Long selected the wooded, sandstone bluffs, called La Belle Pointe by the French, as the ideal site for the post. Major William A. Bradford, veteran of the War of 1812, had been ordered to construct the fort. By December 1818, the camp, named in honor of General Smith, became Fort Smith. Bradford's temporary construction, combined with that of Major Long's, included officers' quarters, barracks, a hospital, a sutler's store, a kitchen, and various shops and sheds. (Hamilton, Fort Smith National Historic Site.)

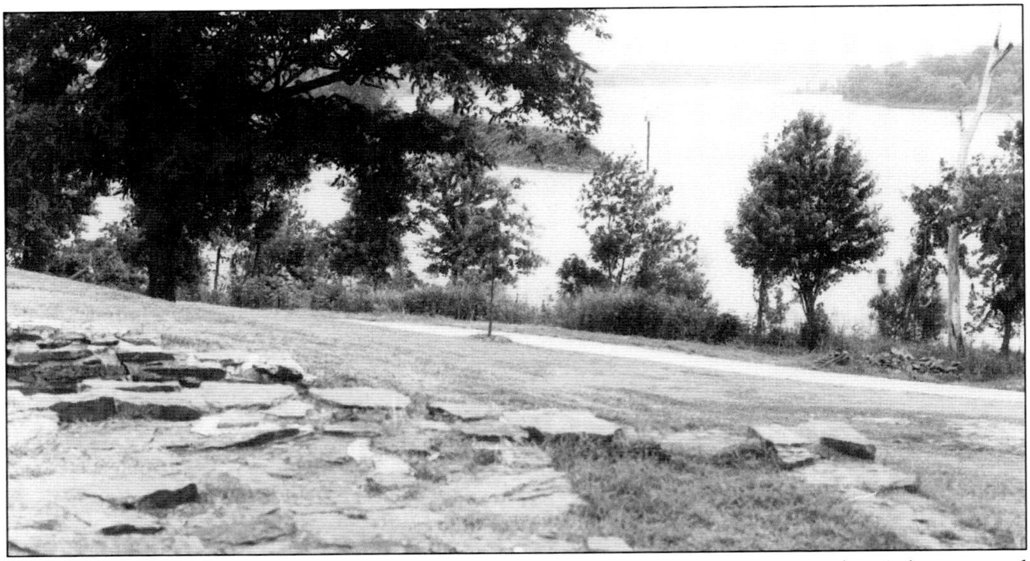

Base stones for the first fort, built in 1817, are seen in this 1998 image. The Arkansas and Poteau Rivers are visible in the background. Except for the heavily timbered, sandstone bluff, this scene remains much as when soldiers first viewed it. The fort consisted of a stockade of heavy square timbers driven closely together into the ground. The buildings were arranged to form a hollow square, and one blockhouse faced the river. (Author.)

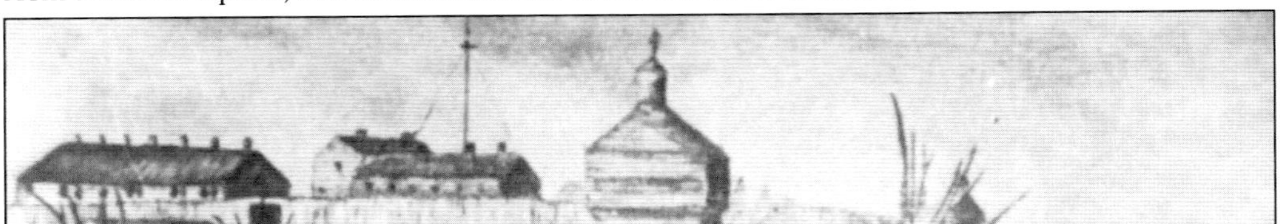

In 1898, R.H. Mohler sketched this image, which is not completely accurate, of the first Fort Smith, its settlers, and the Indians. It is similar to what Major William A. Bradford encountered while in performance of his duties. His progress in building the fort was slower than expected. He and his men were forced to raise most of their food, in addition to keeping the peace among the various Native American tribes and settlers. (Fort Smith Public Library.)

Lieutenant Colonel Matthew Arbuckle, shown in this sketch, arrived at Fort Smith on February 26, 1822, to relieve Major Bradford's command. The following August 9, at Belle Point, the Osage and Cherokee chiefs signed the Treaty of Fort Smith. This treaty attempted to restore peace between the two nations. On April 2, 1824, Colonel Arbuckle received orders to abandon Fort Smith and establish Fort Gibson at the junction of the Verdigris and the Arkansas Rivers. (Fort Smith National Historic Site.)

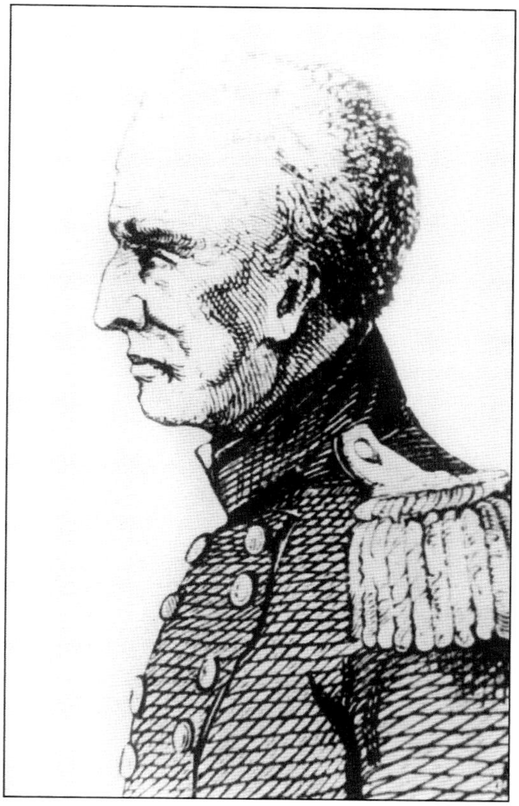

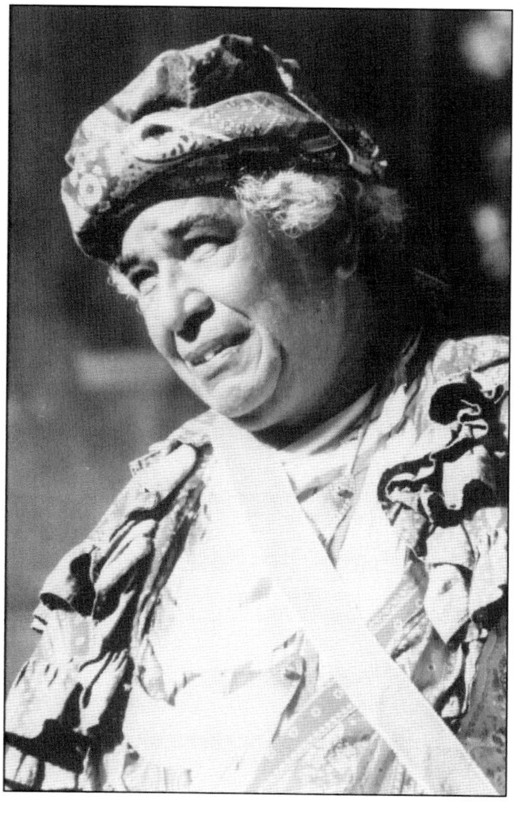

Many contemporary Native Americans of the "Five Civilized Tribes" continue to wear the traditional headdress and colorful garments worn during the settling of the frontier. This Creek Indians likeness was captured at the Fort Smith Art Center's Annual Native American Festival in 1997. The Creek, Cherokee, and other eastern tribes were removed to this area, claimed by the Osage, soon after 1800. Treaty councils of 1808–1809 provided lands on which the Native American could settle. The Cherokee's problems with the Osage and white man began immediately upon arrival. It was decades before the Cherokees would know peace in this new homeland. Native peoples today, through federally funded school programs and festivals such as the one at the Art Center, continue to preserve the native culture through fine arts exhibitions and demonstrations of native crafts. (Gus Thompson, Fort Smith Art Center Collection.)

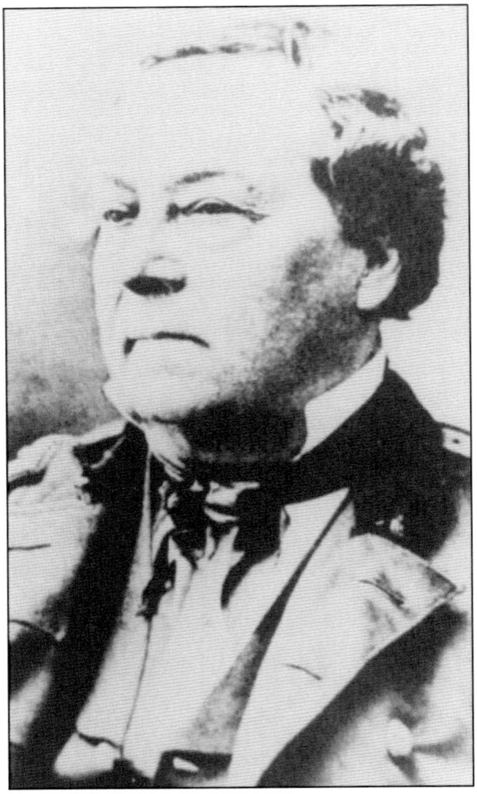

General Benjamin L.E. Bonneville, shown here, was born in France in 1795. He graduated from West Point in 1817, took leave from the United States Army in 1831, and distinguished himself in exploring the great trails of the west. Washington Irving published the story of Bonneville's journeys in a book entitled *Adventures of Captain Bonneville, USA*. Bonneville's diaries, maps, and information, gleaned from his travels, have been a priceless historic legacy for generations. (Fort Smith Public Library.)

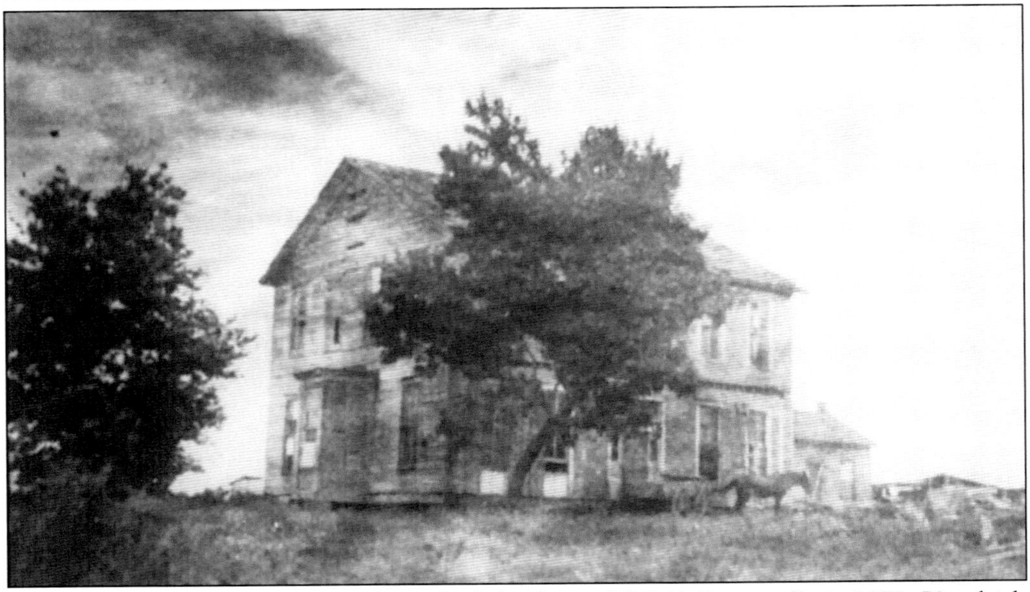

This is a ghostly image of the residence built by General B.L.E. Bonneville in 1871–72, which was located between the present North "O" Street and Kelley Highway. Bonneville and his 24-year-old bride, Sue Neis Bonneville, lived here. They had beautifully landscaped grounds, with exotic flowers, large vegetable gardens, wheat fields, and a large vineyard. Bonneville died June 12, 1878, leaving Mrs. Bonneville an extensive estate. Left unoccupied for some time, the house deteriorated and was demolished in the 1950s. (Fort Smith National Historic Site.)

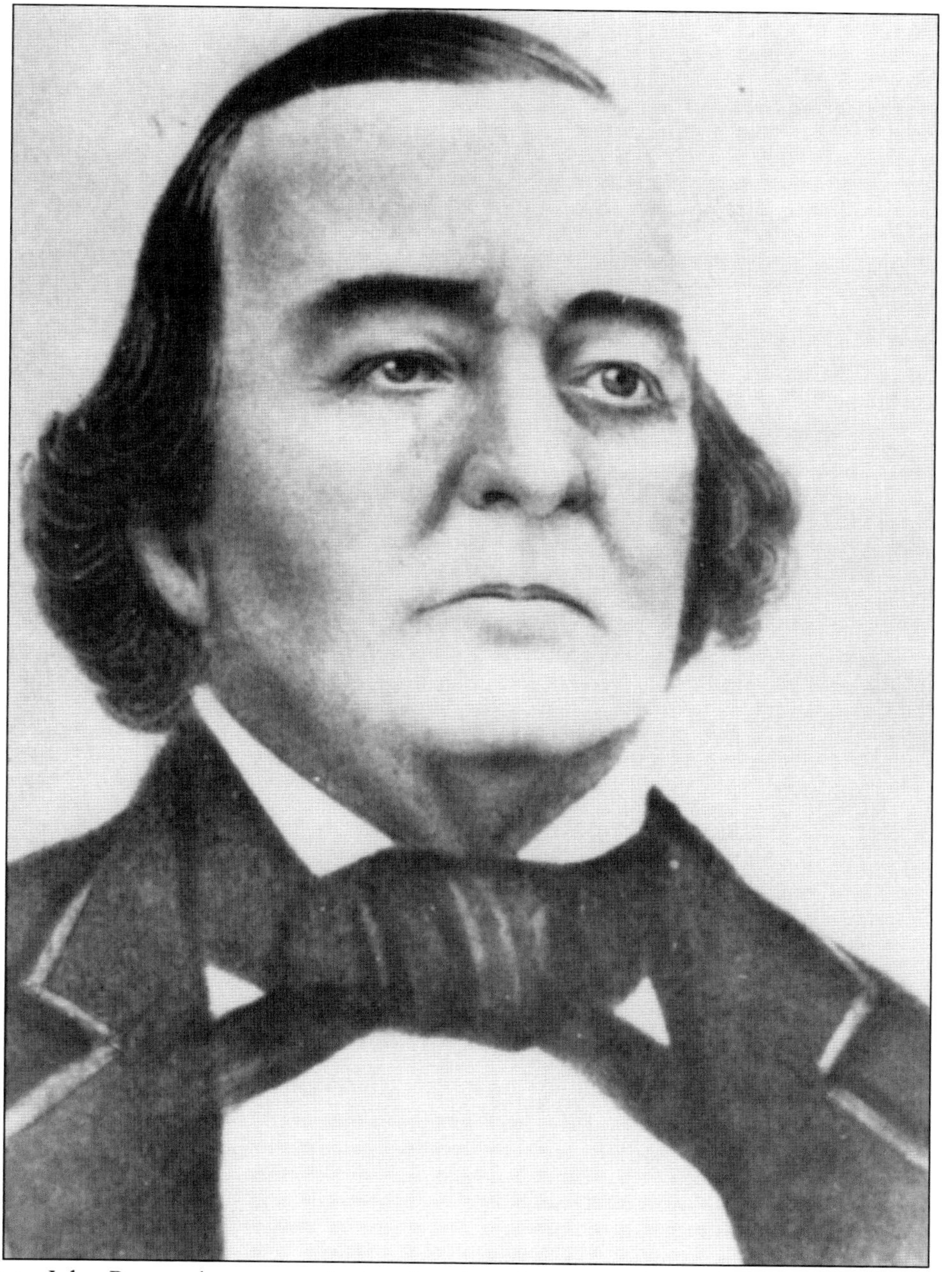

Captain John Rogers, long recognized as founder of the city of Fort Smith, arrived in 1822, acquired property in the area, and sold 296 acres to the U.S. Army for $15,000. He and Colonel John Nicks were partners as post sutlers of the first fort. The Fort Smith post exchange was the only store within 50 miles. Stocked in the store, among other necessities, were salt, sugar, coffee, flour, beans, rice, thread, needles, locks, knives, powder, lead, tobacco (both twist and cut), molasses, clothing, bacon, cheese, shovels, hammers, saws, iron kettles, and medicines. Whisky was the most popular item stocked. When the fort was abandoned in 1824, Rogers and Nicks continued to maintain a store in a blockhouse of the old fort. Rogers also became the postmaster on March 29, 1829, a position he held until 1855. Construction on the new stone fort began in 1838. (Fort Smith National Historic Site.)

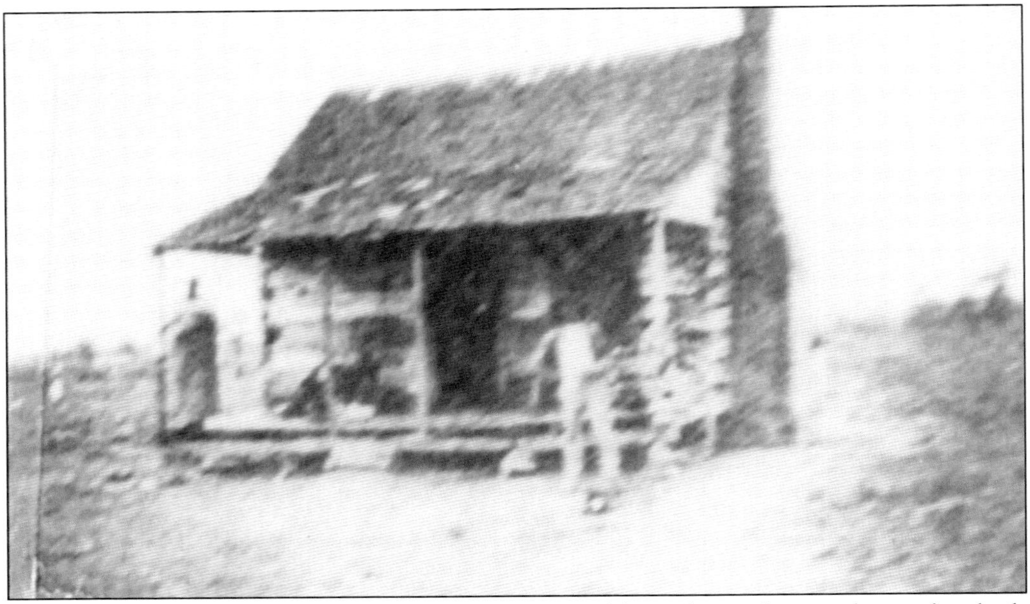

This unidentified log home, in Fort Smith, is comparable to the modest residences first built in the city. In 1837, John Rogers advertised his intention to sell 160 acres in town lots, and Crawford County Surveyor George Herald laid out the original town in 1839. Soon pioneer families were traveling up the Arkansas River to Belle Point. The first buildings were erected on Front or Water Street, along the river bank. (Fort Smith Public Library.)

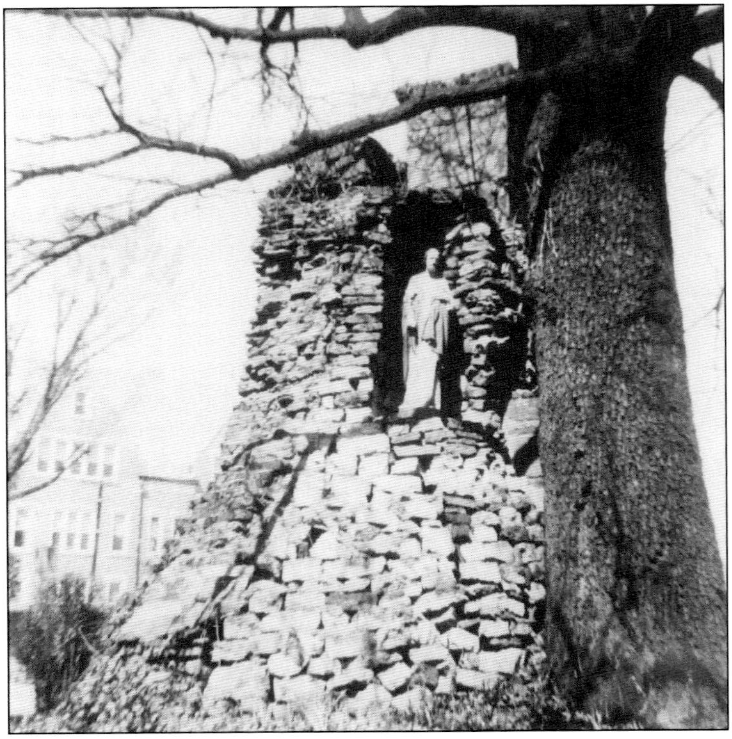

This beautiful metal statue of St. Joseph, patron of the dying, was donated by the Church of the Immaculate Conception Parish. Facing south on the triple shrine, enclosing the General Zachary Taylor headquarters chimney, it was adjacent to the church. Taylor left Fort Smith in 1845 to take command of the American forces in Mexico. He was elected President of the United States in 1848 and died in office two years later. (N.J. Kelly, Fort Smith Public Library.)

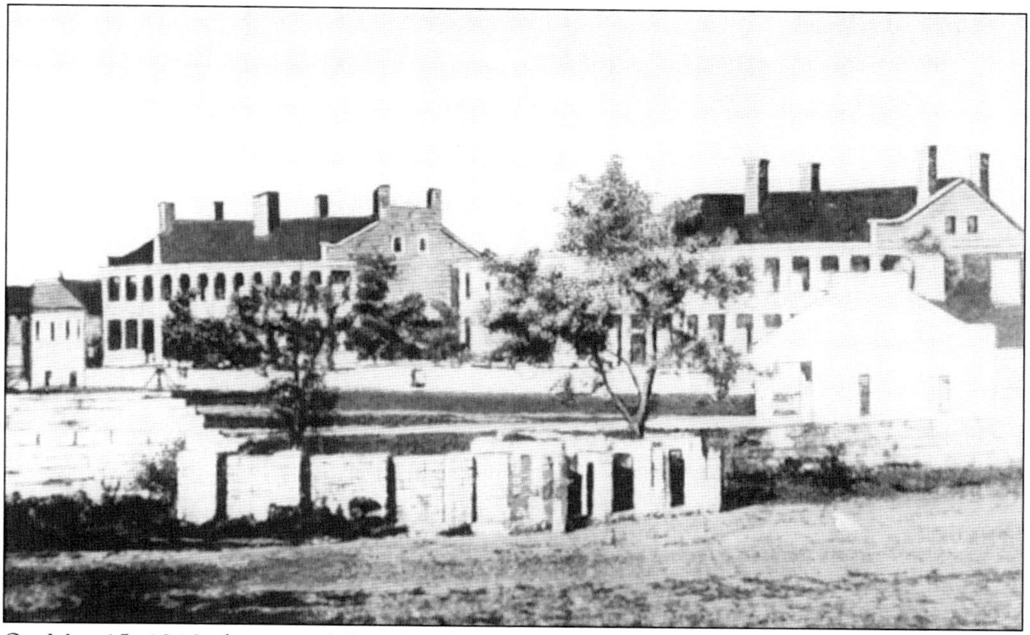

On May 15, 1846, the second Fort Smith was occupied by officers and men of companies D and F, Sixth Infantry, from Cantonment Belknap. This beautiful fort had cost the taxpayers nearly $300,000. Until the outbreak of the Civil War, the post was a supply station for the southwestern frontier. This picture postcard shows the fort *c.* 1863. The magnificent brick barracks to the left accidentally burned in 1865, and the one on the right burned in 1870. (Fort Smith Public Library.)

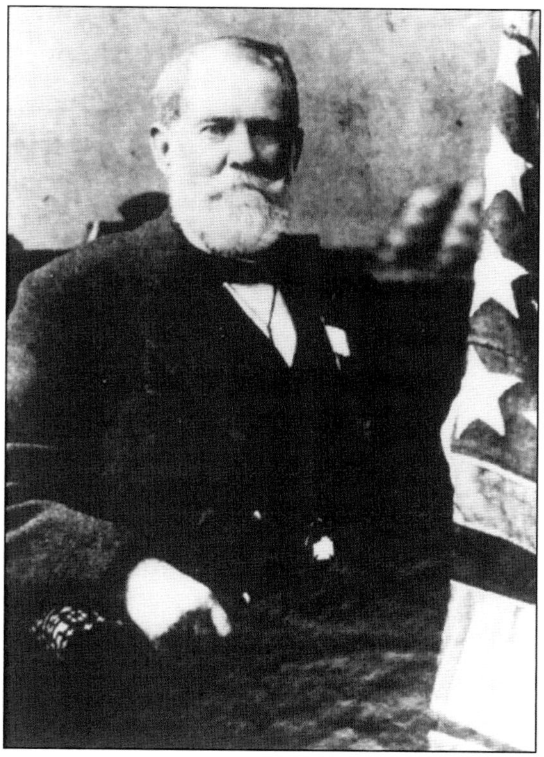

In 1839, stonemason Willard R. Ayers came to Fort Smith from Vermont to work on the second fort. He served in the Mexican War with an Arkansas regiment. Three of his sons, Willard, C.C., and J.T., became highly competent deputy marshals who rode for Judge Parker. Willard was shot and killed while attempting an arrest. J.T., the youngest, accidentally shot himself in the left leg and died of complications. (Fort Smith National Historic Site.)

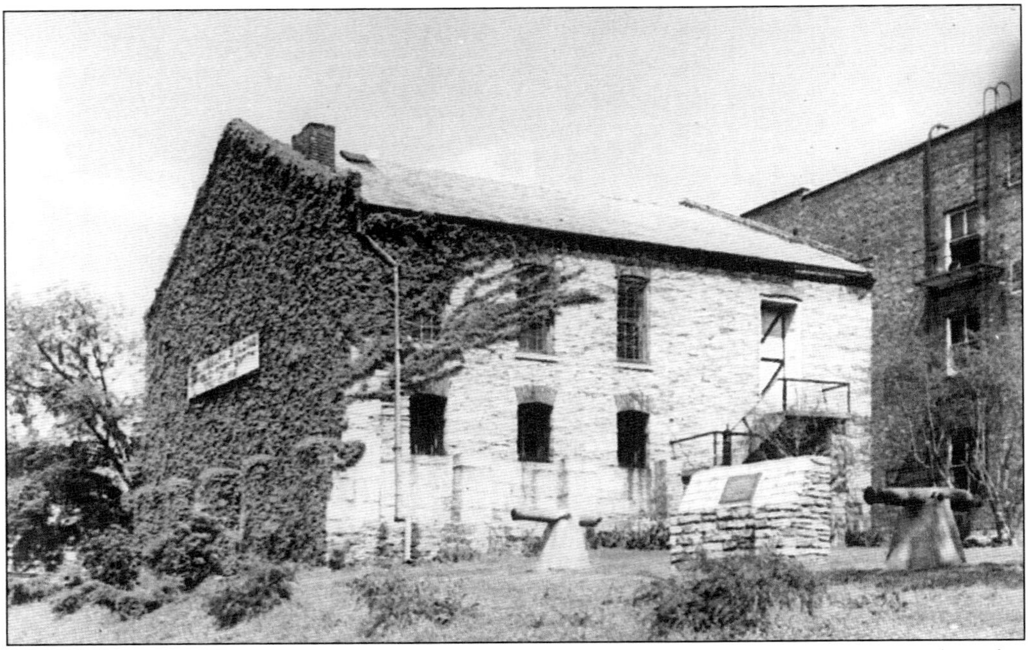

Fort Smith's Commissary was soldiers' barracks during the Civil War, and subsequently Judge Isaac C. Parker's office and library. After the 1900s, the city planned to demolish it. Members of the City Federation of Women's Clubs, headed by Mrs. George Lyman, intervened and saved it. It was a museum until 1979, when it reverted to the National Park Service as part of the Fort Smith National Historic Site. (Fort Smith National Historic Site.)

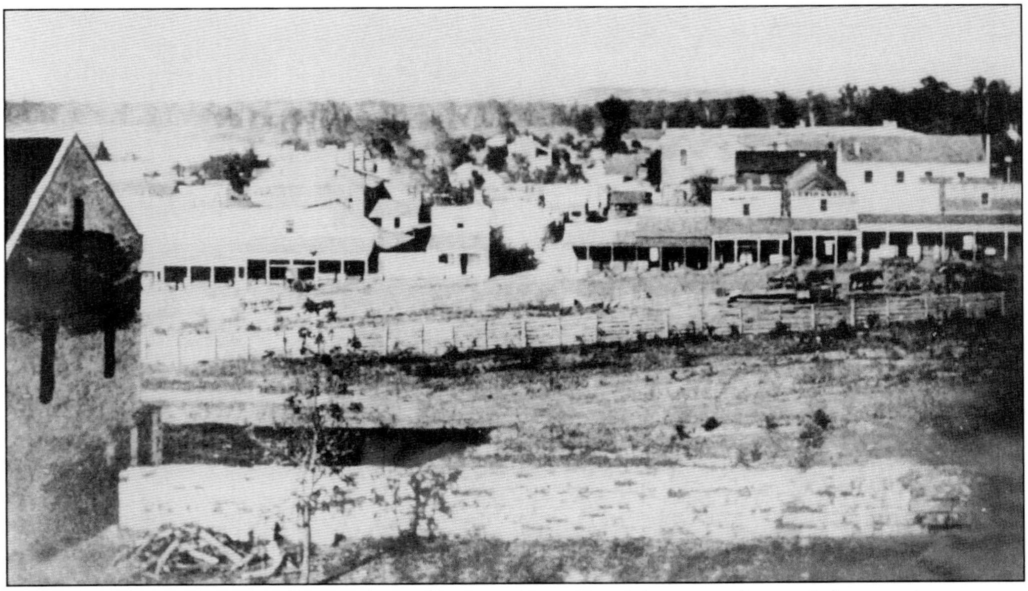

This photo was taken in the early 1860s from Fort Smith's upper floor of the northern-most barracks. The river can be seen in the background. In the center of the photo is a large gate which led to the fort. The post had excellent accommodations for officers and families. The river provided a means of communication with the outside world. Here in what was a wilderness, surrounded by dangers, were scores of refined ladies and gentlemen from every walk of life. (Riggs Studio, Fort Smith National Historic Site.)

The Honorable Thomas Boles, Republican Congressman from Arkansas, is seen here with his wife in a photo taken by Matthew Brady in Washington, D.C., 1868–72. Judge Boles, born in Clarksville, Arkansas c. 1837, studied nights while working on his father's farm. After the Civil War he was a United States Marshal, circuit judge, private attorney, and a United States Commissioner. (Fort Smith National Historic Site.)

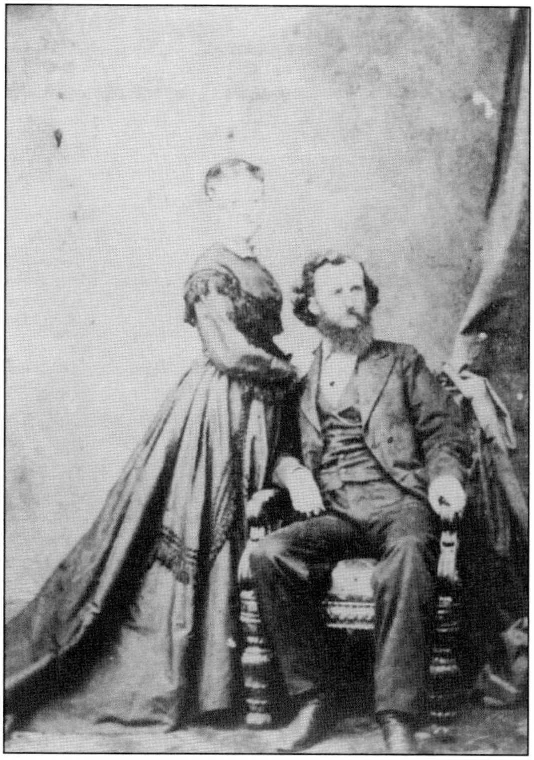

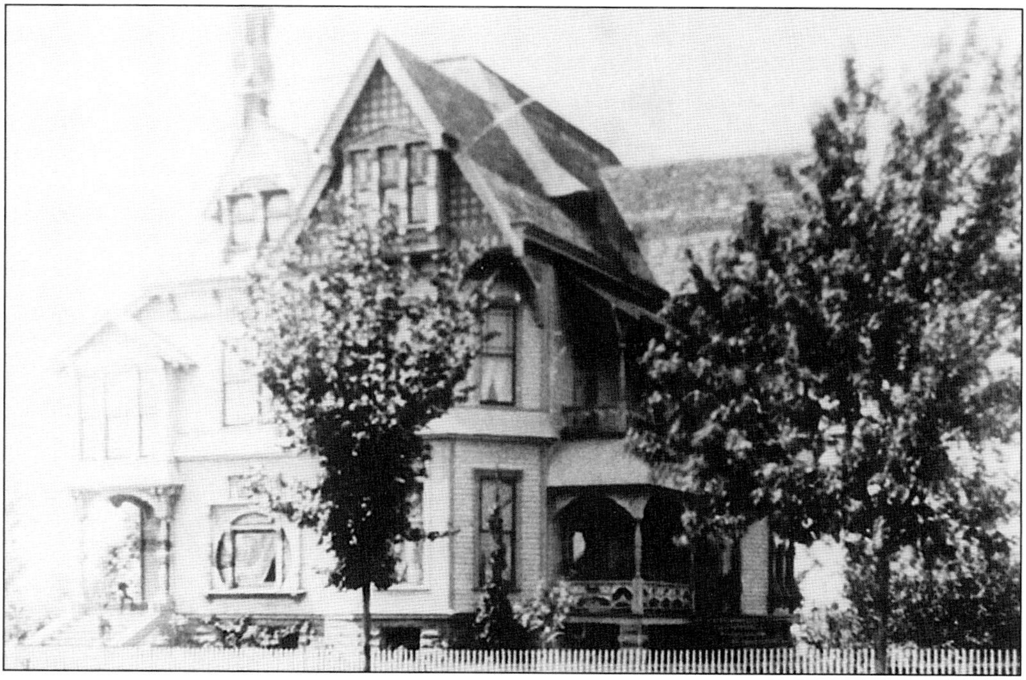

Fort Smith became known for its gracious and lovely homes. This unique, storybook house was built on South Knox (Sixth Street), also known as the Reserve, c. 1880s, by Judge Thomas Boles. It sustained a great deal of damage from the cyclone of 1898. The Reserve addition to the town was mapped, and the streets identified, in July 1884. (Fort Smith Public Library.)

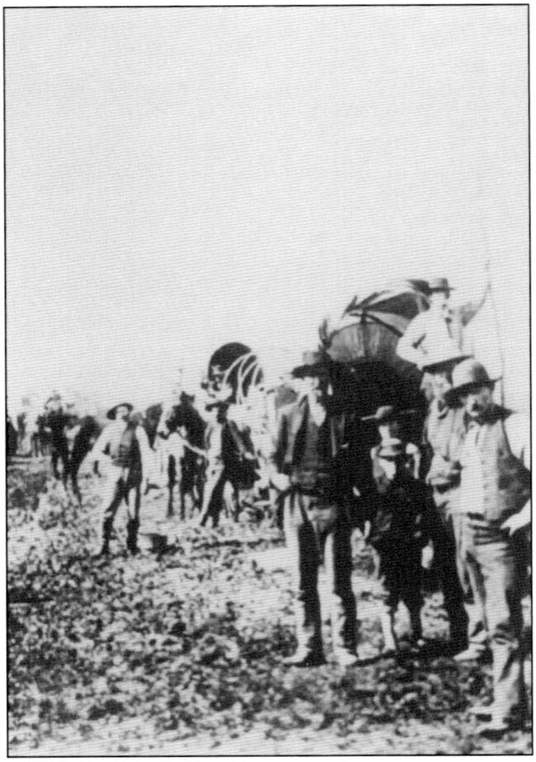

This is an unidentified photo of the Westward movement. In 1849–50, eastern companies arrived in Fort Smith and bought oxen, mules, wagons, and other equipment to outfit their wagon trains for their journey to the gold fields of California. Many city merchants became wealthy during this period. An estimated 5,000 persons passed through Belle Point in the 1850s. The migration lasted for three years. A company commanded by Captain John Dillard numbered over 500 people. (Fort Smith National Historic Site.)

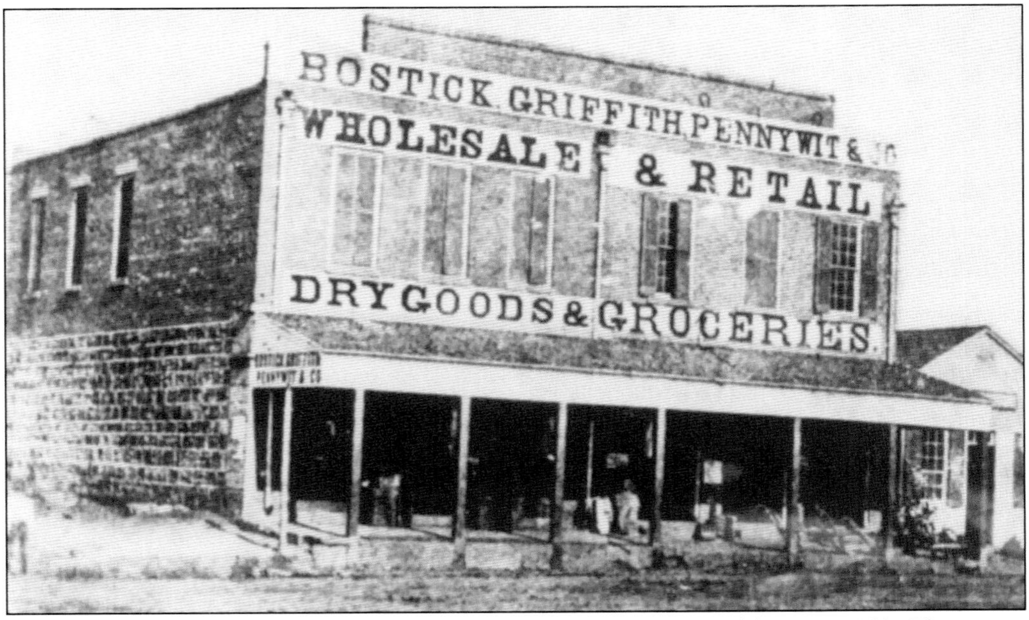

The store of Bostick, Griffith, Pennywit, and Company is pictured here *c.* 1850. This was a mercantile and manufacturing business on the Avenue, near the riverfront, in Fort Smith. Captain Phillip Pennywit commanded one of the first steamers, the *Facility*, to ever ascend the Arkansas River. In 1851, a side-wheeler and steamer, *Pennywit*, struck a snag and sank in the Cherokee Bend. Asa Clark's house, at North Fourth and B Streets, was built of lumber taken from that wreck. (Fort Smith Public Library.)

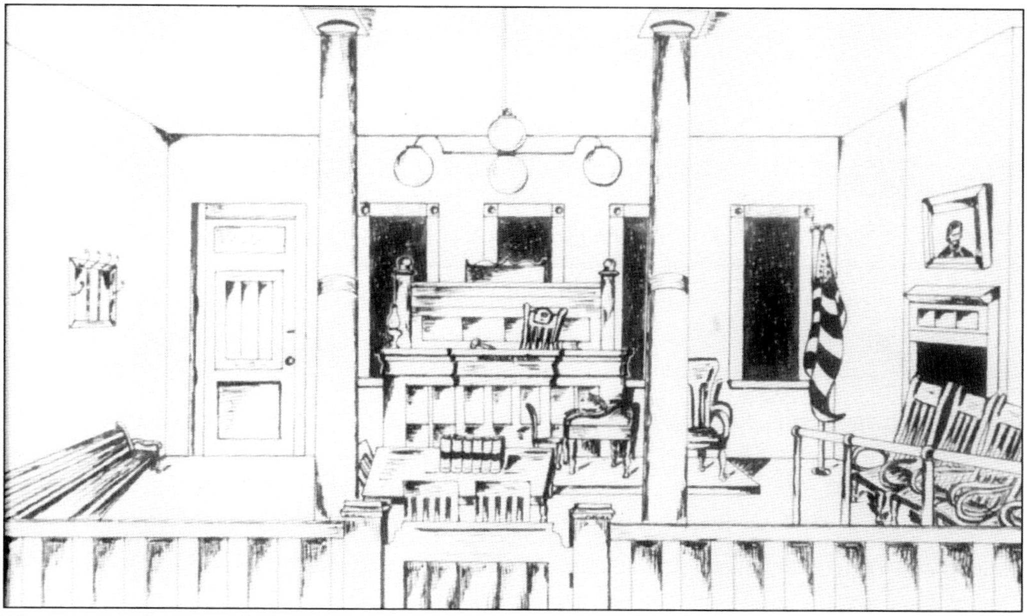

There is no known photo image of Judge Isaac Parker's first courtroom. This sketch by an unidentified artist, as shown, gives us an idea of how the courtroom in the old officer's quarters appeared upon Parker's arrival in Fort Smith on May 2, 1875. It was fitted with a jury section; tables and chairs for attorneys, witnesses, and prisoners; and a gallery for spectators. The court for the Western District of Arkansas was first located in Van Buren. When Federal troops left the garrison in September 1871, Congressman Thomas Boles introduced a bill to transfer the seat of the courtroom from Van Buren to Fort Smith. The bill was approved on March 3, 1871. Also removed were the offices of the judge, marshal, district attorney, and court clerk. (Fort Smith National Historic Site.)

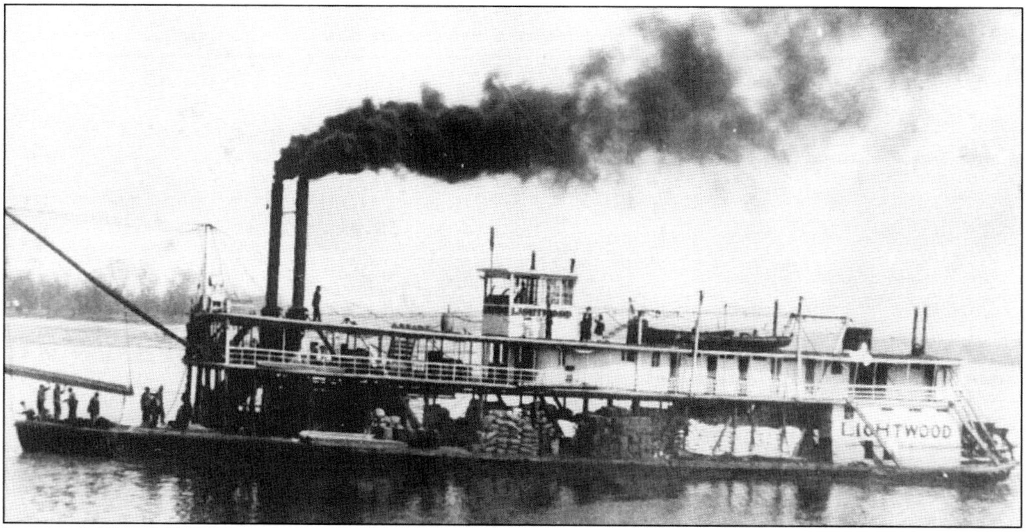

The Steamboat *Lightwood* is shown here at the foot of Garrison Avenue, commanded by Captain B.C. Blakely in the pilothouse. The gangplank is being hauled in with a crane. In those days, with the coming of the railroads, and for years afterward, steamboats made the Arkansas River the main artery of commerce to Fort Smith. Native Americans called steamboats "houses that could swim on water." (Fort Smith Public Library.)

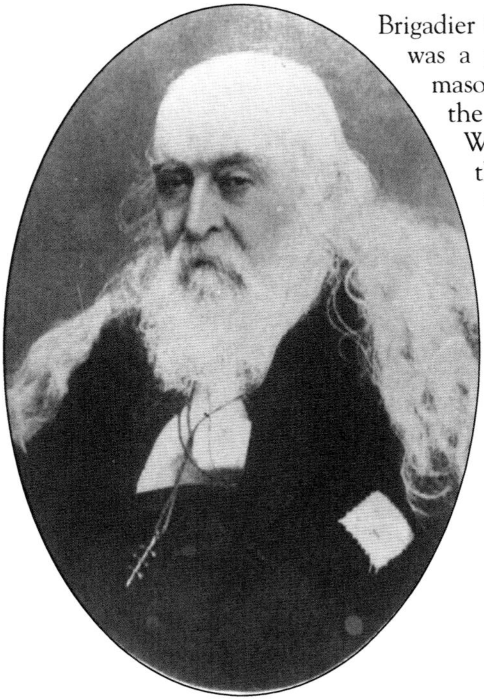

Brigadier General Albert Pike, about 80 years of age here, was a poet, an adventurer, a lawyer of some note, a mason, an Indian commissioner, and commander of the Confederate Indian Brigade during the Civil War. He negotiated treaties of alliance between the "Five Civilized Tribes" and the Southern Confederacy in 1861. He fought a duel, puffing a cigar the entire time, with John Seldon Roane, who became the fourth governor of Arkansas. No one was seriously injured and they became good friends. (Author.)

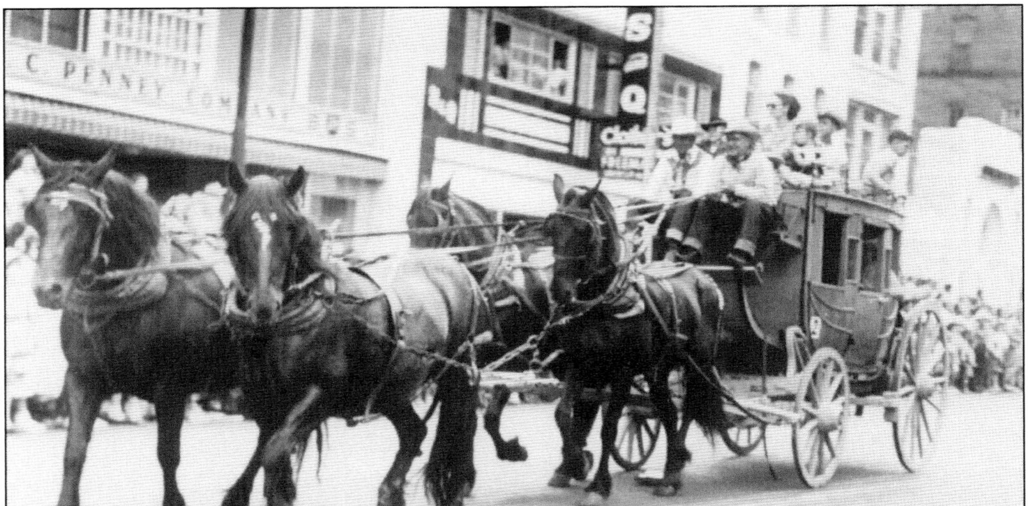

This replica stagecoach, commemorating the arrival, in Fort Smith, of the Butterfield Stage and Overland mail on September 19, 1858, was exhibited in a 1950 rodeo parade. The coach is part of a collection of wagons and coaches on display at Kay Rodgers Park. The stage routes from Memphis and St. Louis merged at Fort Smith and continued southwest to El Paso and San Francisco. The first coach was met and escorted into the city by a musical band and a party of young men. They arrived at John Rogers City Hotel at North Second and A Streets. Hundreds of people joined in the celebration. There was a parade, the inevitable speeches, and a circus for everyone. John Butterfield, a passenger on that first stage, was guest of honor at a ball and banquet that evening. An even larger, official ceremony was held October 13, 1858, when the mail arrived from San Francisco. (Fort Smith Chamber of Commerce.)

James H. Clendening, attorney at law, shown here c. 1860s, was a leading civil attorney in Fort Smith from 1867 to 1898. He organized the Fort Smith Chamber of Commerce, helped build the first sewer system, helped with street paving, played a role in having the United States Weather Bureau office located here, and helped to establish a fire department. He also led a successful, humorous campaign to keep livestock from roaming the streets. President Grant appointed him postmaster of Fort Smith in 1875. He worked to construct a courthouse and helped in construction of the first theater. During the Civil War he was wounded 14 times, and his horse was shot from under him at the Battle of Vicksburg. He died December 21, 1898. (Clendening Collection, Fort Smith National Historic Site.)

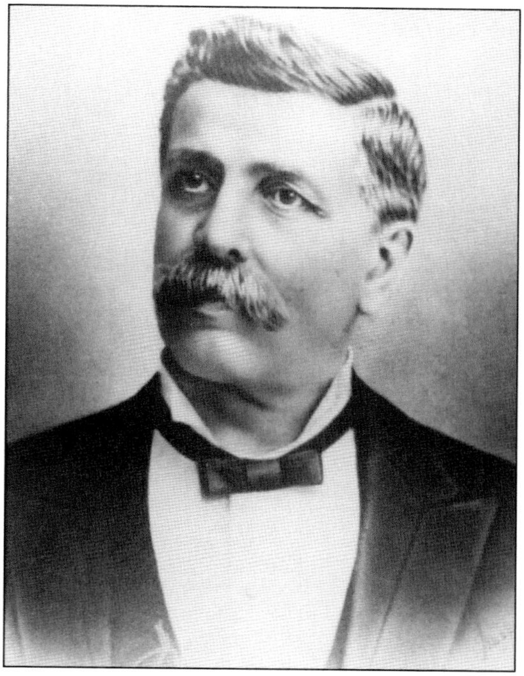

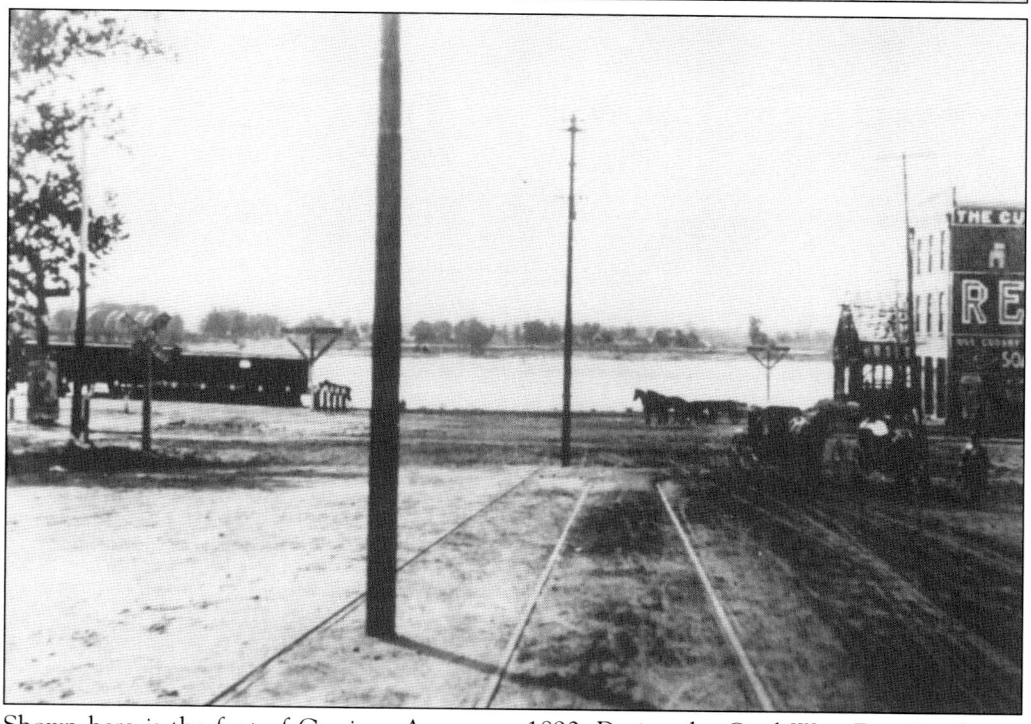

Shown here is the foot of Garrison Avenue c. 1890. During the Civil War, Fort Smith was known as a strategic location in possession of storehouses and magazines. It was supplied by steamers, which docked here in 1860 and 1861, from St. Louis, Cincinnati, and New Orleans. On April 23, 1861, former United States Senator Solon Borland took command of Fort Smith. The fort remained a Confederate outpost until September 1, 1863, when Union forces took over. (Fort Smith Public Library.)

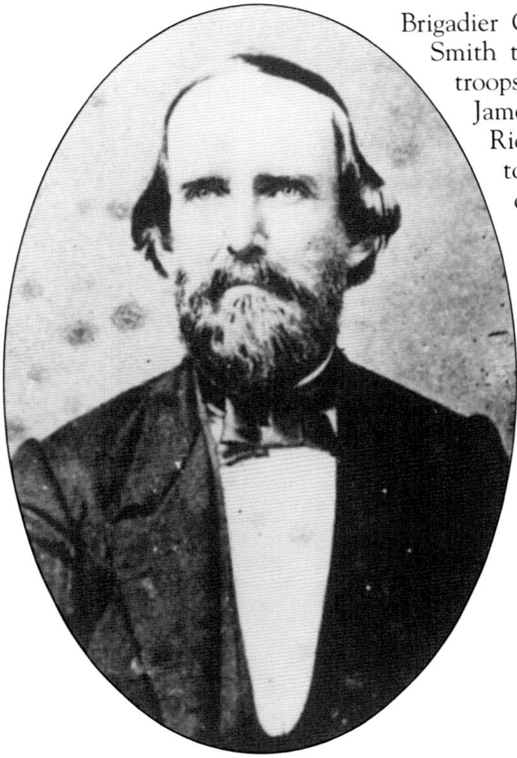

Brigadier General Ben McCulloch was linked to Fort Smith through his men. He was commander of all troops in western Arkansas. McCulloch and General James McIntosh lost their lives at the Battle of Pea Ridge, March 7, 1862. Their bodies were returned to Fort Smith for burial in the government cemetery. They were carried to their graves on two cannon of the battery and buried with military honors. McCulloch's body was later disinterred and taken to Texas. James McIntosh's body still lies in the Fort Smith National Cemetery. (Author.)

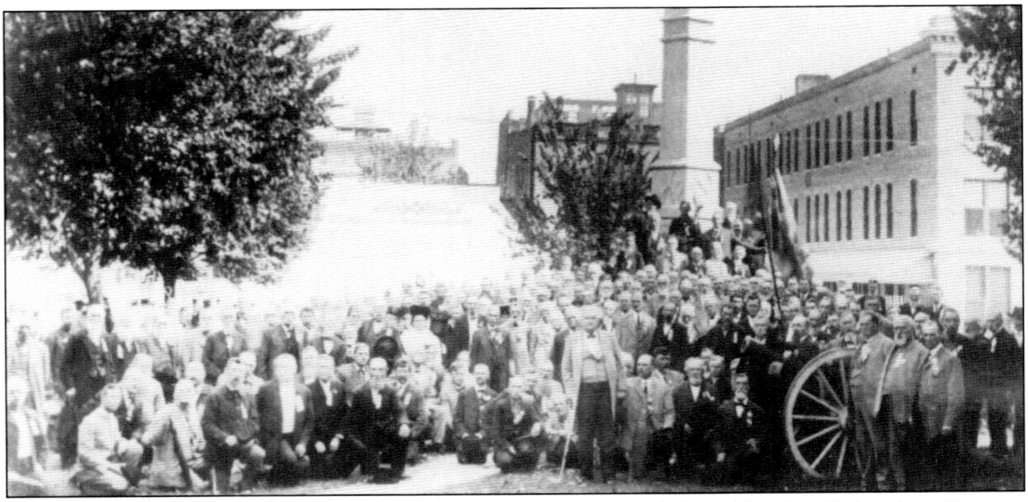

The Confederate Monument was erected on the lawn of Fort Smith's Sebastian County Courthouse by the Varina Jefferson Davis Chapter Daughters of the Confederacy. More than 300 Confederate soldiers lie buried in Fort Smith's National Cemetery. Confederate veterans, shown here in June 1903, are grouped in front of the monument at the unveiling. To the left of the monument, in front with a cane, is Confederate Brigadier General William L. Cabell of Civil War fame. On September 1, 1863, Cabell, in command of a small number of Confederate forces at Fort Smith, retreated to Backbone Mountain, 25 to 30 miles south, while pursued by General James G. Blunt's Federals. At Backbone, Cabell sharply repulsed Blunt. After three hours, Cabell withdrew his command to Waldron. Losses were 14 Federals and 17 Confederates killed and wounded. (Fort Smith Public Library.)

Two

LAW AND ORDER

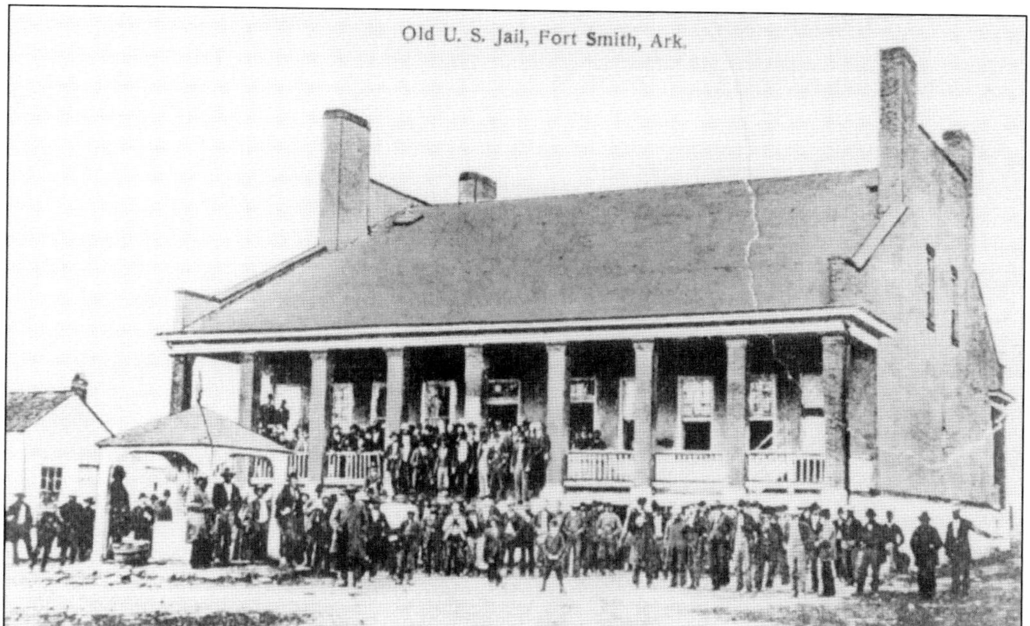

The old soldiers' barracks, as seen prior to the Civil War, became a courtroom and jail before Judge Parker arrived in Fort Smith. Regardless of crimes committed, all prisoners were kept together in the basement jail, sometimes staying there for months before coming to trial. The lice-ridden and rat-infested jail hosted as many as 110 men at one time. In the summer, when court was in session, the stench of over-flowing toilet wastes permeated the courtroom directly above. Judge Parker's court received much bad press before more sanitary conditions were met in the old jail. In 1887–88 a new, three-story brick jail was constructed adjoining the courthouse. (Fort Smith National Historic Site.)

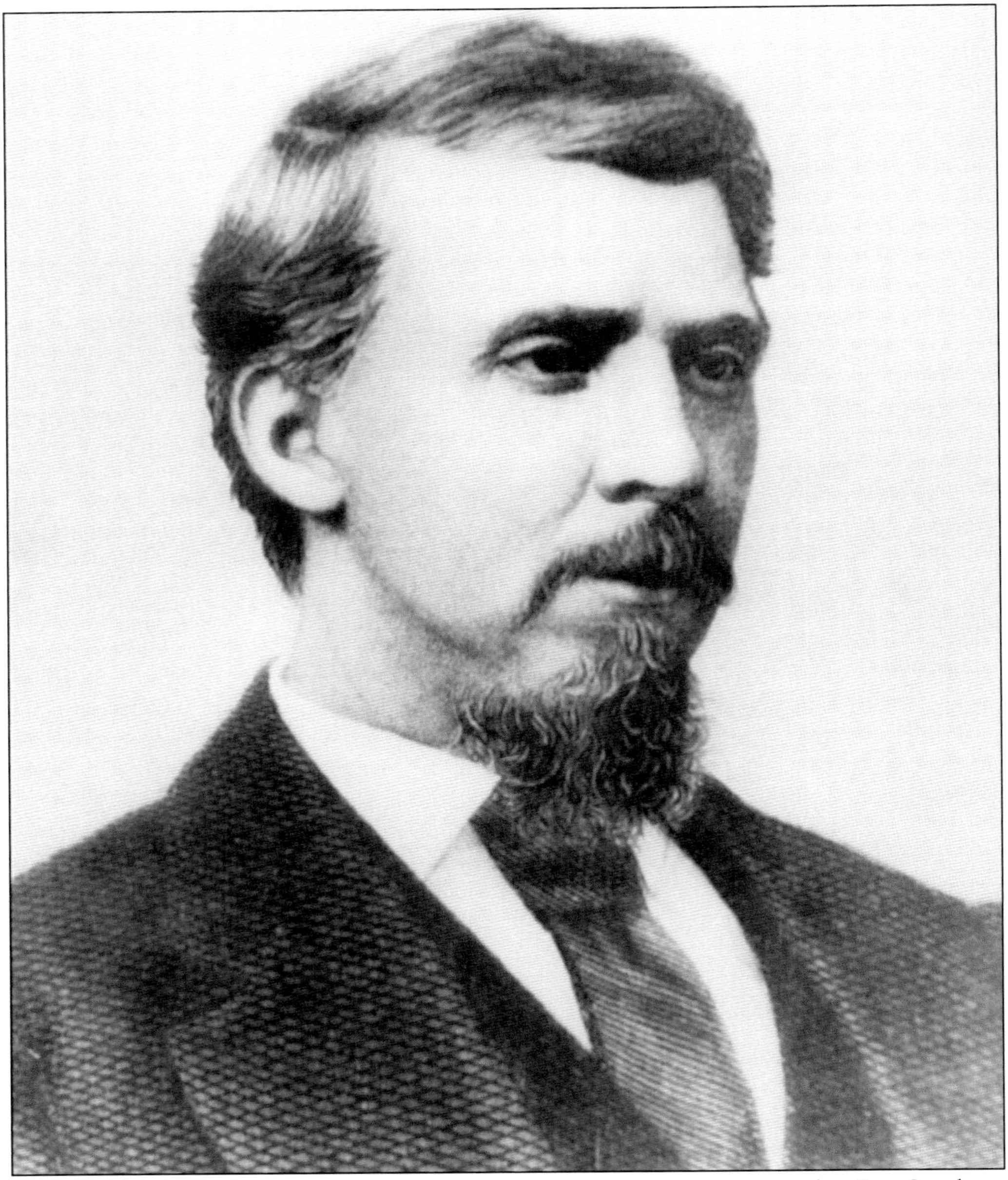

This photo of Isaac C. Parker was taken at approximately the time he arrived in Fort Smith on May 2, 1875. Parker was born in Ohio in 1838. He began practicing law in St. Joseph, Missouri in 1859 and became a corporal in the Civil War. Parker was a city attorney, prosecuting attorney, and a circuit judge. As a congressman he served two terms. For 21 years, from 1875 to 1896, Parker was the federal judge of the United States Court for the Western District of Arkansas, holding jurisdiction over the people of Arkansas and Indian Territory. Judge Parker's tribunal was unique. His court had criminal jurisdiction over Indian Territory for any crime that involved a non-tribal member. His court broke up the gangs and meted out immediate justice. During Parker's tenure, over 12,000 criminal cases were tried. Parker, his marshals, and deputies made it possible for citizens to live in safety. He appeared strict and inflexible, but was actually kind and gentle in his private life. (Fort Smith National Historic Site.)

Ex-slave George Winston, pictured here at an unknown date, was Judge Parker's special bailiff. He kept order in the court and often transported prisoners. Parker was an abolitionist prior to the Civil War, and he felt each individual should be judged on his own merits, regardless of color. He saw in George Winston a man who was efficient and competent. Winston enjoyed an amount of prestige uncommon for an African-American man in post-Civil-War times. (Fort Smith National Historic Site.)

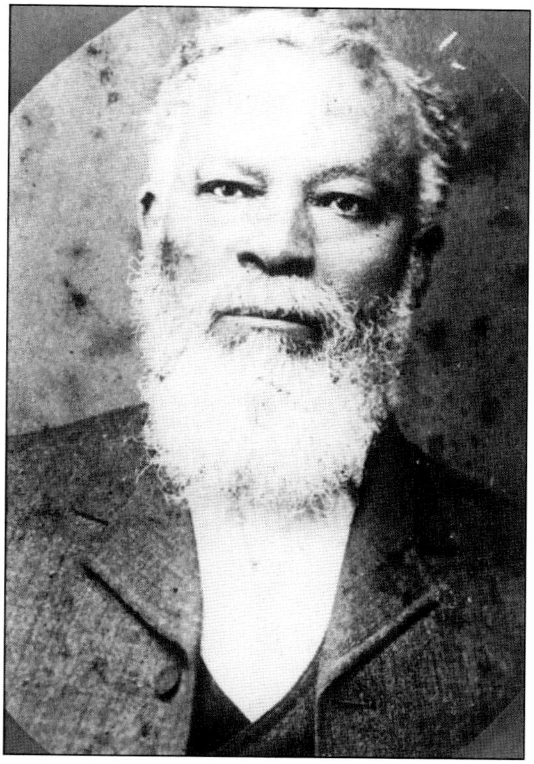

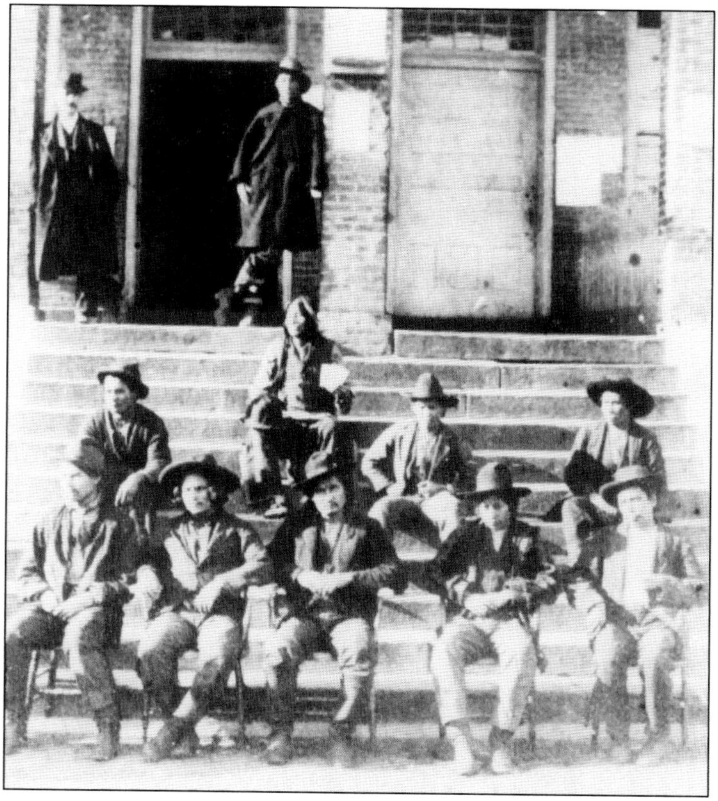

Federal prisoners are pictured here on the steps of the old jail, *c.* 1890. The Fort Smith Federal Court convened at 7:30 a.m. and adjourned at 5 p.m. The night sessions often ran until nearly midnight. Prisoners were brought from the basement jail in leg shackles for their date with the judge. Those incarcerated dreaded the jail almost as much as they did Parker's stern pronouncements. One prisoner, when caught in Indian Territory, said, "Just shoot me now, don't take me to Ft. Smith." (Fort Smith National Historic Site.)

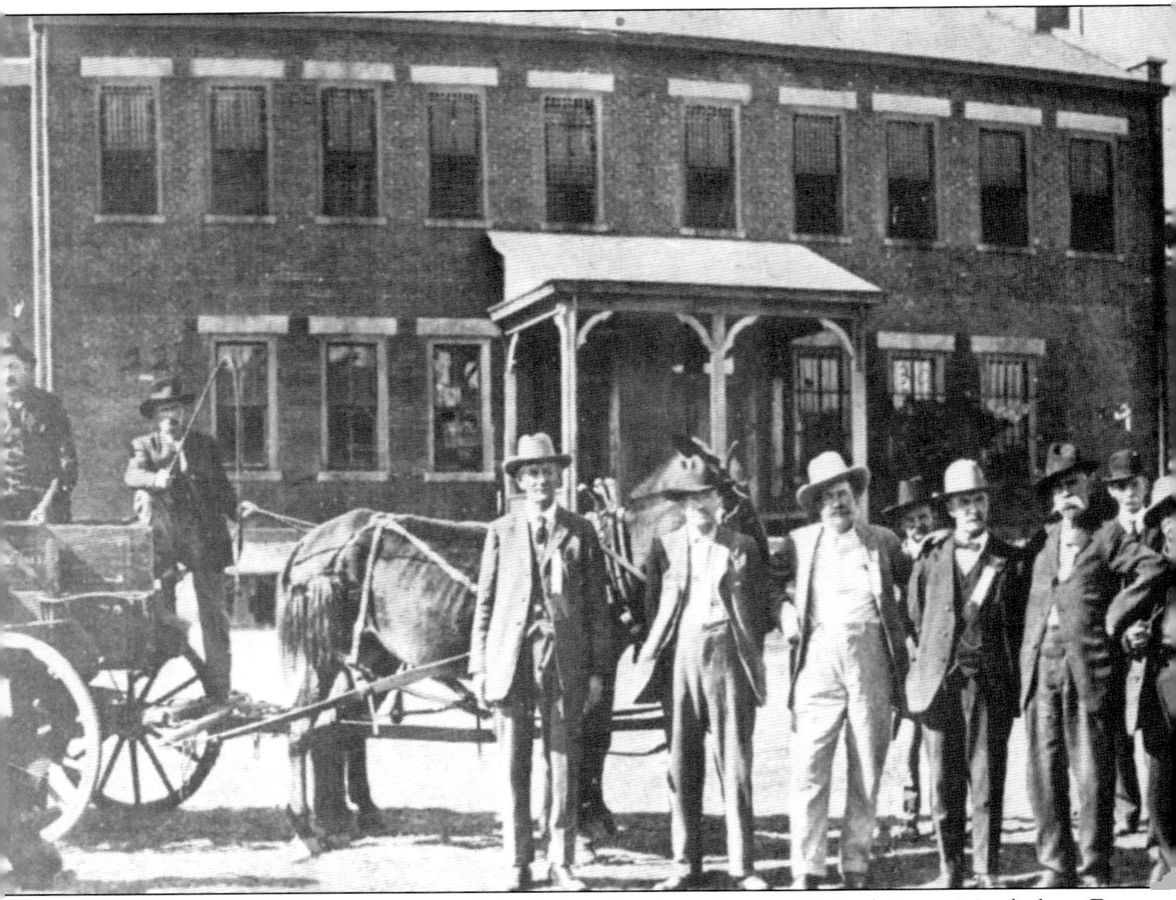

Shown here is the last reunion of the Indian Territory Deputy United States Marshals at Fort Smith in 1908. At that time, a memorial service was held for 65 deputy marshals killed in the line of duty. These are the men who prepared Indian Territory for statehood. The building to the rear is Judge Parker's courtroom. Deputy Marshals worked long hours for little pay. If the suspect was killed, and the family did not claim his body, the deputy had to pay for his burial.

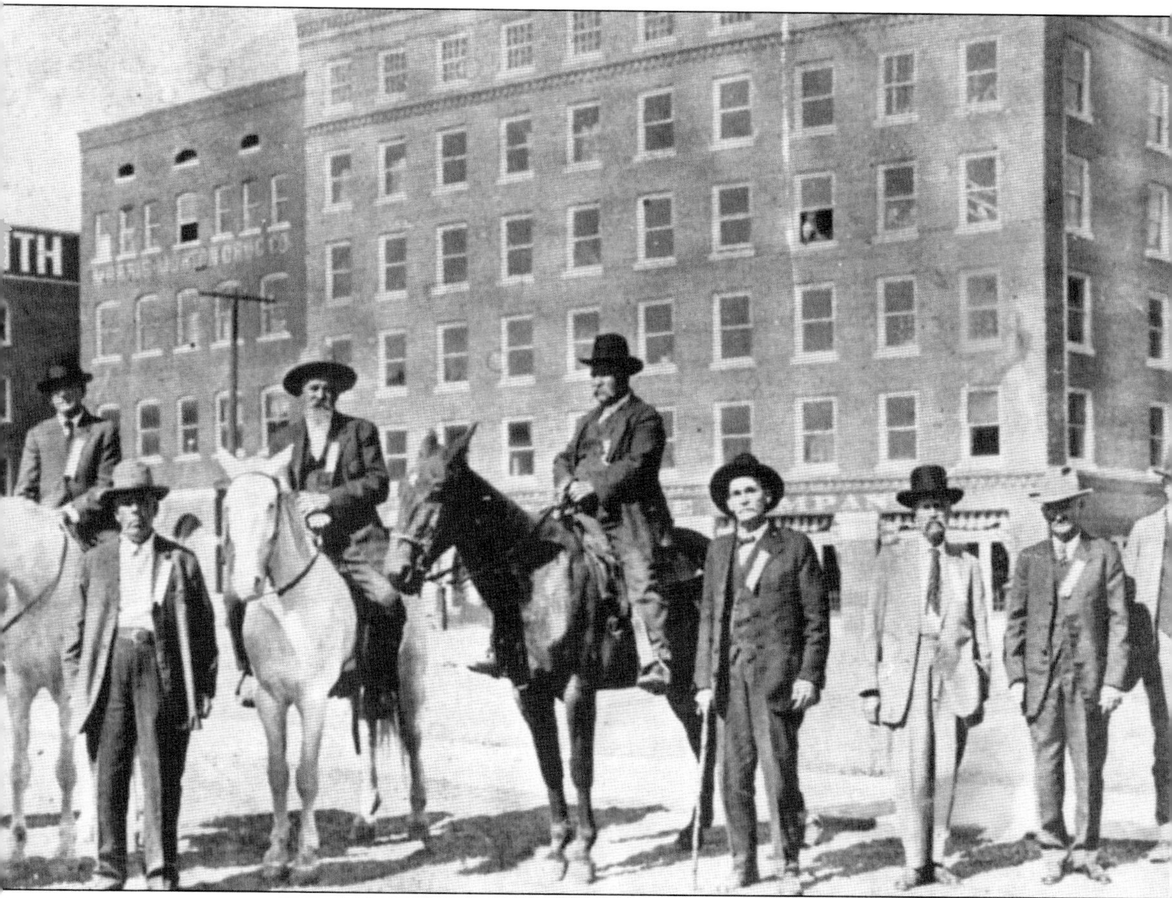

If he did not bring in his suspect, he was not even paid for his time. A list of United States Marshals for the Western District of Arkansas, succeeding Marshal Sarber, is as follows: James F. Fagan (1874), D.P. Upham (1876), Valentine Dell (1880), Thomas Boles (1882), John Carroll (1886), Jacob Yoes (1890), and George J. Crump (1893–1897). (Author.)

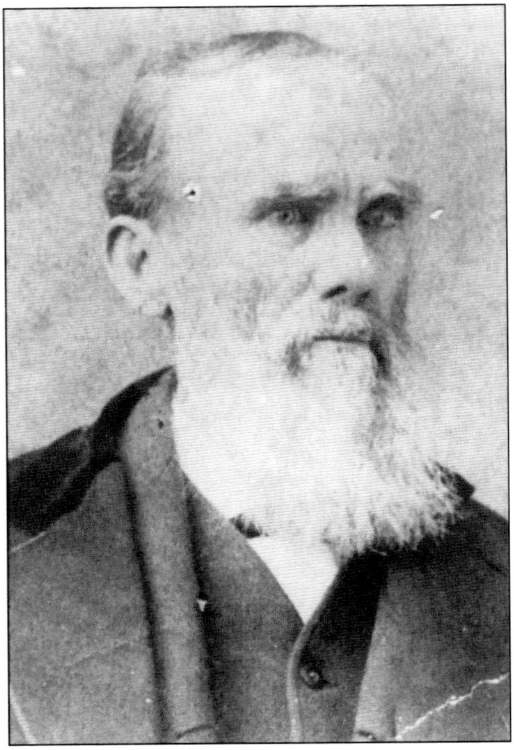

George Maledon was the "prince of hangmen," due to his expertise with the hangman's noose. He hanged approximately 40 men. To avoid undue suffering in those he executed, he prepared each noose with care. He claimed that a large knot, when placed under the left ear in the hollow of the jawbone, would throw the head sidewise when the rope snapped taut. This cracked the neck in a "jiffy," and death came instantly. He also incorporated a slip-knot into the noose to avoid having to cut the rope. The attending physician pulled the slip knot to release the corpse. One tale, and there are many, is that he would walk from his home with the hanging rope in a basket. The great tragedy of his life was the murder of his daughter Annie. Maledon retired, in failing health, in 1890. He was born in June 1823, in Bavaria, and died in 1911 at the Soldiers' Home in Johnson City, Tennessee. He is buried near there. Cavalry Cemetery in Fort Smith contains the remains of a brother, also named George. (Bernice Kizer, Fort Smith Public Library.)

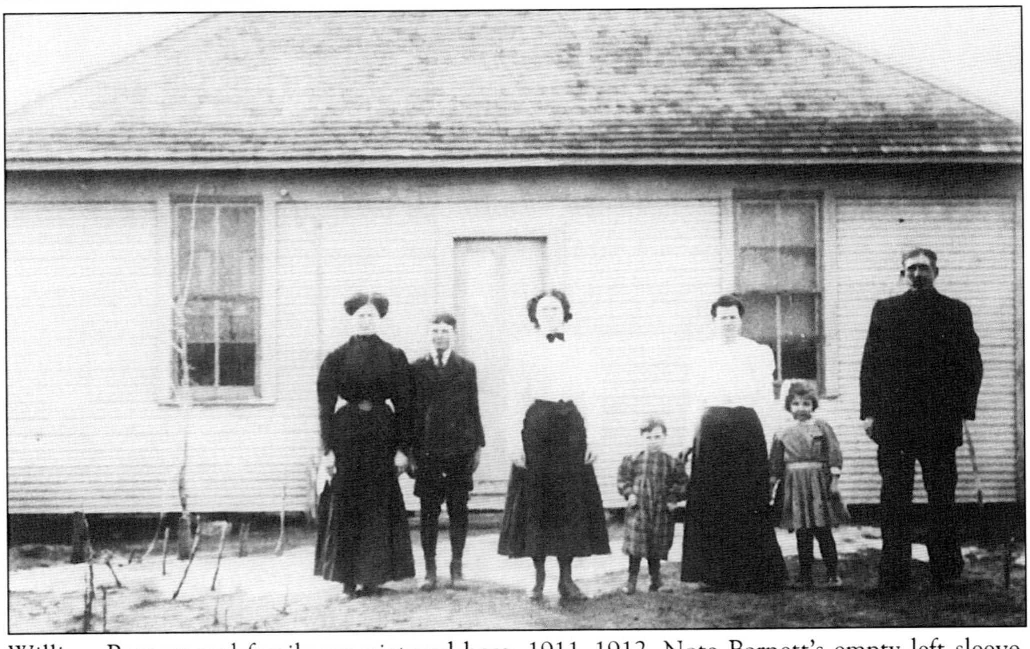

William Barnett and family are pictured here, 1911–1912. Note Barnett's empty left sleeve. Amos and Abner Manley shot Ellis McVay, their overnight host, as he cared for his sick, twin babies. When hired man William Barnett attempted to intervene, they attacked him with an ax, chopping off his left hand. Mrs. McVay was to be next, when a dog began to bark and scared them off. Barnett's testimony, the stump of his hand, and the bloody ax sent the Manleys to the gallows. (Royce Waltrip, Fort Smith National Historic Site.)

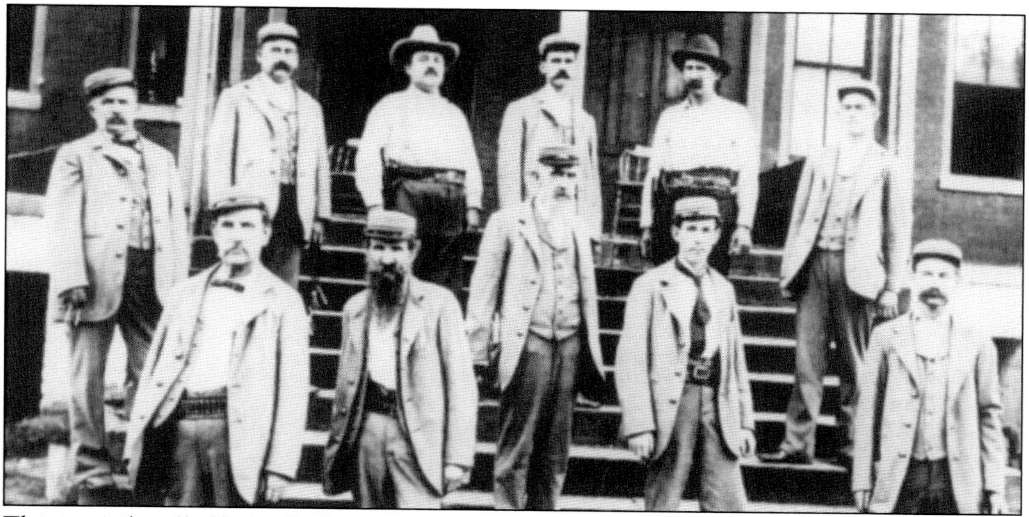

This is a jail staff of Judge Parker's Court. Shown here, from left to right are: (front row) W.H. McConnell, guard; Robert Jackson, guard; J.H. Berry, jailer; Tom Parker, guard; and Con Berry, turnkey; (back row) Duke Brown, night guard; Campbell Eoff, turnkey; Clarence Owensby, death guard; Will Lawson, guard; Bros Parker, guard; and William Franklin, guard. When the Pierce brothers were scheduled to hang, Turnkey Campbell Eoff, due to lack of time, proceeded with the hanging even after discovering a rotted gallows cross-beam. (Fort Smith National Historic Site.)

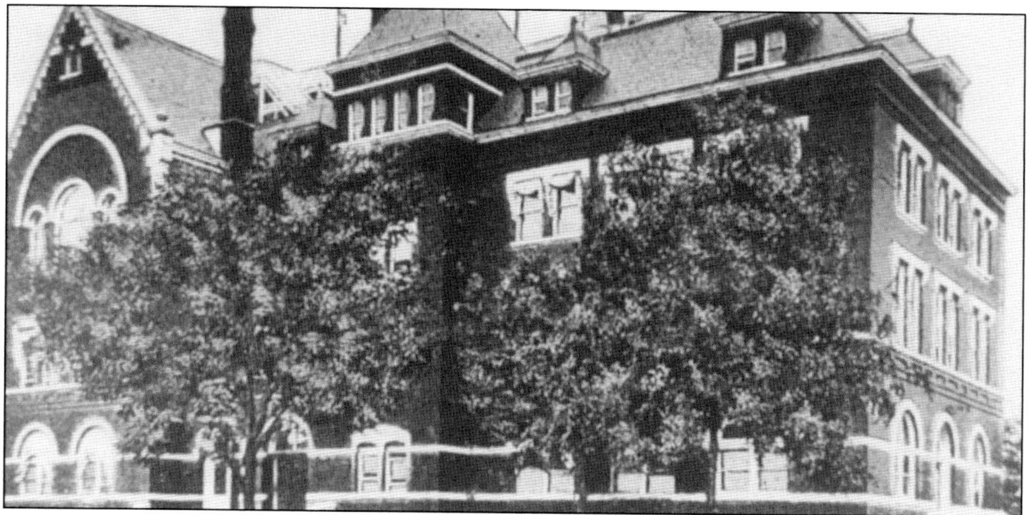

In 1887, $100,000 was designated for a federal courthouse and post office. It was completed in 1889, as shown in this picture postcard. The post office was on the first floor, and Judge Parker's Federal Court was on the second floor. It was here that Parker pronounced that Cherokee Bill and the Buck Gang were to hang. Sentencing Rufus Buck he said, "May God, whose laws you have broken, and before whose tribunal you must then appear, have mercy on your soul." It was also here that Judge Parker's court was closed forever. One of the first air mail stations in the world was established at this post office. Approximately 25,000 specially stamped postcards were dropped on its lawn in 1911. The mail was flown about 3 miles from League Park on Midland Boulevard, Eleventh and Plum Streets, by commissioned Mail Carrier Lincoln Beachey. A couple of months earlier Beachey also carried the first air mail in the world and dropped it on an ocean liner in New York City Harbor. (Wayne Bledsoe.)

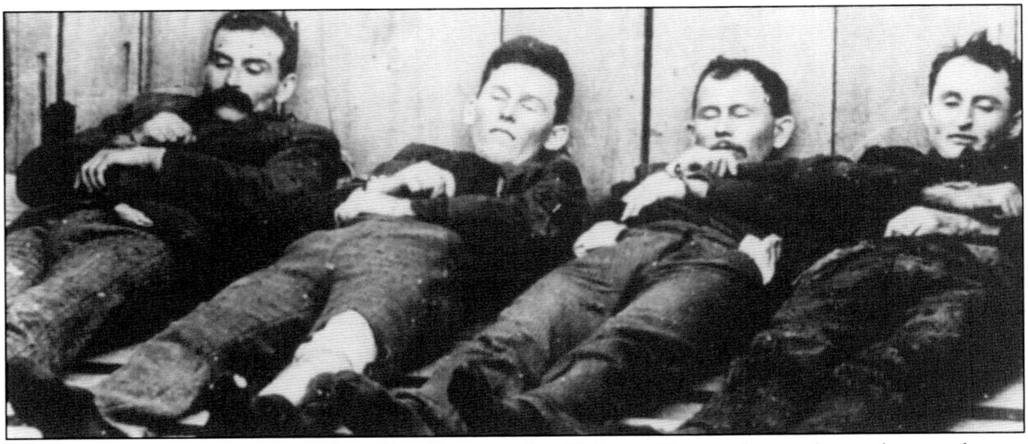

On October 5, 1892, in Coffeyville, Kansas, the Dalton Gang, shown here deceased, was killed attempting to rob two banks at once. From left to right are Bill Power, Bob Dalton, Grat Dalton, and Dick Broadwell. Emmett Dalton recovered from his wounds. Grat, Bill Powers, and Dick Broadwell entered C.M. Condon and Company Bank at 9 a.m. Bob and Emmett simultaneously entered the First National Bank across the street. The townspeople were alerted and the shooting began before the robbers exited the banks. Eight men died and three were wounded. Almost all the money was recovered. The next day, the First National had a surplus of $1.98 and the Condon had lost $20. Parents Lewis and Adeline Younger Dalton had 15 children. Frank Dalton, a Parker deputy, was murdered in 1887 while attempting to arrest a whiskey runner. Three other brothers followed a life of crime after serving Judge Parker's court. Deputies Grat and Bob served under Marshal John Carroll. Emmett served as posseman. Bill, another notorious brother, was killed in Texas by Deputy-Marshal Selden Lindsey. (Kansas State Historical Society.)

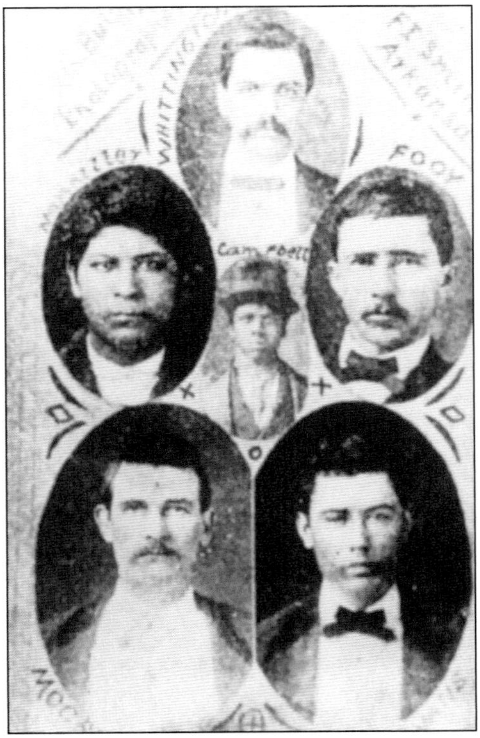

Five thousand people witnessed the first sextet hanged by Parker's Court on September 3, 1875. All six men were convicted of heinous crimes. They are Daniel Evans, William Whittington, James Moore, Smoker Mankiller, Samuel Fooy, and Edmund Campbell. At the gallows, they lined up with their feet on the death trap. Their nooses were adjusted, black hoods pulled over their heads, and the trap door sprung. Four died instantly, but it took longer for the other two. (Fort Smith National Historic Site.)

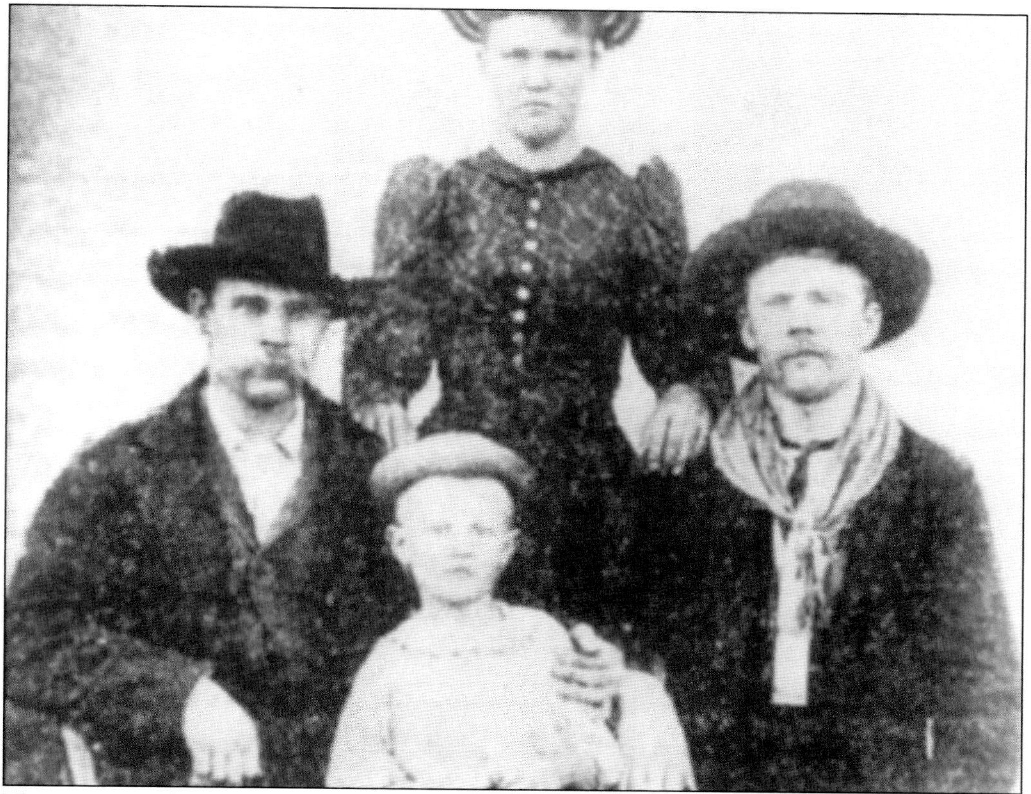

This innocent-looking photo of John and George Pierce, their sister, and John Pierce's son, was taken the day before the Pierces were hanged for murder on April 30, 1896. Webber Isaacs was hanged at the same time. Isaacs had tried to burn his murder victim, but the victim was identified by his chin whiskers, which failed to burn. The Pierces, when arrested, were traveling with the horse, colt, and $100 they had killed for. (Fort Smith National Historic Site.)

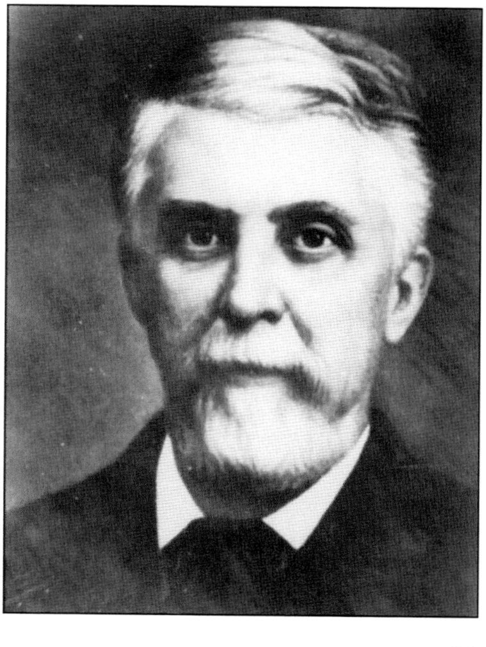

The Honorable Isaac C. Parker, pictured here a short time before his death, died on November 17, 1896. This aged image, taken when he was 57, reflects the Bright's Disease with which he suffered and the wear and tear from his 21 years on the bench. Heads of state came to his funeral services, but the greatest tribute to this champion of Indian rights came from the Creek Chief Pleasant Porter, who placed a simple garland of wildflowers on his grave. (Fort Smith Public Library.)

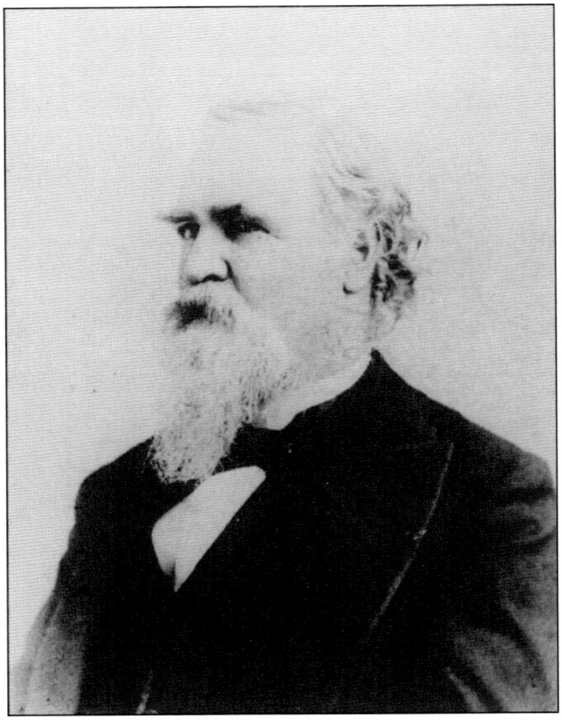

It was the sad duty of Court Crier J.G. Hammersley, on September 1, 1896, shown here, to announce the closing of the court in this manner "Oyez! Oyez! The Honorable District and Circuit Courts of the United States for the Western District of Arkansas, having criminal jurisdiction of the Indian Territory, are now adjourned, forever. God bless the United States and the honorable courts!" Already gravely ill, Judge Parker died soon afterward. (Fort Smith National Historic Site.)

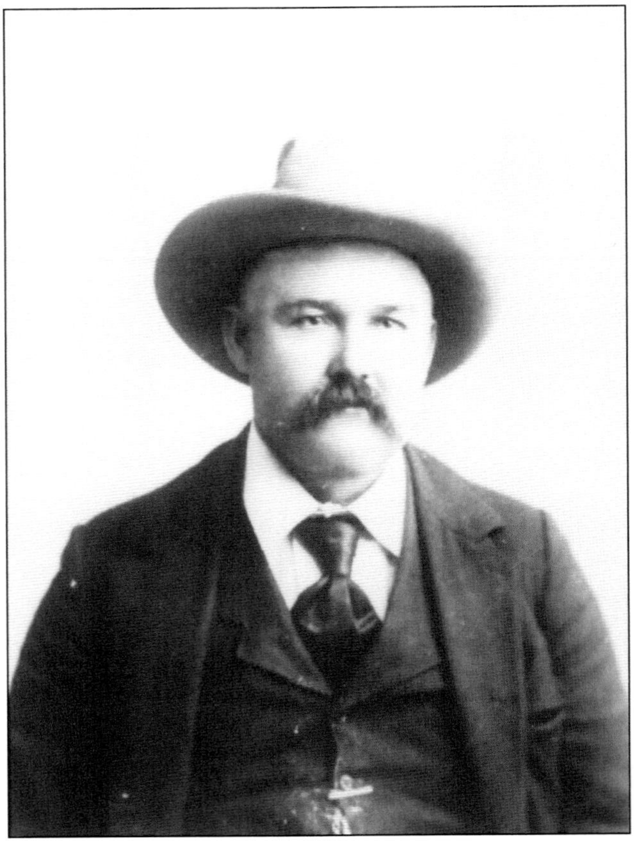

Deputy Marshal George Lawson was the executioner of Cherokee Bill and the Rufus Buck Gang. It has been said that 12 of the 79 executions of Judge Parker's court were performed by Lawson. One dark and lonely night, Deputy Lawson requested help in investigating some mournful sounds issuing from the old gallows. The other deputies recalled convicted murderer Lewis Holder's pleas, to anyone who would listen, to spare his life. Realizing he would hang anyway, he threatened to haunt those who hanged him. Fearing it was Lewis Holder's ghost, no one would accompany Lawson that night. Lawson went alone and found a highly intoxicated man, weeping, on the floor of the scaffold. (Fort Smith National Site.)

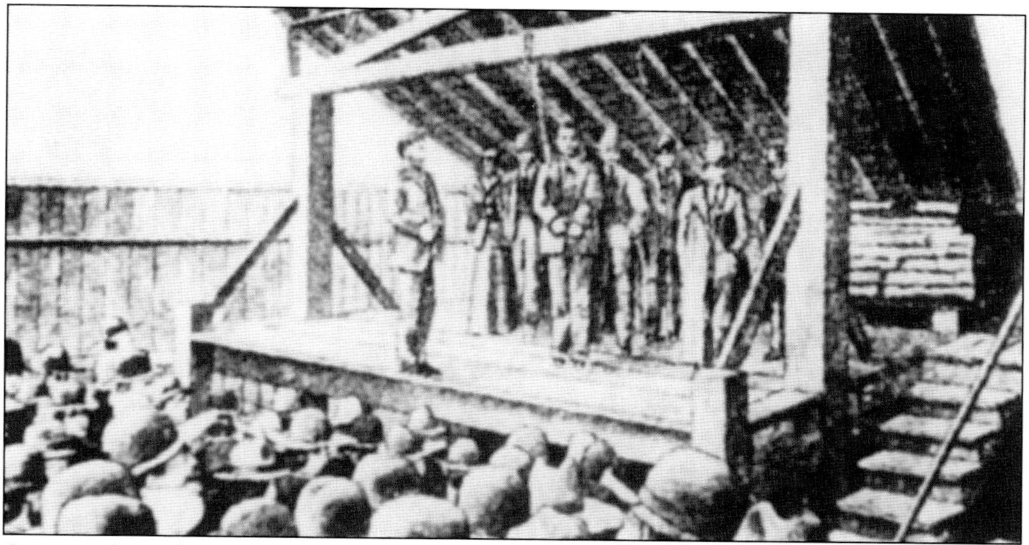

Convicted murderer Cherokee Bill, at his hanging on March 17, 1896, requested that no photos be taken. Instead, someone sketched the scene. Walking to the gallows, Bill remarked that it was as good a day as any to die. Bill's mother, Ellen Lynch, stands among the men to the left. When Bill objected, she replied, "I can go anywhere you are." She hugged him before they put the black hood over his head. (John B. and Leon Williams, Fort Smith National Historic Site.)

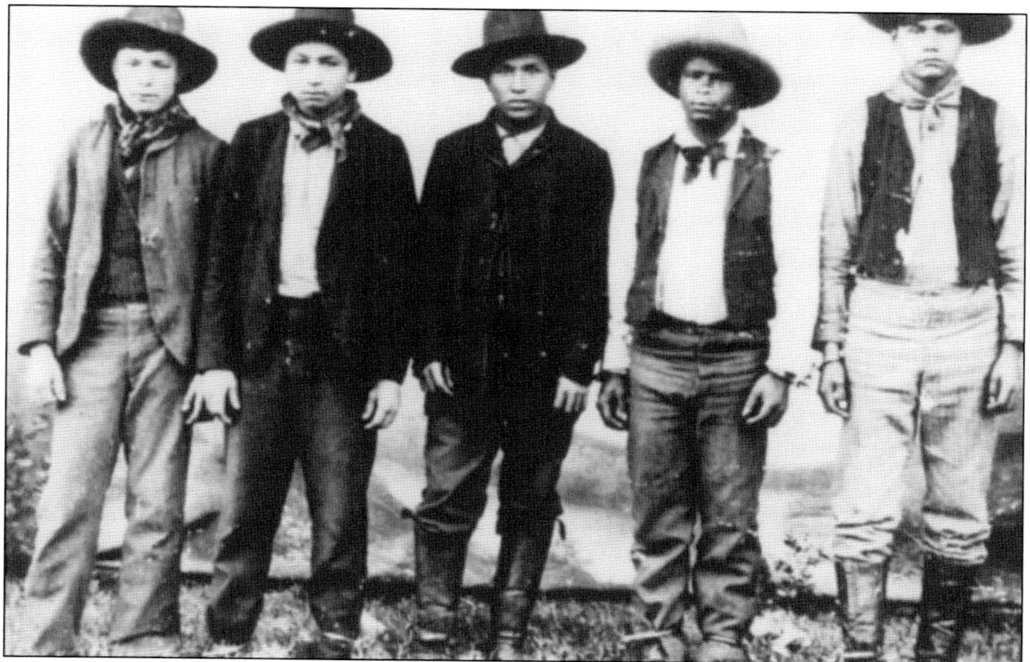

The Rufus Buck gang were Creek Indians. Pictured from left to right are: Maoma July, Sam Sampson, Rufus Buck, Luckey Davis, and Lewis Davis. They were convicted of a five-day crime spree, and all five hanged together July 1, 1896. The gang disagreed on the hour they should hang. Luckey Davis wanted to be hanged at 10 a.m., so his body could be shipped on the Cannon Ball Express at 11:30. However, the others held out for 1 p.m. (Fort Smith National Historic Site.)

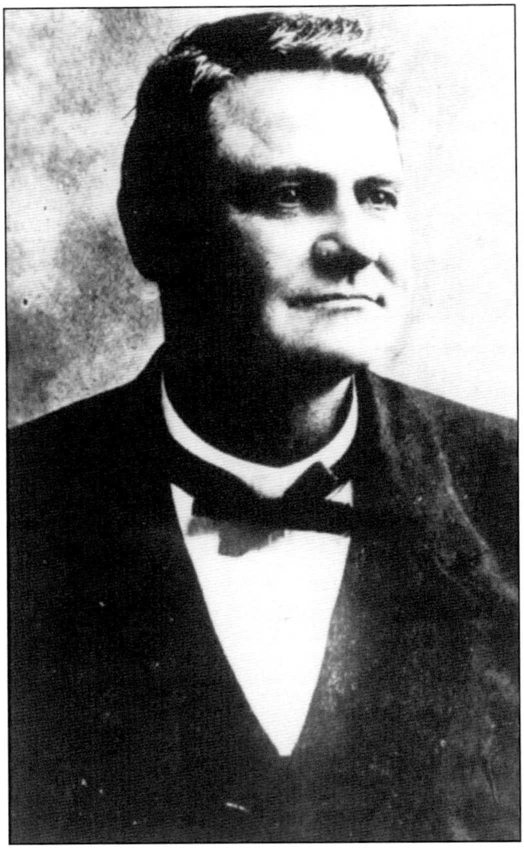

Colonel Jacob Yoes was marshal when Ned Christie was blasted out of the fort he built in the Cherokee Hills. Yoes was a sergeant in Companies D and F of the First Arkansas Cavalry. He was appointed United States Marshal for the Western District of Arkansas and Eastern District of Oklahoma on May 18, 1889, under Judge Isaac C. Parker. Yoes was so well liked that people honored him with the title of Colonel. (Fort Smith National Historic Site.)

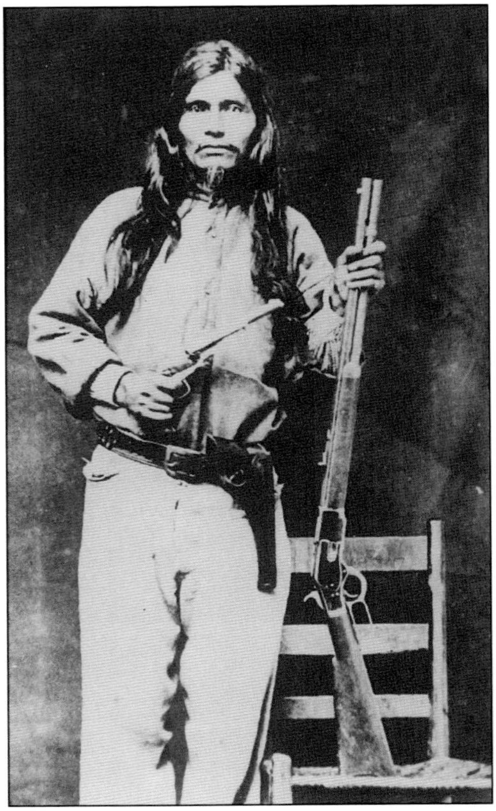

Ned Christie, who served as a member of the Indian Legislature, was intelligent and competent. He claimed innocence in the murder of a deputy marshal and vowed "never to be taken to Fort Smith." Judge Parker's deputies waged a four-year war against him. They burned him out of his fortress on November 3, 1892, using dynamite and a cannon, then shot him as he fled. To this day, a martyred Christie is believed innocent by the Native American community. (Photographer Johnson, Fort Smith National Historic Site.)

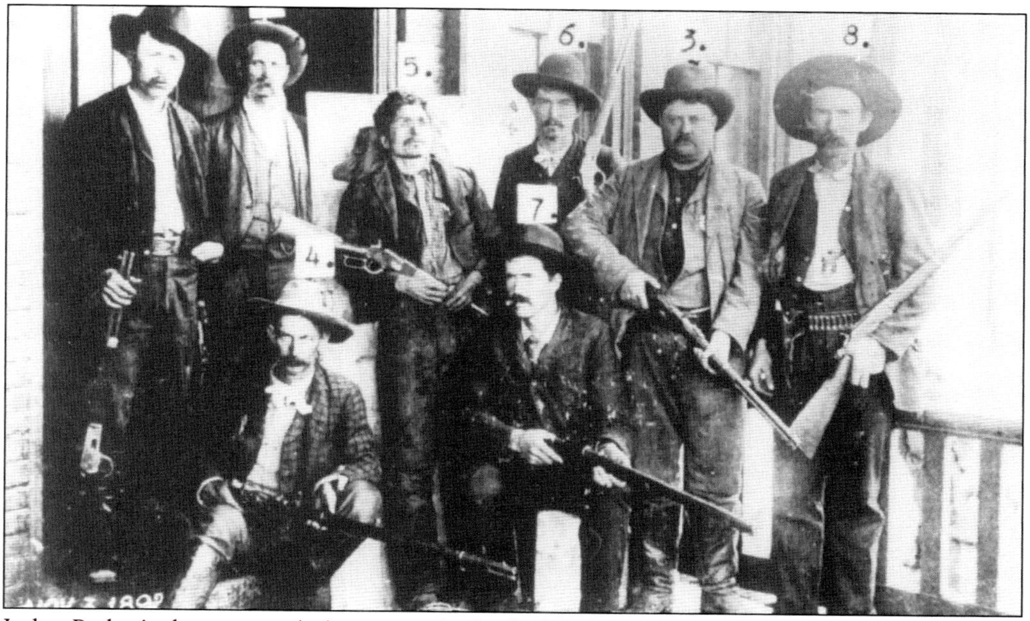

Judge Parker's deputy marshals pose with the body of Ned Christie. He was killed in Indian Territory on November 3, 1892. Pictured here, from left to right, are: (bottom row) Thomas Johnson, Charles Copeland, and Heck Bruner; (top row) Paden Tolbert, Captain G.S. White, Coon Ratteree, Enoch Mills, and Ned Christie, deceased. It was typical in those days for law enforcement to secure the outlaw to a slab (Christie was on a door here) and pose with him. (Fort Smith National Historic Site.)

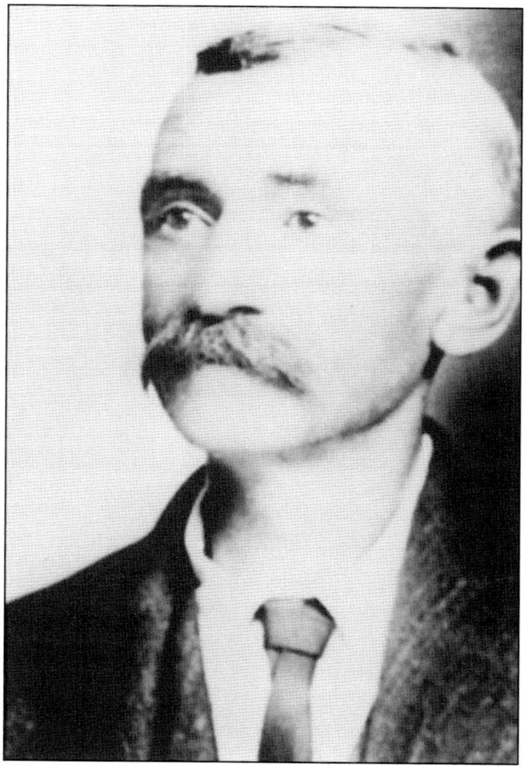

On October 12, 1882, Deputy L.W. Marx arrested Belle and Sam Starr and charged them with horse stealing in the Cherokee Nation. They planned to sell the horses on the McAlester market. Belle accompanied Marx willingly. She felt sure she could prove her innocence in court. A newspaper reported that she looked at Judge Parker with a "bold and fearless glance." Despite this, she was found guilty and sentenced to one year in prison. (Fort Smith National Historic Site.)

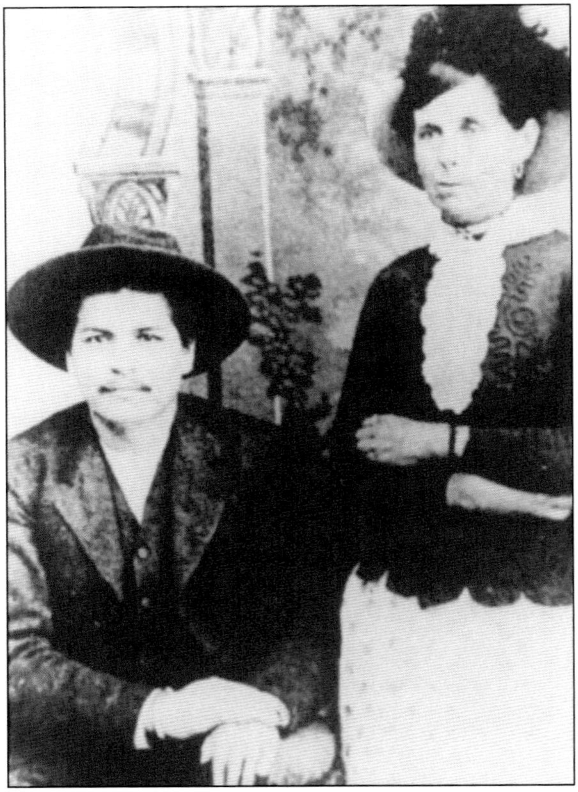

Pictured here are Belle Starr and "Blue" Duck in 1886. Some claim that Bluford "Blue" Duck was another of Belle's suitors; others claim that he was just a friend. Sometimes Belle spent her own money hiring lawyers for her outlaw friends. Duck served eight and one-half years in prison. He developed consumption. When doctors gave him one month to live in March 1895, President Cleveland issued a pardon so he could go home and die among friends. (Fort Smith National Historic Site.)

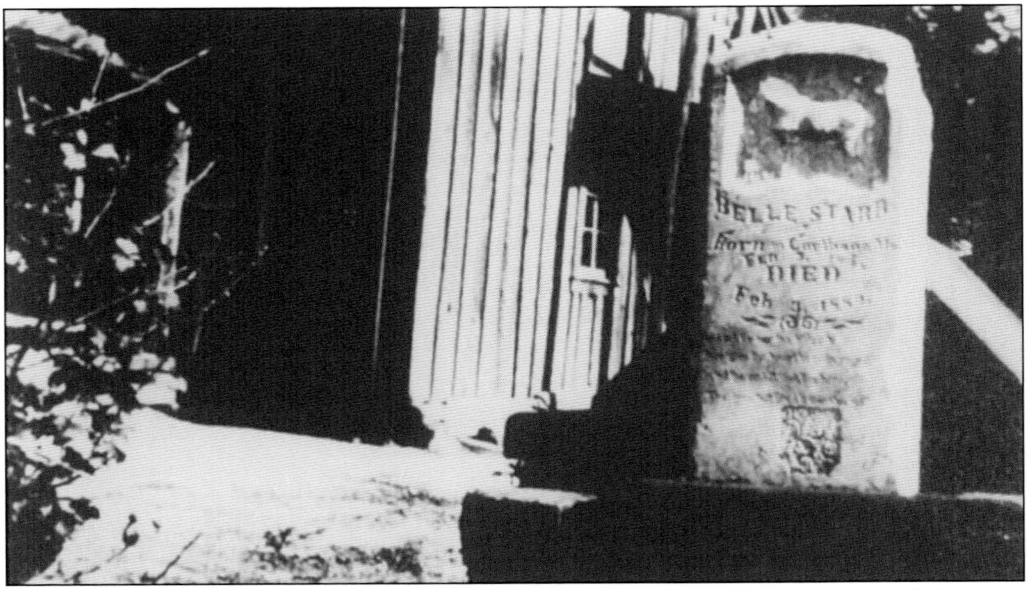

Belle Starr's grave inhabits a lonely, windswept field near Lake Eufaula in Porum, Oklahoma. Belle named it Younger's Bend. The log cabin is gone, but pieces of tin and logs still lie about. Her tombstone simply says, "Belle Starr Born in Carthage, Missouri, February 5, 1848, died February 3, 1889," and these words, "Shed not for her the bitter tear, Nor give the heart to vain regret; Tis but the casket that lies here, The gem that filled it sparkles yet." (Fort Smith Public Library.)

Ed Reed, son of Belle Starr, is believed by many historians to be his mother's murderer. Ed said he would kill Belle for beating him with her horse whip. Ed had abused her prize horse. Although he was convicted and served time for horse stealing, after Belle's death, Ed was appointed a Deputy United States Marshal in 1893. He was murdered on December 14, 1896, by two saloon keepers. Belle's murderer was never brought to justice. (Fort Smith National Historic Site.)

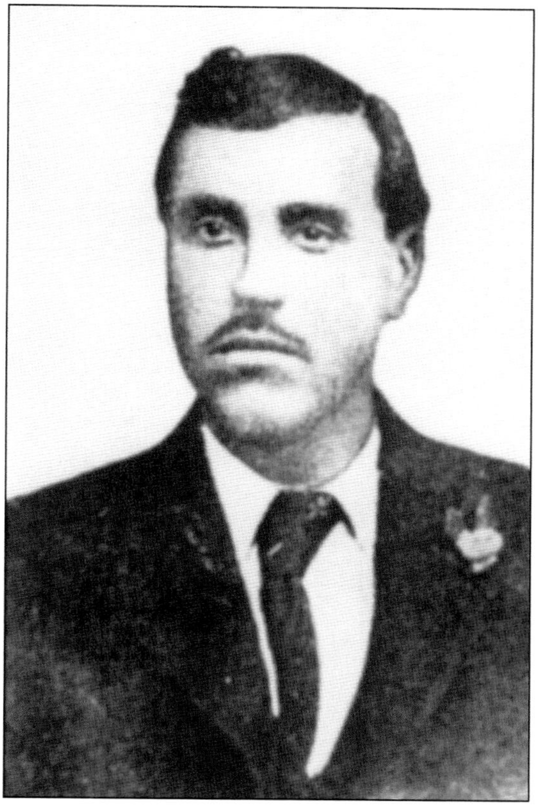

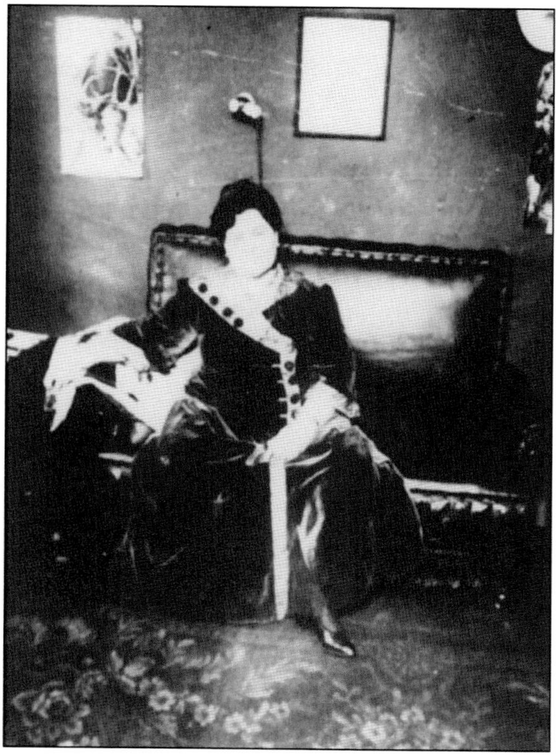

Pearl Starr possessed, among other talents, a shrewd business sense. She purchased and sold property around Fort Smith at a profit. She bought a swanky boardinghouse, "The Flats," on South Fourteenth Street and operated it legally for awhile. When she drifted back into prostitution, she was asked to leave town. Pearl, owner of the first neon sign in Fort Smith, designed for the entryway to her "house" a large, red star and a string of pearls, and outlined them in electric lights. (Fort Smith Public Library.)

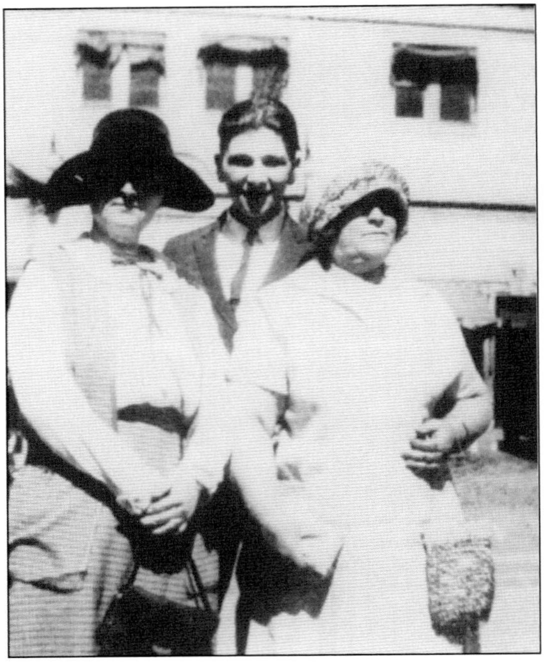

In 1924 Flossie Hutton, on the left, met her mother Pearl Starr for the first time since she was six-months old. Belle Starr, Pearl's mother, took an illegitimate Flossie and put her up for adoption. As a result, Pearl couldn't locate her daughter. The young man in the photo is Robert Hutton, Flossie's son. Pearl died in Douglas, Arizona, in July 1925. She is buried as Rosa Reed. Flossie didn't know Pearl was her mother until she was an adult. (Fort Smith Public Library.)

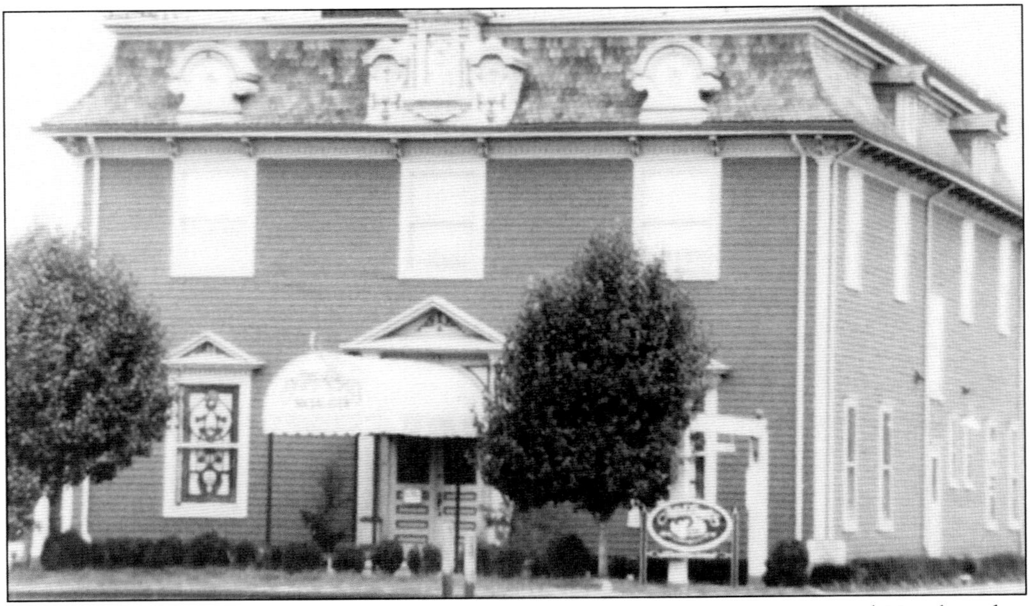

In 1903, Laura Ziegler opened a brothel, known as the Riverfront or Commercial Hotel, with a loan from a local banker, which she paid off in 17 months. That hotel, pictured here in 1977, is known today as Miss Laura's Social Club and Visitor Information Center. It is the only bordello listed on the National Register of Historic Places. The downstairs was used for dancing, singing, and visiting. There are nine bedrooms upstairs. Champagne was chilled in an upstairs bathtub, and guests listened to Fort Smith's first player piano. Open prostitution in Fort Smith has been illegal since about 1915. During "the night of the lingerie parade," in 1910, winds blew flames from an exploded oil tank of the Fort Smith Light and Traction Company and burned three of the brothels. The incident sent partially dressed ladies and customers into the street. (Author.)

Three

Calamity and Opportunity

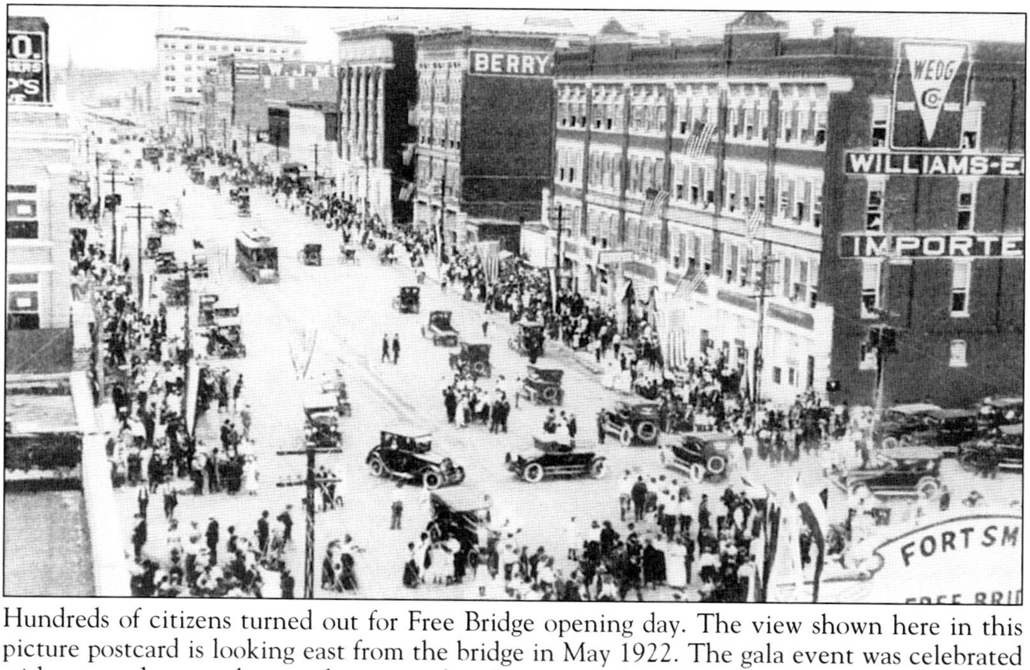

Hundreds of citizens turned out for Free Bridge opening day. The view shown here in this picture postcard is looking east from the bridge in May 1922. The gala event was celebrated with a parade, speeches, and a street fair. It appears that the parade has just concluded. American flags flew from almost every floor, and red, white, and blue bunting decorated the avenue. Prior to the construction of the bridge, people could pay a toll and cross on the railroad bridge from Oklahoma to Arkansas. Money was hard to come by, though. Some families waited until they saw a farmer coming across with a wagon and asked to ride, so they wouldn't have to pay. Before the railroad bridge, folks had to ride the ferry or come across in a row boat. (Fort Smith Public Library.)

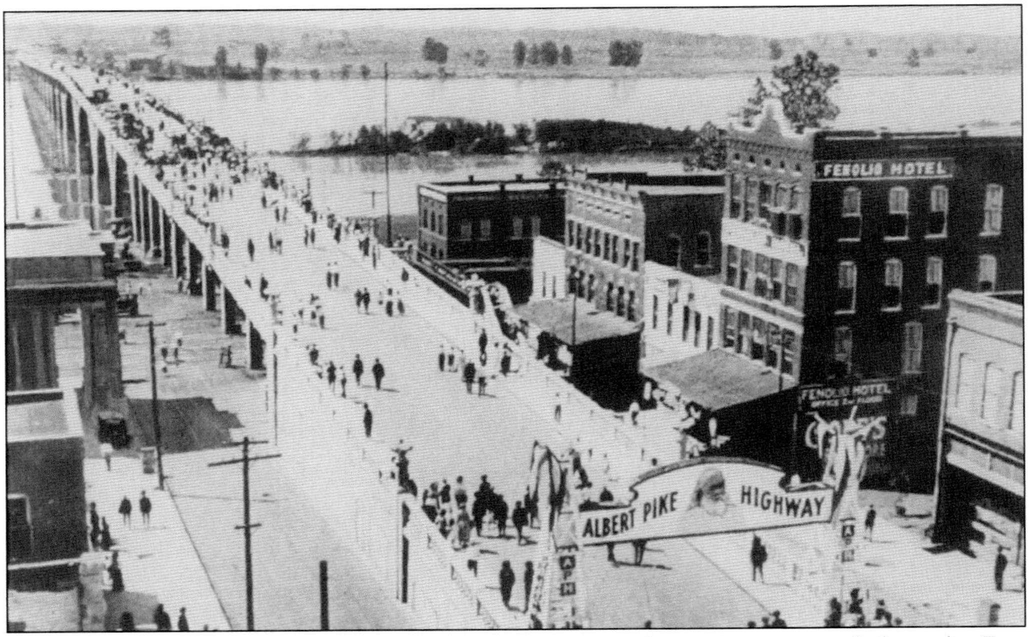

The Free Bridge from Arkansas to Oklahoma is seen in this picture postcard, from the Fort Smith side of the bridge, on May 21, 1923. The view is looking west into Oklahoma. Just five years later, during the flood of April 15, 1927, the Missouri Pacific Railroad pushed 25 loaded coal cars onto the bridge to keep it from being swept away on the swiftly rising water. (Fort Smith Public Library.)

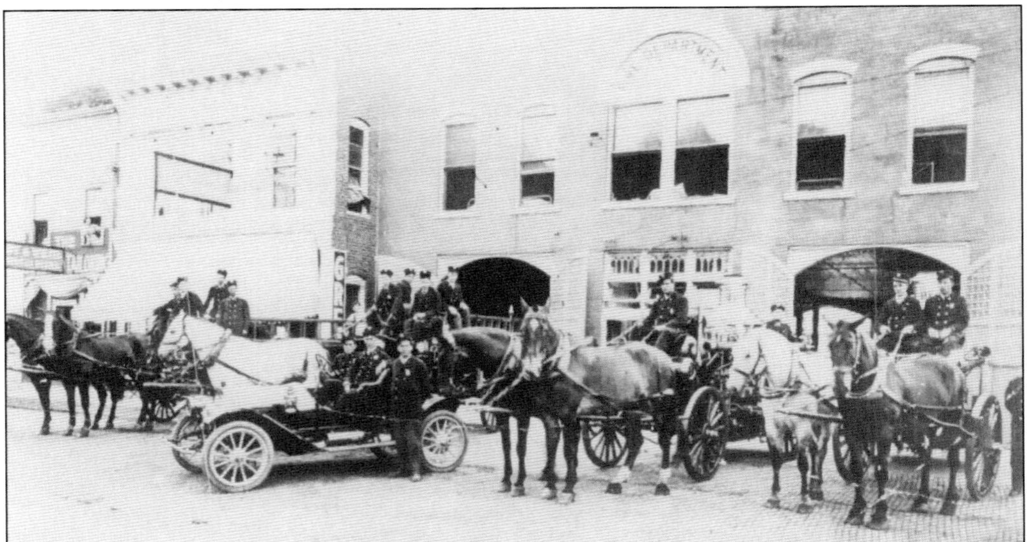

On April 25, 1877, the first volunteer fire department was organized, with James Brizzolara as foreman. J.J. Little was elected Fort Smith's first fire chief. Little continued in that capacity for many years. The first fire department building was constructed in 1879 on North Sixth and Walnut (A) Street. That building is still there today. It was called the Sebastian Fire Company. Shown here is the first chief's car, along with horse-drawn fire wagons, in 1907. Note the people watching from the windows next-door in West and Weir Cleaners, Dyers, and Tailors. (Fort Smith Public Library.)

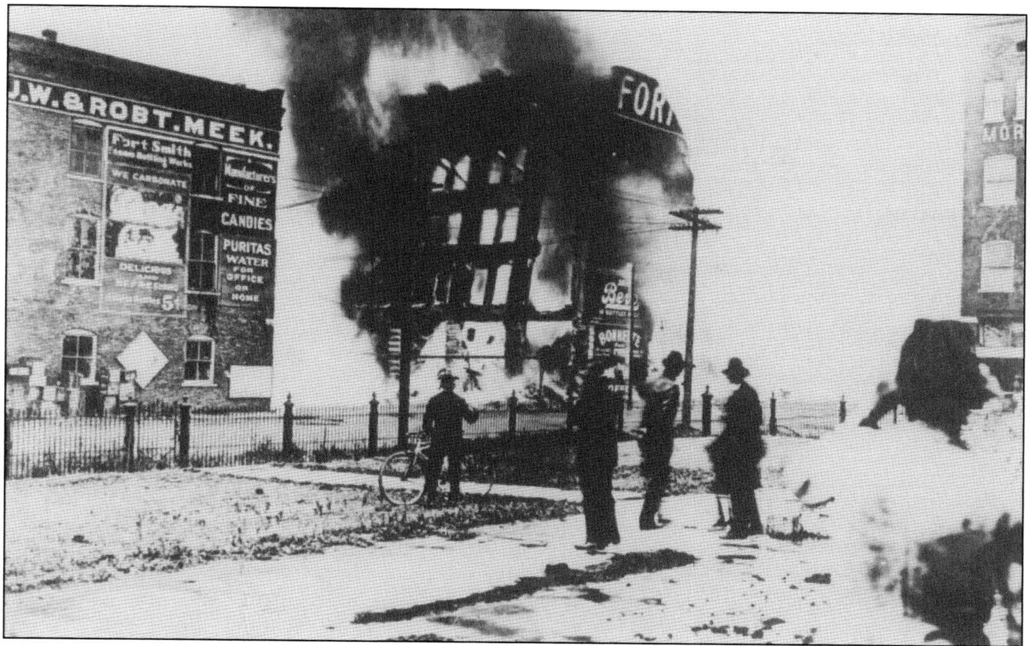

The building of the Fort Smith Commission Company was collapsing when this photo was snapped on October 23, 1918. The blaze was a 32-hour and 10-minutes working fire at South Second and Rogers. The fire spread to the Echols Dry Goods building, where three people lost their lives. Note the J.W. and Robert Meek manufacturers of fine candies to the left. (Fort Smith Public Library.)

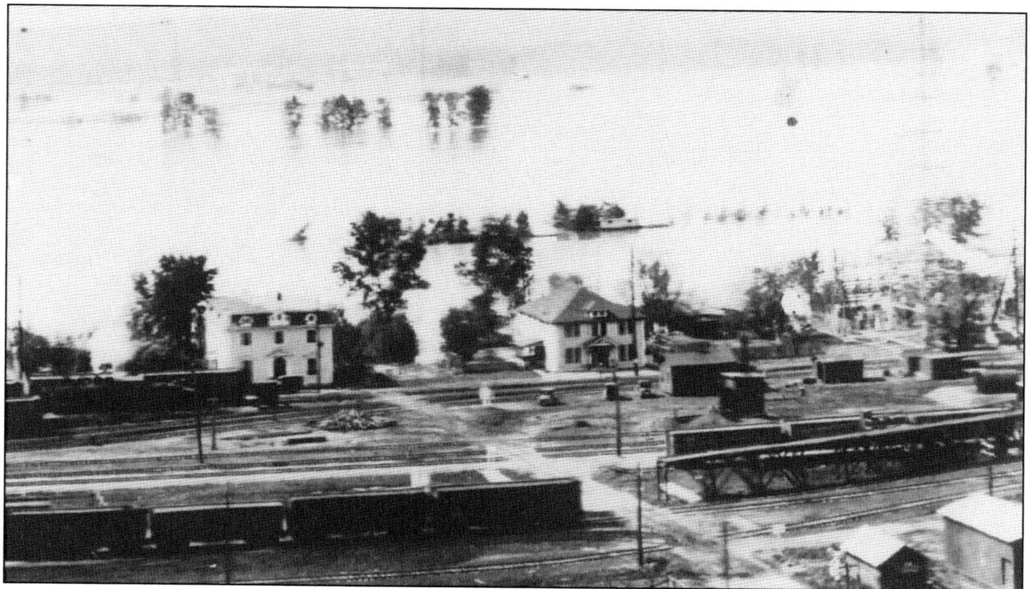

On April 15, 1927, 2 million acres along the Arkansas River were flooded. The majority of the flooding was in eastern Arkansas. As can be seen from this photo, the town of Moffett was under water. The Red Cross aided 166,781 victims of the disaster. The crest of the river flood at 36.7 feet broke the previous record of 1833. All levees between Fort Smith and Little Rock were washed away, and more than 50,000 animals drowned. (K.C. Studio, Fort Smith Public Library.)

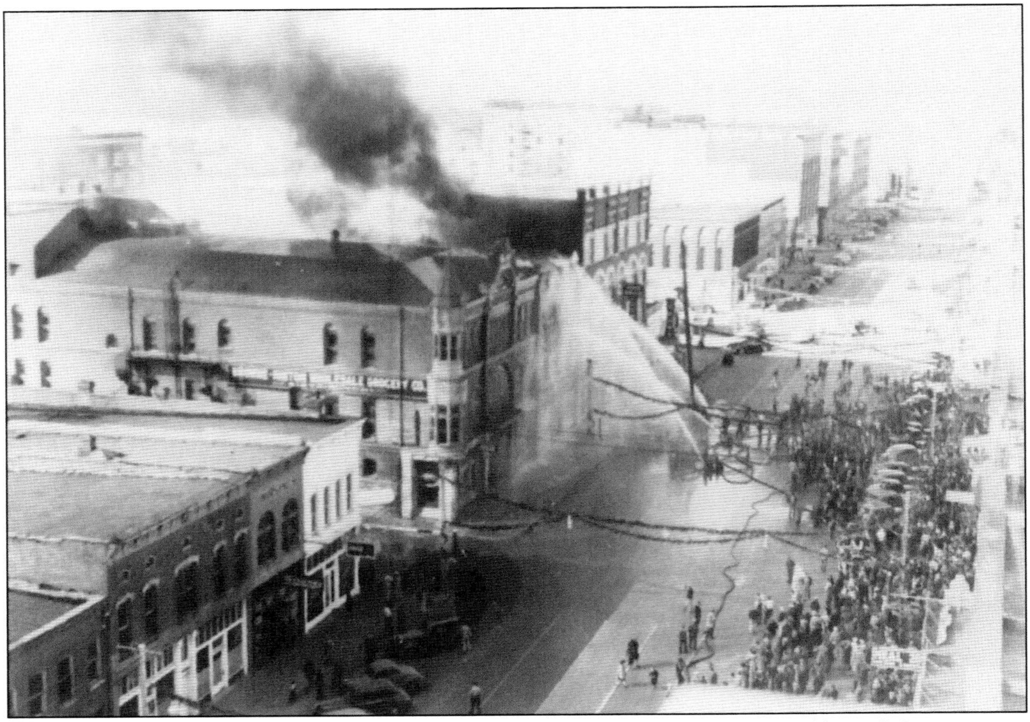

Pictured here is the Stein and Company Wholesale Dry Goods fire, at Fifth and Garrison, in 1941. The building on the corner was once the Grand Opera House, where some of the biggest names in show business performed. At this time it was known as Browne-Hinton Wholesale Grocery Company. Note the large crowds. Fort Smith's disasters have always been well attended. (Fort Smith Public Library.)

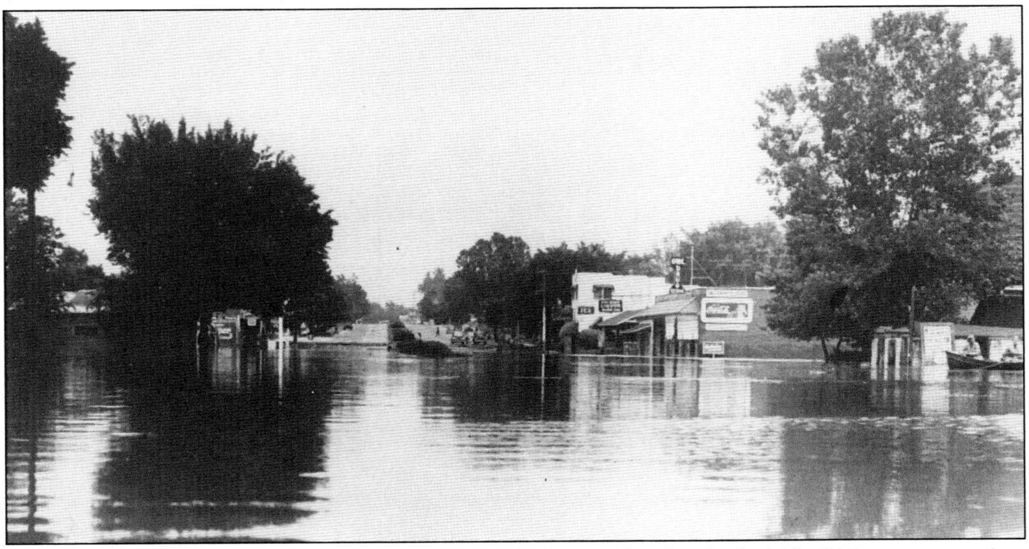

Shown here is the downtown area of Fort Smith during the flood of 1943. Old-timers say that Sixth Street was under water frequently. A total of 19,000 troops were used from the Arkansas National Guard, Camp Chaffee, Camp Robinson, and Camp Livingston to battle the river which crested in Fort Smith at 41.7 feet, more than 4 feet higher than the previously recorded highest crest. (L.V. Marks.)

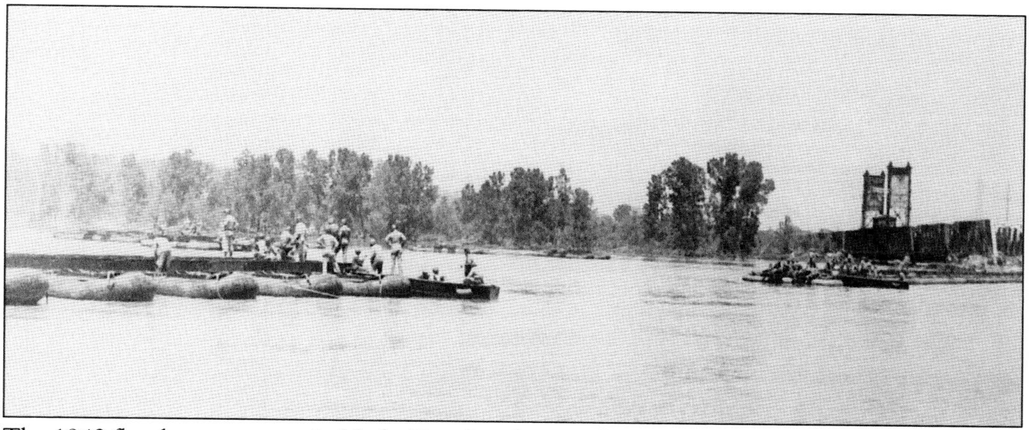

The 1943 flood swept away vital Lake Fort Smith water lines, washed out the south approach to the Van Buren highway bridge, tore out a chunk of the railroad bridge between Van Buren and Fort Smith, and flooded about 600 blocks of Fort Smith property. The Army from Fort Chaffee laid water lines across a pontoon bridge on the Arkansas River, so that Fort Smith and Camp Chaffee could once again have water. (Fort Smith Public Library.)

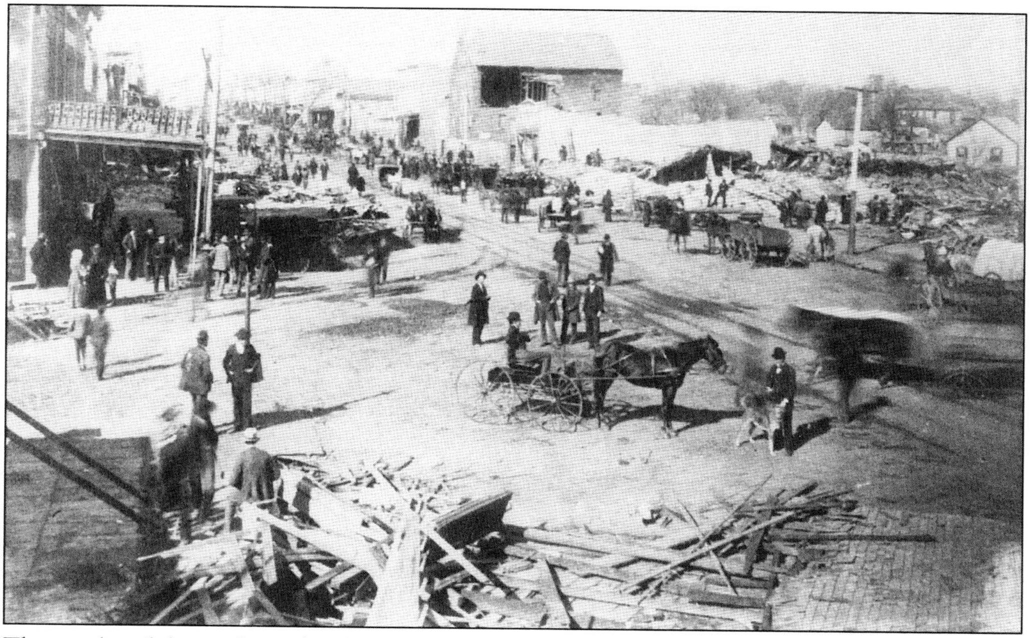

The results of the cyclone that hit the area on January 11, 1898, at 11 p.m., are shown in this photo. The view is looking south at the intersection of what is now Towson and Garrison. At that time it was called Texas Corner, due to the presence of the old Texas Road. The storm progressed through the National Cemetery, from the old Belle Point site, and collided with the avenue between Texas Corner and the Arcade Building. It destroyed Judge Parker's home, now the location of the present KFSM-TV Studio. It made kindling wood of the First Baptist Church on Thirteenth and D, and almost demolished the three-month-old Fort Smith High School building on Fifteenth Street. Fifty-one people were killed. The greatest loss of life occurred in business buildings located on the north side of Garrison Avenue, near Texas Corner. Those buildings had apartments on the second floors. The next day there was a long line at Birnie's Funeral Home, as citizens identified deceased family members. (Fort Smith Public Library.)

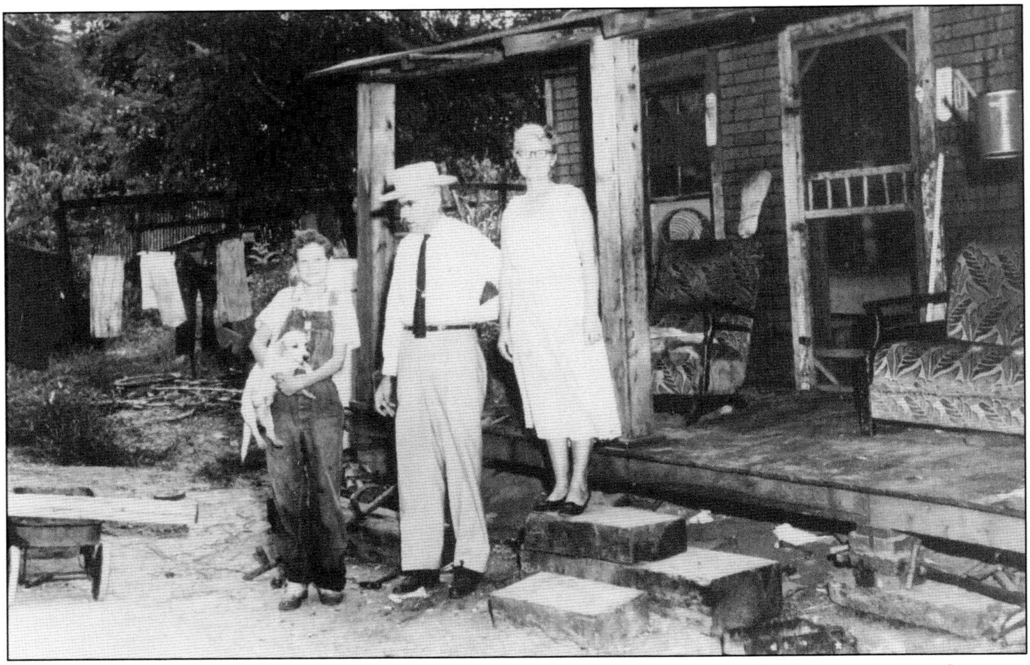

In the beginning, the strip of land called Coke Hill was part of the Choctaw Nation. Since it was on the Arkansas side, it became a no-man's-land, and squatters began to build homes there. Shown here are residents of Coke Hill and R.K. Rodgers, *c.* 1950. Rodgers was chairman of the Coke Hill Clearance Committee. Note the toy army truck near the steps. Coke Hill fell before the bulldozer in 1958. (Fort Smith National Historic Site.)

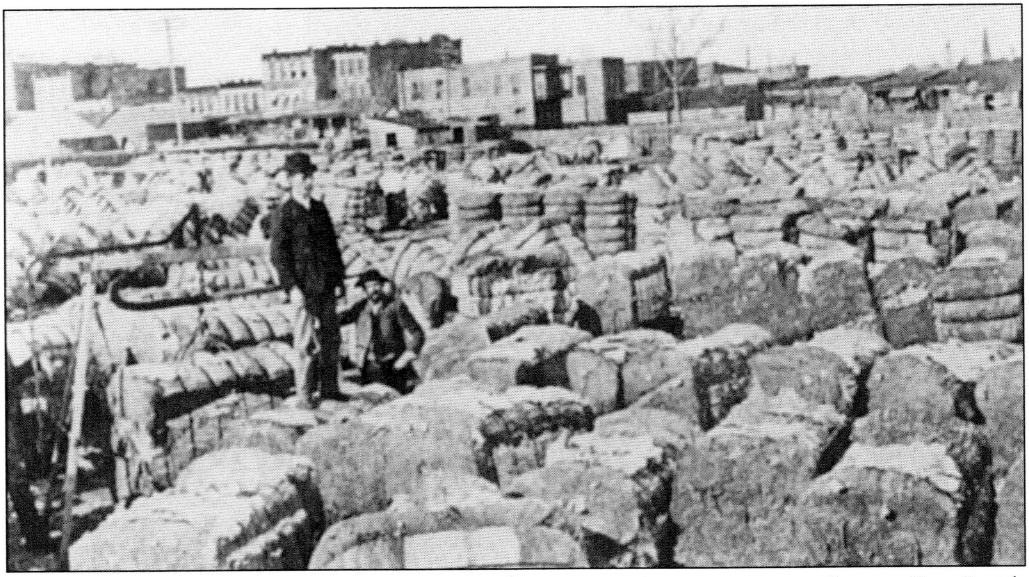

Shown here in a picture postcard is a Fort Smith cotton yard, covering several acres. Fort Smith had the largest cotton compress in the world before the turn of the century. The compress processed 40 bales of cotton per hour in May 1882. One of the old cotton company buildings still exists near the riverfront. The DuVal Family was involved in the cotton compress business and owned their own wharf due to the high level of cotton traffic they handled. Note the church spire in the distance. (Fort Smith Public Library.)

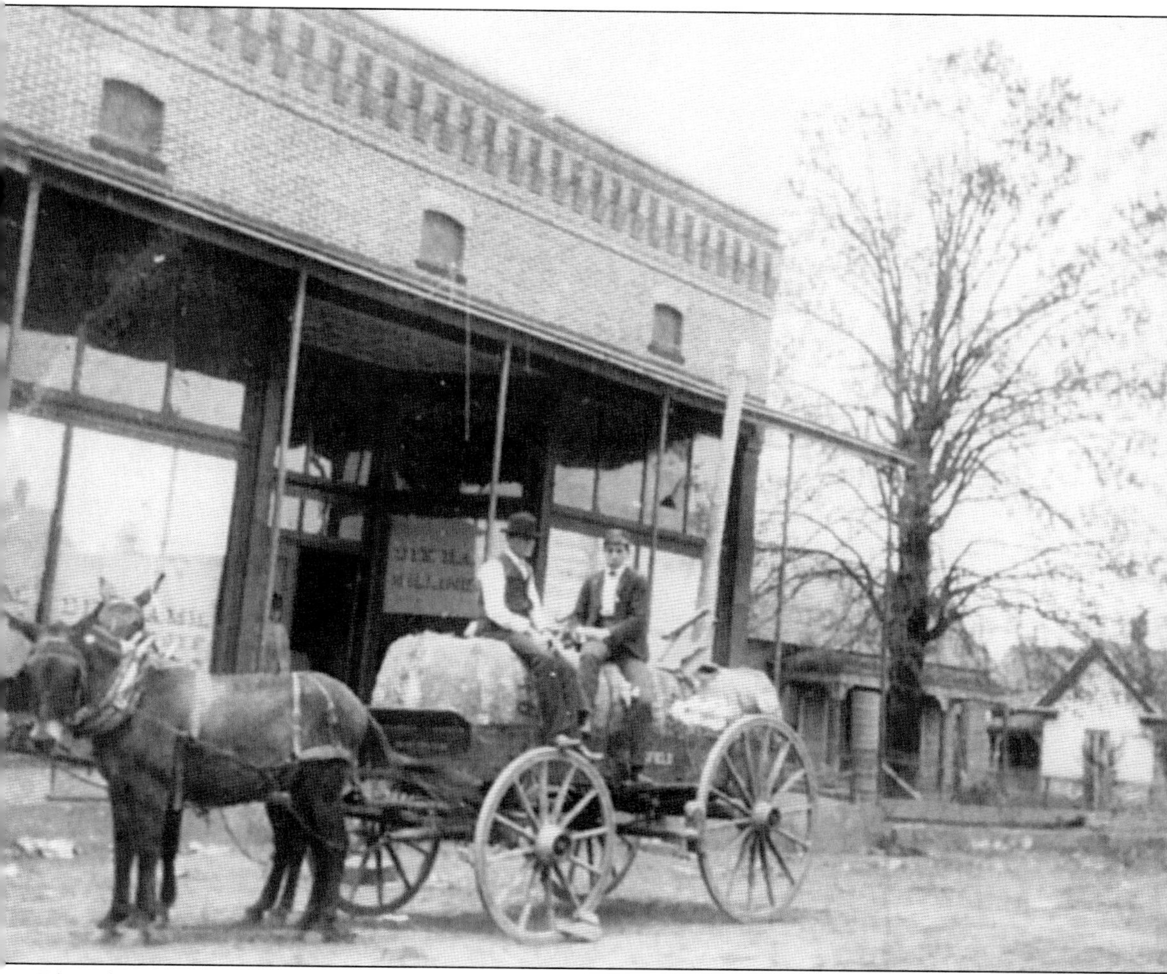

This photo is of two young farmers, identity and date unknown, bringing their cotton crop to one of Fort Smith's many cotton factories. In July 1884 alone, 200 bales of cotton were shipped to Liverpool, England, from Fort Smith. A cotton compress burned in the 1940s, and flames spread to a large portion of the downtown area. (Fort Smith Public Library.)

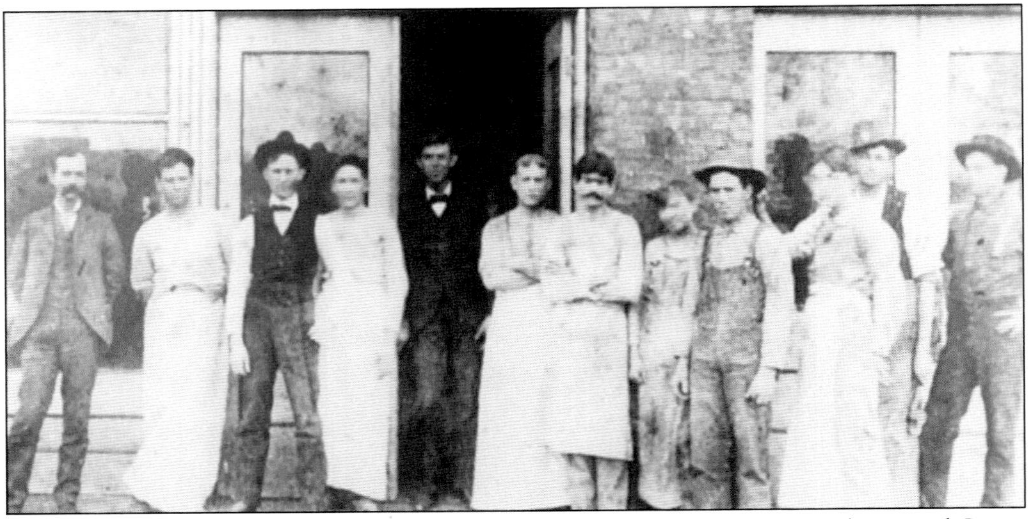

In 1899, the Meek family constructed a three-story factory building at South Second Street and Rogers Avenue. It was the J.W. and Robert Meek Manufacturing Confectioners and Fort Smith Steam Bottling Works. It later became the Coca-Cola Bottling Company. The building was constructed over portions of the barracks and reserve of the old fort. Meek's employees are shown here at the turn of the century, with J.W. Meek to the extreme left and Robert in the doorway. (Coca-Cola Bottling Company.)

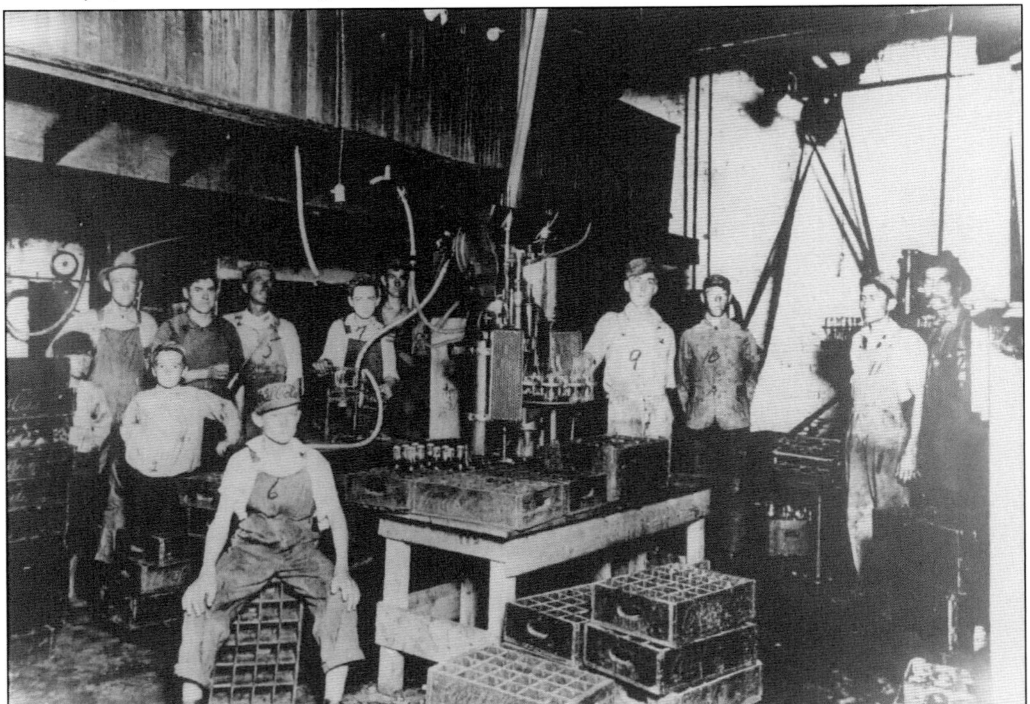

This is a photo of the interior of Meek's bottling works. The boy with the number nine is George Wolfe, and number 11 is John Lampkin. Note the youth of some of the workers. The plant was first known as the Fort Smith Steam Bottling Works, and they were the original bottlers of Coca-Cola in the area. Bobby Meek and Roger Meek, grandsons of the company's founders, are today the managing partners. (Coca-Cola Bottling Company.)

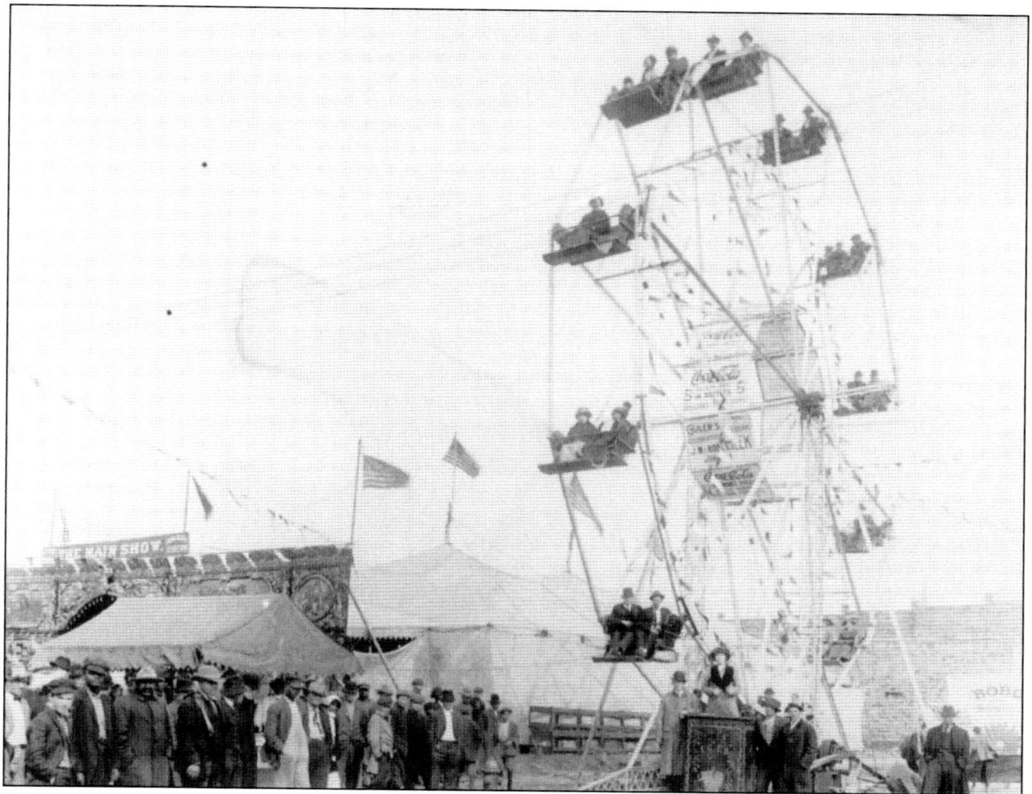

This circus was set up on Texas corner at Tenth and Garrison Avenue. The Ferris wheel seems to have been sponsored by Coca-Cola. Signs encircling the center of the wheel advertise J.W. and Robert Meek Soda Water Pure Food Products, and Gulers Celebrated Ice Cream, and Coca-Cola made with Puritas water. Those riding the wheel are probably the executive staff of Meek Bottling Company. Note the bird dog on an upper seat of the Ferris wheel, and the cultural diversity of the crowd. (Fort Smith Police Department.)

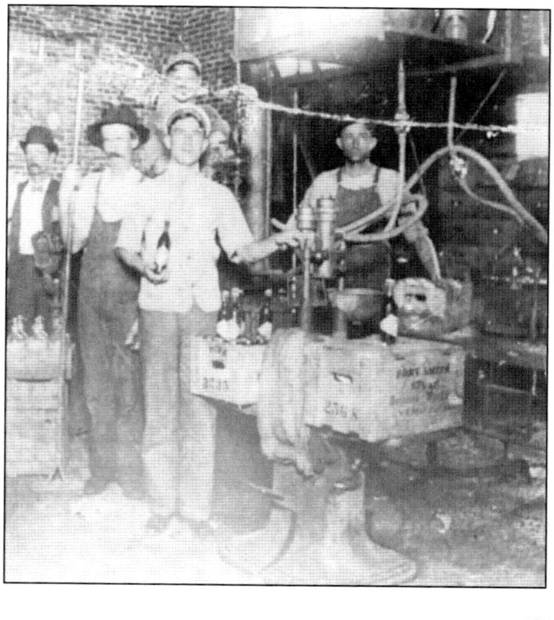

This image, taken *c.* 1916, shows the foot-powered bottling machine, inside the Coca-Cola Bottling plant on South Second and Rogers Avenue. The young man is holding a turn-of-the-century bottle of Coca-Cola. It looks like a Tabasco sauce bottle. The box says Fort Smith Steam Bottling works. This is the third floor of the plant, and the two gentlemen in the front are Barney and Tom. Obviously, the bottling conditions were not as sanitary as they are today. (Coca-Cola Bottling Company.)

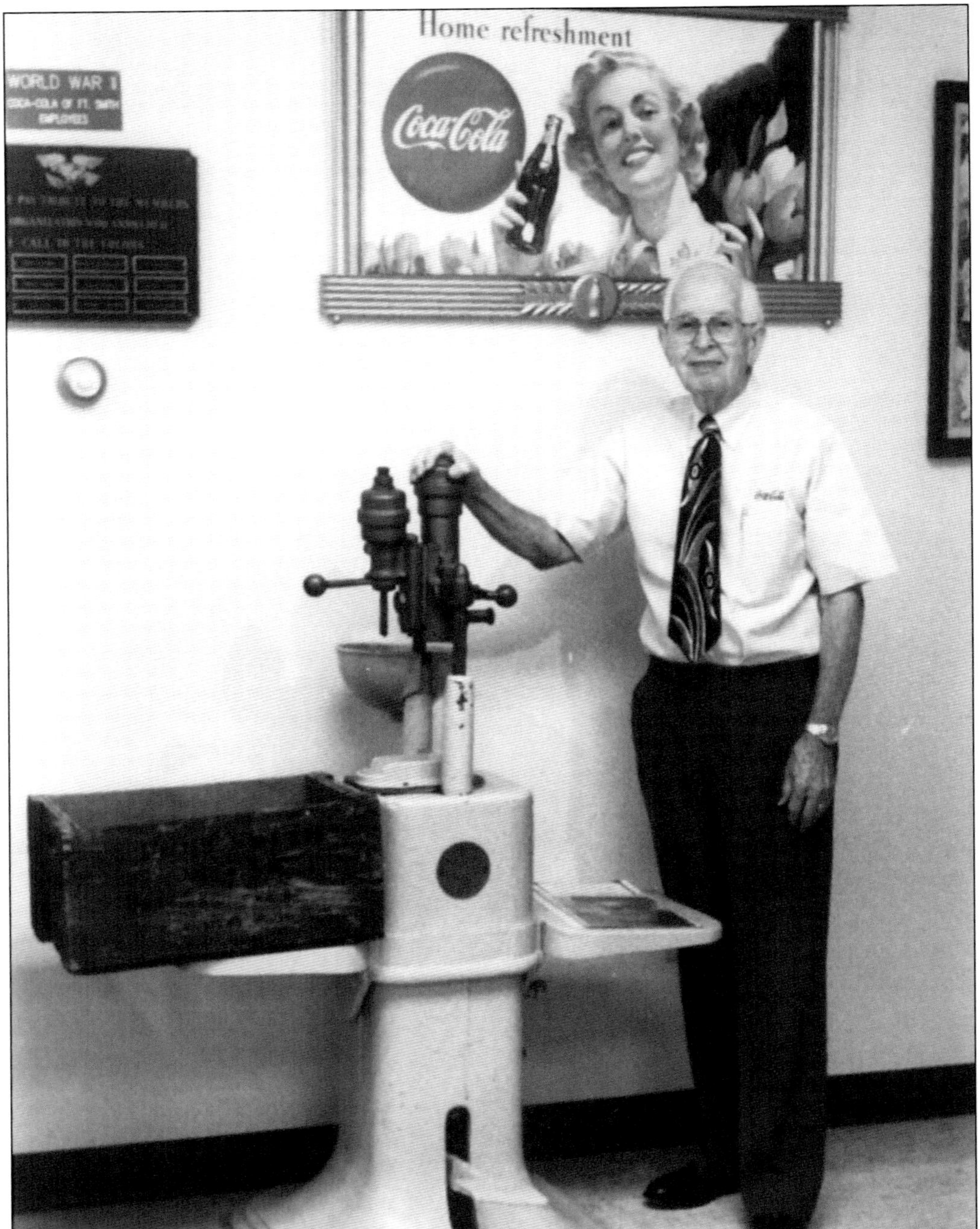

A foot-powered bottling machine, or step bottling machine, is shown here in 1998 with consultant Fred Kirkpatrick. The machine, or one like it, was used in the Coca-Cola plant around 1916. It can be seen at the Museum of Coca-Cola Memorabilia on Phoenix Avenue, at the plant. Kirkpatrick is retired from Coca-Cola and devotes his time to the collection and maintenance of the artifacts of the Museum of Memorabilia. In the museum can be seen such items as metal serving trays distributed by Coca-Cola, calendars with featured models, Coca-Cola radios, commemorative and presentation bottles from around the country, many signs used by Coca-Cola, and other items too numerous to mention. (Author.)

Anna Heim Sharum and Bernadine Merkle Werner pose for a promotional photo under the Coca-Cola sign at the plant on South Second Street. They are standing on the front bumper of an old Dart Automobile around 1917. (Coca-Cola Bottling Company.)

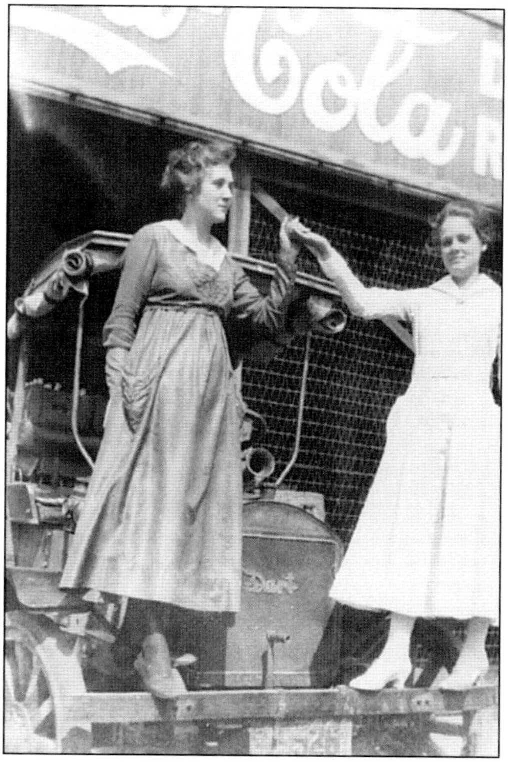

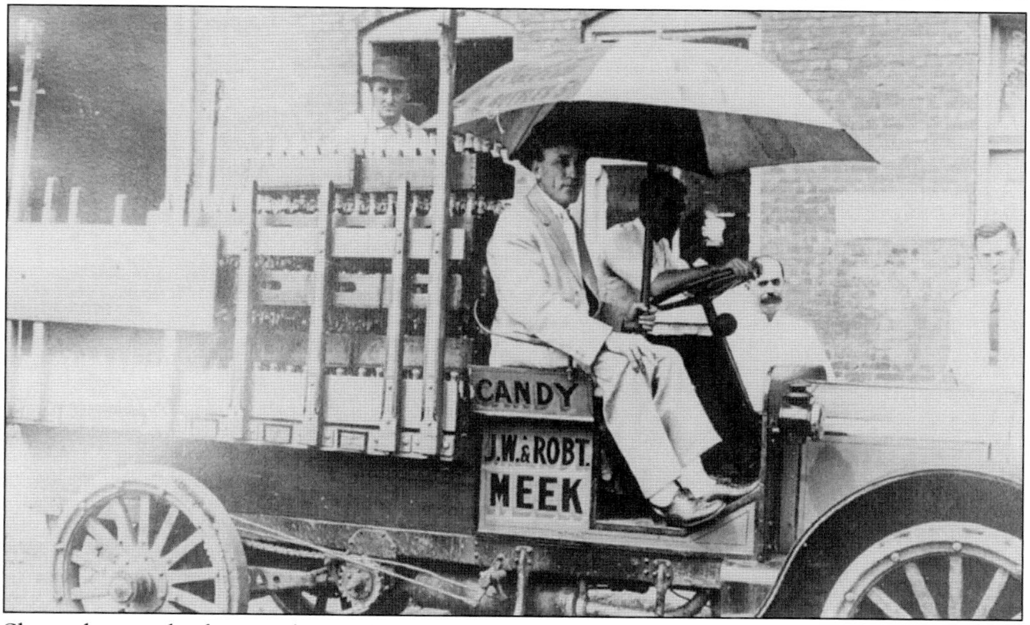

Shown here is the first mechanized Coca-Cola delivery vehicle in Fort Smith, *c.* 1915. Note the chain-driven wood and rubber wheels. J.W. Meek, with mustache, is shown here at the Second Street bottling works. The first deliveries were made by horse and wagon. Deliveries to some out-lying towns were made by rail prior to the trucks. Barrels of 18-dozen bottles, with the glass much thicker and heavier than now, and in cases of three- and six-dozen bottles, were shipped. (Coca-Cola Bottling Company.)

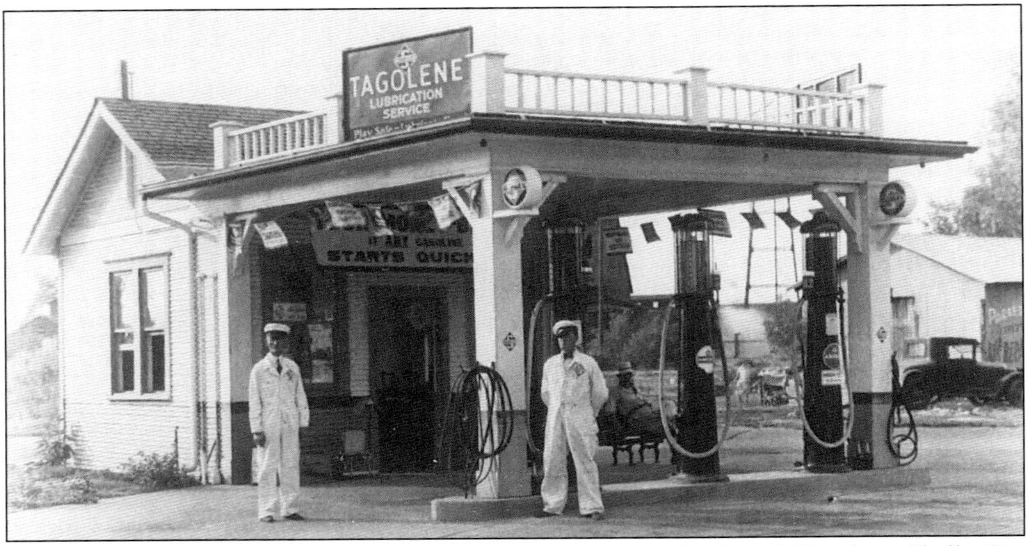

Frank Golden, on the left, and Don Bias were partners in this leased Tagolene Skelly Gas Service Station, which faced Midland Boulevard, *c.* 1935. The gentleman in the background is unknown. Next door was Harding Glass at Midland Boulevard and Kelley Highway. Service station attendants took great pride in their well-starched and ironed uniforms. The service stations were also neat and clean. Note the gasoline pumps with glass containers on top. (Lillian Golden Hissom.)

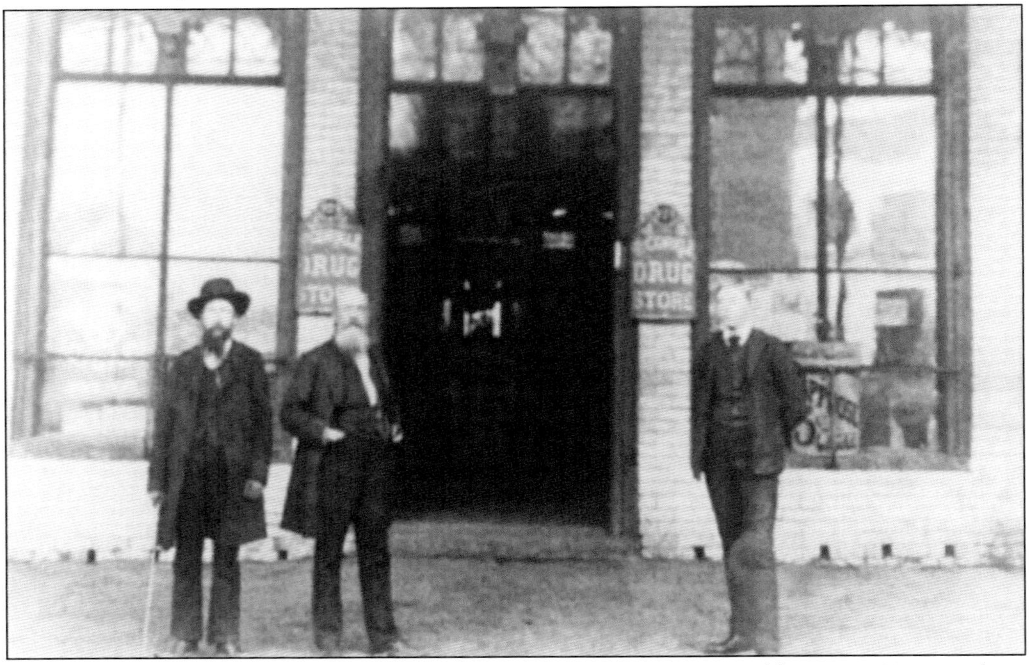

McCorkle's Drug Store was located at 1006 Garrison Avenue. Pictured here, *c.* 1904, are, from left to right: unknown, Dr. Jacoburn Stewart McCorkle, and Will Cruse. Dr. McCorkle was born *c.* 1835 in Mississippi, and attended Jefferson Medical College in Philadelphia. He graduated from the Nashville University in Tennessee in 1860. Dr. McCorkle's license was recorded in Sebastian County on March 16, 1895. He was a physician, druggist, and dentist. (Fort Smith Public Library.)

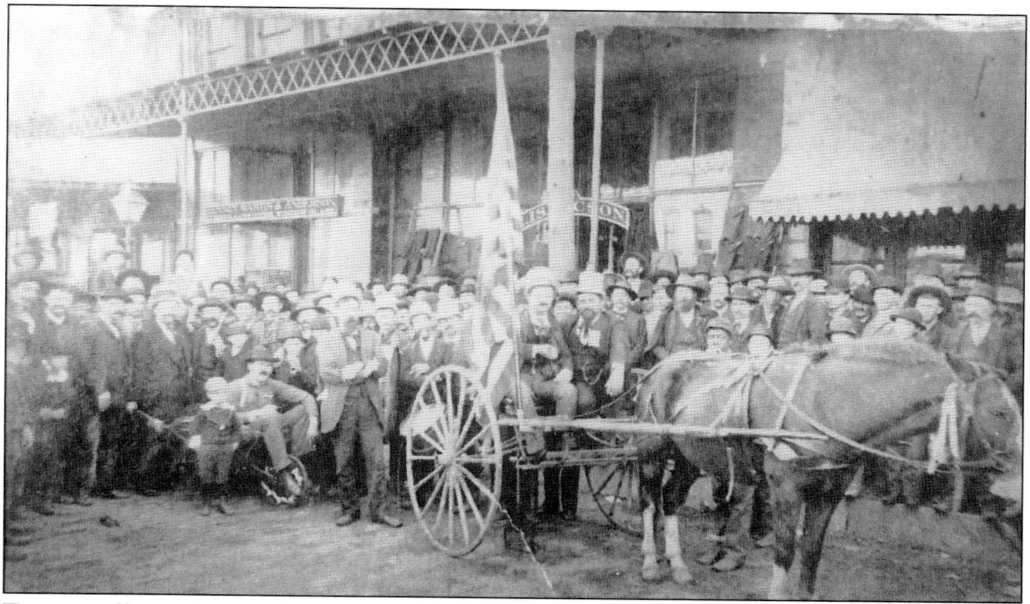

To pay off an election bet, Mayor James Brizzolara had to drive John Fuller, seated in wheelbarrow, up Garrison Avenue, *c.* 1880. The man seated in the wagon is Sam Edmondson. At left is Tim Bishop and, holding the handles of the wheelbarrow, is Mayor Brizzolara. Note that only a few people in this photo are bare-headed. (Fort Smith National Historic Site.)

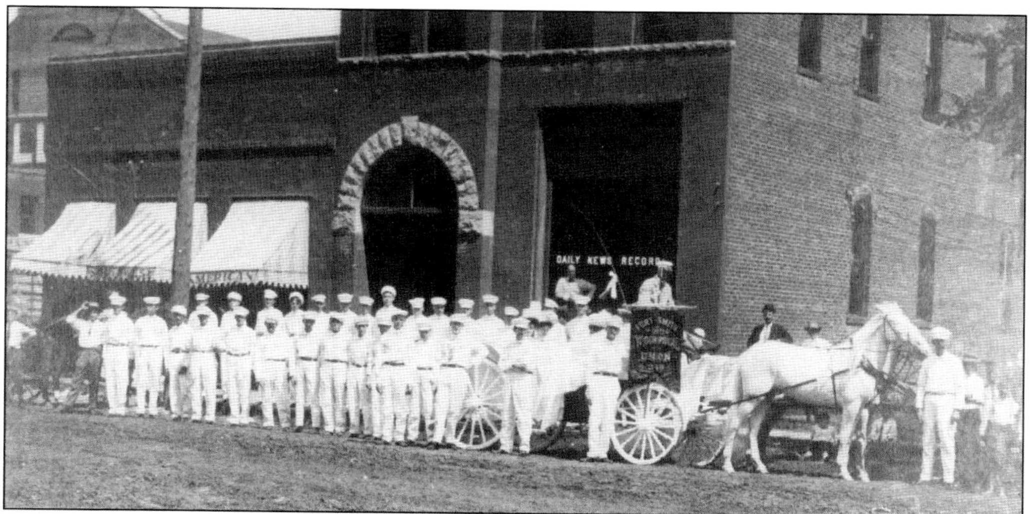

Shown here is the *Times Record* newspaper building, located at 505–507 Rogers Avenue, next door to the Southwest American building. The scene is the September 9, 1908 Labor Day Parade, featuring the queen of the parade, Mrs. Louise Boyd, who is seated. The sign on the wagon says, "Fort Smith Typographical Union 249." Driving his Tally-Ho Wagon is John B. Williams. Employees of the newspaper worked very hard. Over half of the newspaper's reading columns were devoted to flat-plates of type-metal shipped from Little Rock by train. The plates hauled to the depot by horse and wagon contained serial stories, feature articles, recipes, puzzles, jokes, and pictures. This material was called "boiler plate" by printers and newspaper people. It was very heavy. The plates were used, melted, cast into "pigs," and shipped back each day, so the metal could be recycled. (Fort Smith Public Library.)

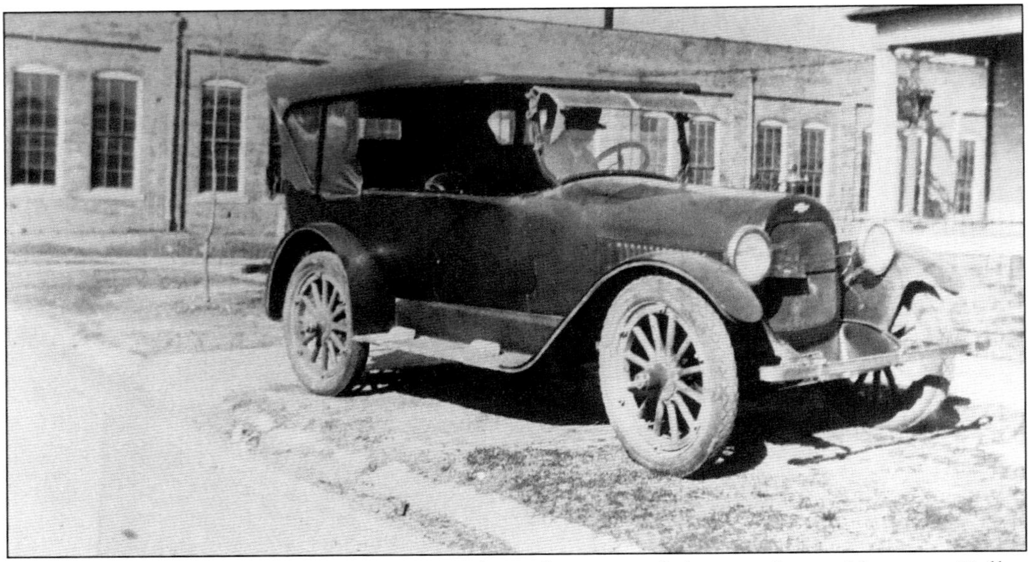

Henry Killion is shown in this c. 1924 Chevrolet automobile near his residence at Kelley Highway and Midland Boulevard, in Fort Smith. Note the trolley barn in the background. Killion was foreman of the pressroom of the local newspaper. He owned many new automobiles, purchasing them the moment they came on the market. (Lillian Golden Hissom.)

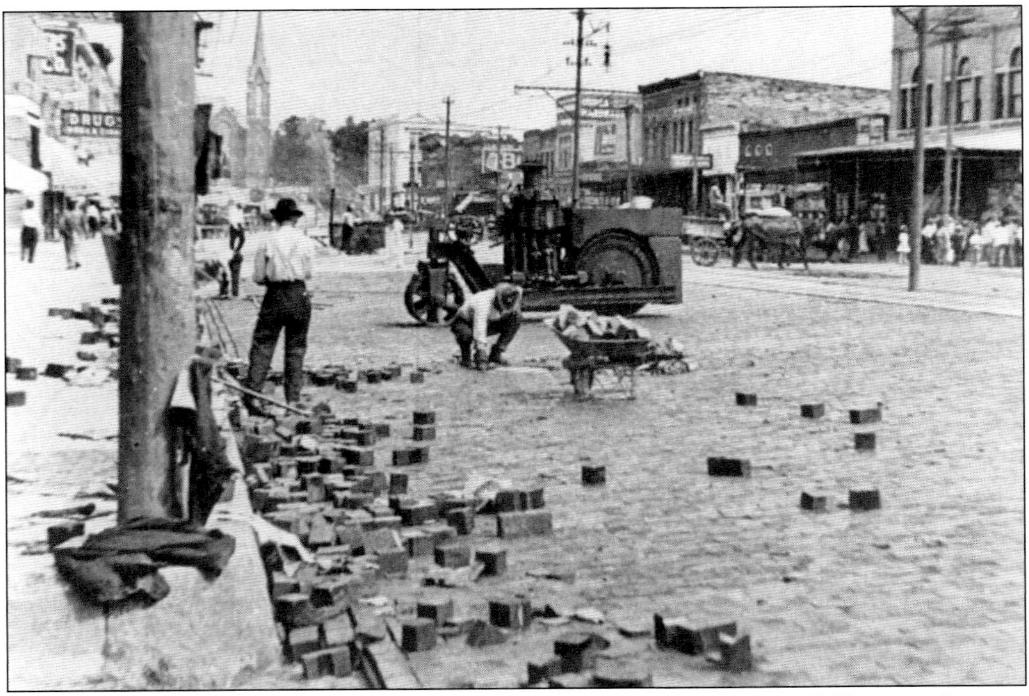

At one time, a creek ran across Texas Corner at Eleventh Street and Towson Avenue. Wooden, creosoted blocks used to pave the streets, would wash out during floods and travel downstream. Afterward they would have to be put back into place. Sometimes they would disappear altogether, and more would have to be made. When the city paved the streets with cement, many of the old wooden blocks were left in place. (Lillian Golden Hissom.)

Four

FAITH AND STRUCTURE

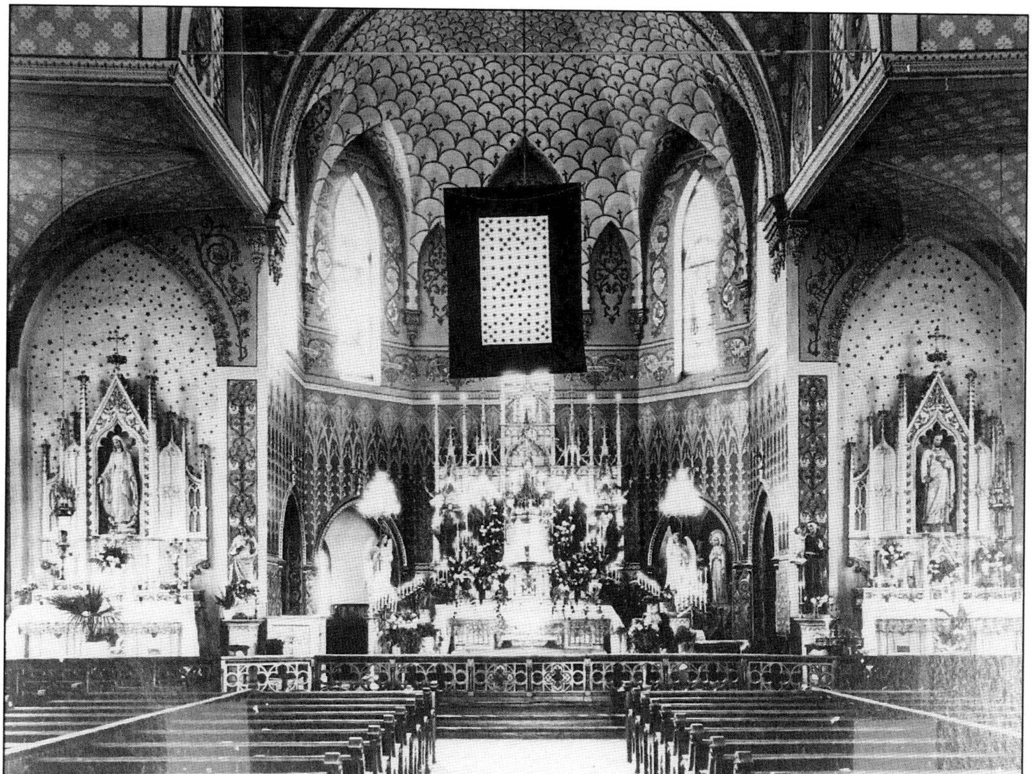

The beautiful interior of the Church of the Immaculate Conception is shown here in 1917. The banner hanging over the altar has a star to represent each soldier from the church who served in World War I. The church has been through several renovations, one of which stripped all vestiges of fine trappings from the vestry, including the side altars. This was done to destroy all show of affluence during the Depression. The location of those altars is a mystery today. (Jerry and Wincie Hendricks.)

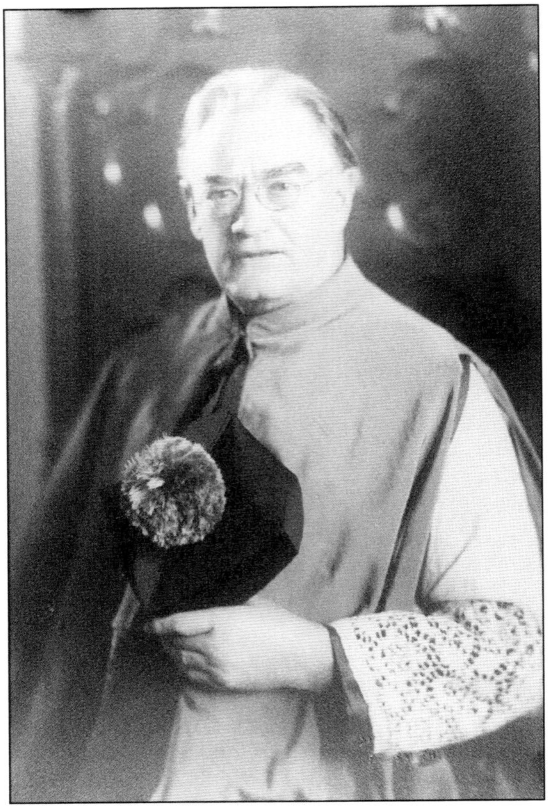

Father Patrick Horan was born on December 2, 1866, in Birr, Ireland, and ordained on June 11, 1892. He became pastor of the Church of the Immaculate Conception in 1906. He did interior redecoration of the church and strengthened the walls, and was responsible for installing the rock wall around the cemetery and for affixing the cross at the church's front entrance. Father Horan was also known for giving away his possessions. One time he gave a needy family his bed and had to sleep on the floor. (Jerry and Wincie Hendricks.)

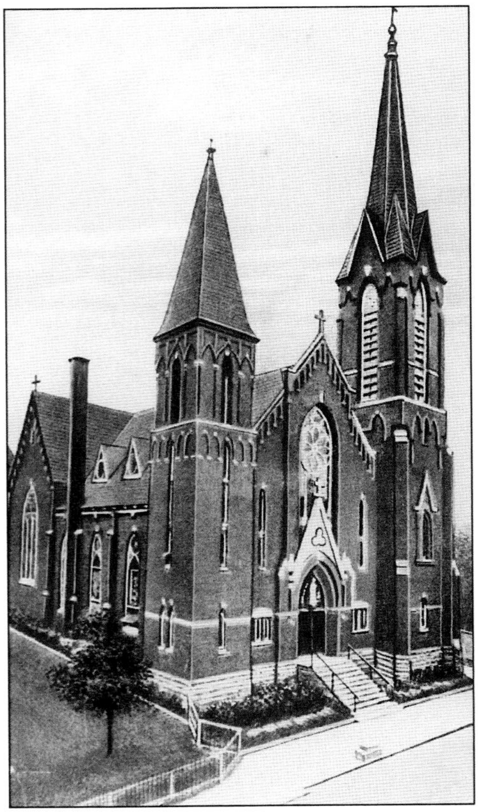

The Church of the Immaculate Conception was built in 1898, during Father Lawrence Smyth's pastorate. He was pastor for 38 years and died in 1900. Immaculate Conception Church, as shown in this picture postcard, is Fort Smith's best-known landmark due to its location at the end of the avenue, its towering spires, and its inspirational beauty. The tallest spire is 110 feet in height, and the other is 85 feet. (Jerry and Wincie Hendricks.)

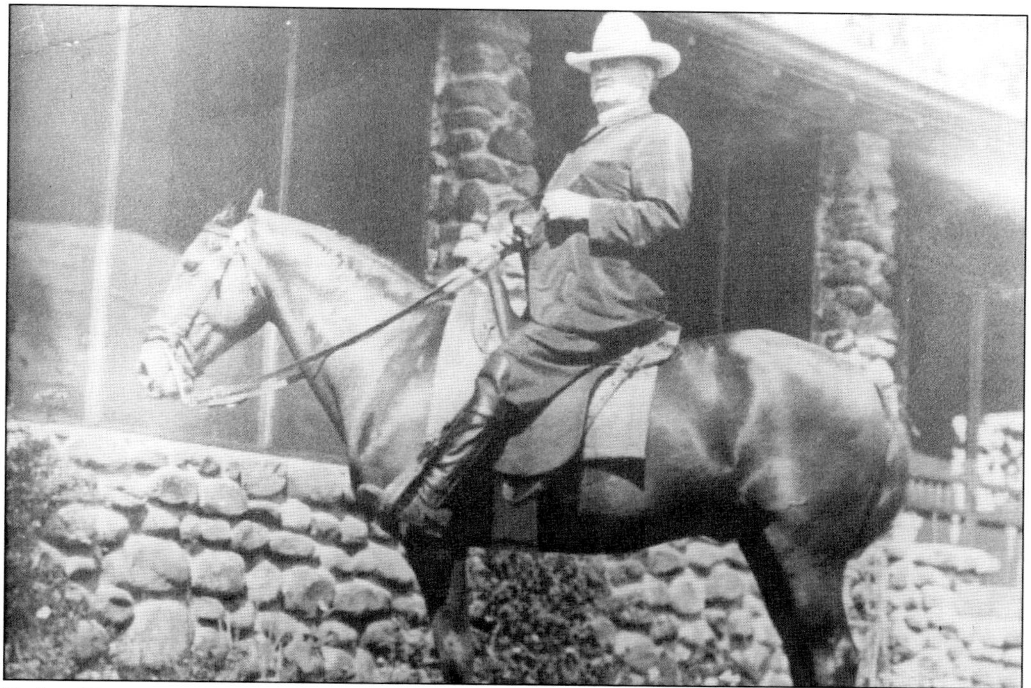

Father Horan spent as much time as he could spare at his rustic home on Wildcat Mountain. Riding his horse Kate was one of his diversions. He was active in all ward drives during WW I. Father Horan's judgment and advice were sought by Catholic and non-Catholic alike. He had a remarkable memory and was fluent in Latin, German, and Italian. He had a huge personal library and was one of the outstanding personalities in the history of Arkansas' Catholic clergy. (Jerry and Wincie Hendricks.)

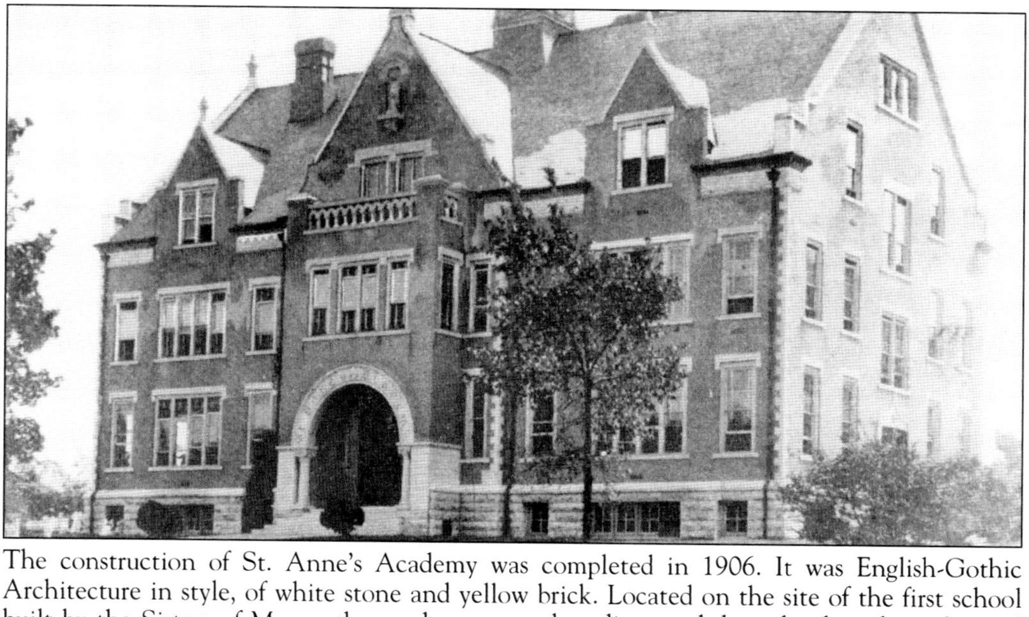

The construction of St. Anne's Academy was completed in 1906. It was English-Gothic Architecture in style, of white stone and yellow brick. Located on the site of the first school built by the Sisters of Mercy, the academy was a boarding- and day school, and was located east of the Church of the Immaculate Conception. It was razed in 1974. (Fort Smith Public Library.)

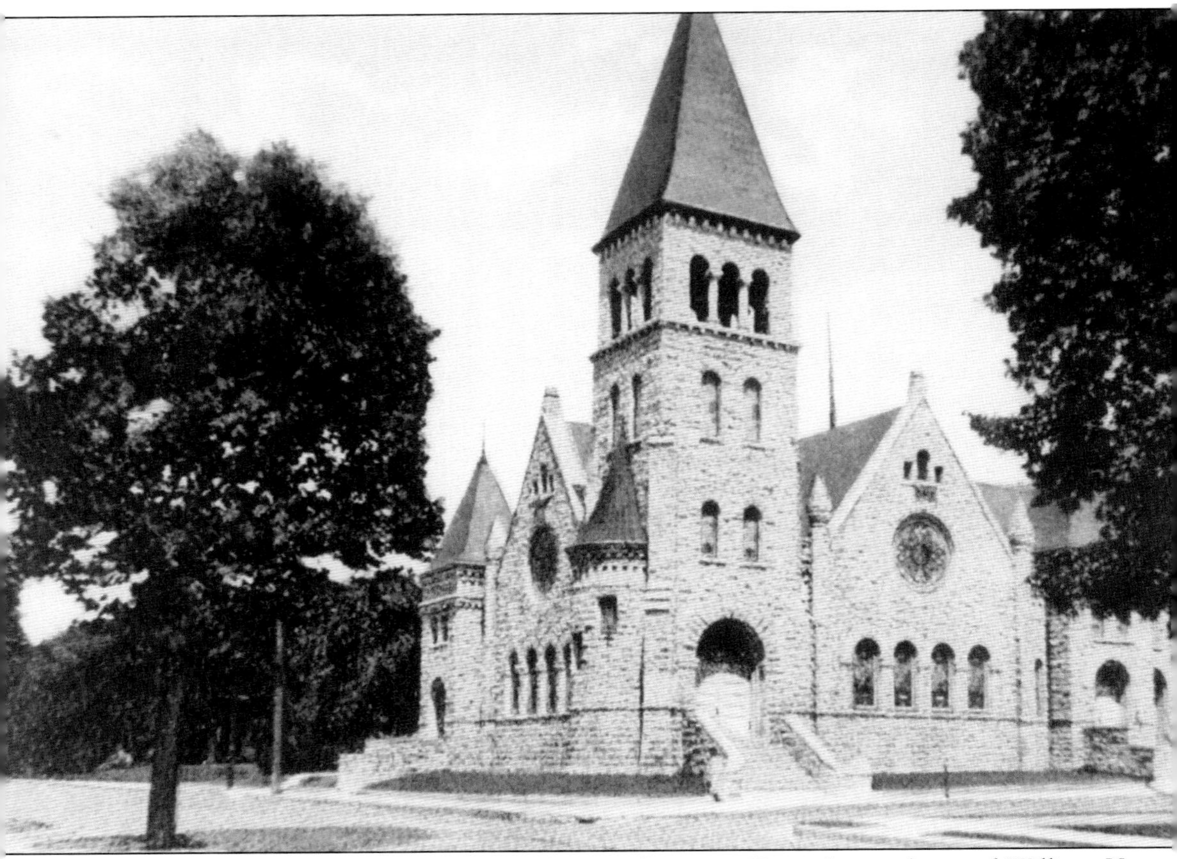

The First Baptist Church was organized December 1, 1857, at the residence of William H. Byers. In 1860, Reverend R.L. Compere was called as pastor of the church. In March 1869, the congregation bought two lots on the corner of North Thirteenth and Grand Avenue and began building their auditorium. Due to the upheaval of the Civil War, the building was not completed until 1885. On Tuesday, January 11, 1898, at 11:15 p.m., a cyclone crossed the city from west to east. It destroyed 100 homes and 4 churches, including the First Baptist Church. A few days prior to the event, a man had announced that God would probably destroy the church because the members refused to repair it. The Baptist congregation met in other churches until the new limestone church, which no longer exists, was completed on October 22, 1899. The Baptists used to preach from the "Cyclone Bible," which had survived the cyclone and served to remind them of what had come to pass. (Fort Smith Public Library.)

The Union Church, built in 1842, was the first house of worship in Fort Smith. Joseph Bennett, a pioneer merchant, was responsible for its construction. The church was used on alternate Sundays by different denominations. Members were called to worship by an old African American, Uncle Majors, who blew a long, tin horn. Uncle Maje, as he was later called, belonged to Joseph Bennett. The building was later owned by the Presbyterians, and then it became the Cleveland Hotel. (Fort Smith National Historic Site.)

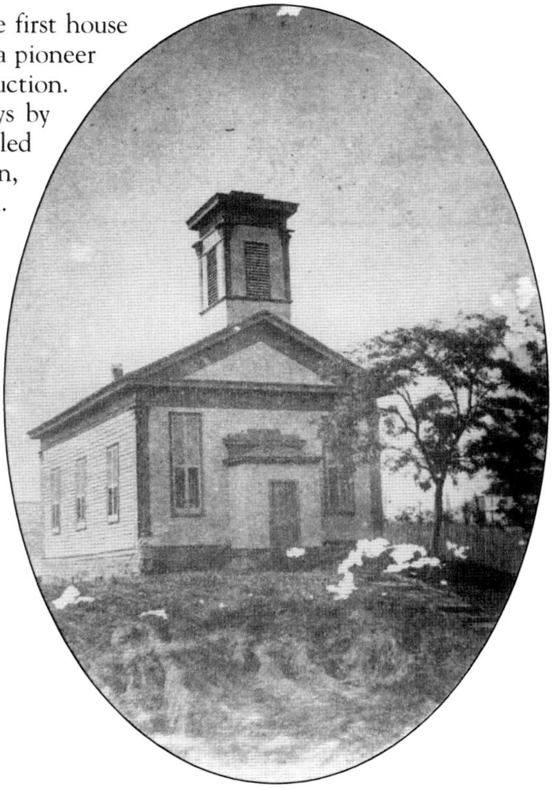

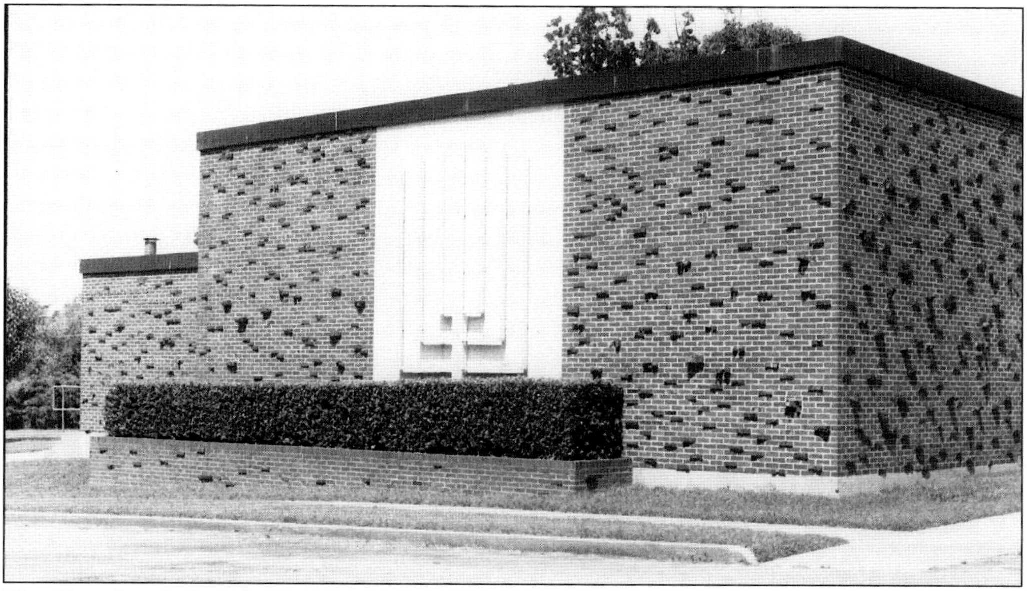

The Fort Smith Jewish Synagogue, located at 1126 North Forty-seventh, was built in 1957. The first temple was erected in 1892, and no longer exists. Since its inception, the Jewish congregation has been Reformed, or Liberal. Jewish settlers migrated to Fort Smith as early as 1845. An early pioneer was Edward Czarniknow. Several businesses were established by Jewish residents. Rudolph Ney was head of Boston Store Dry Goods, and I. Isaacson operated a mercantile business. (Author.)

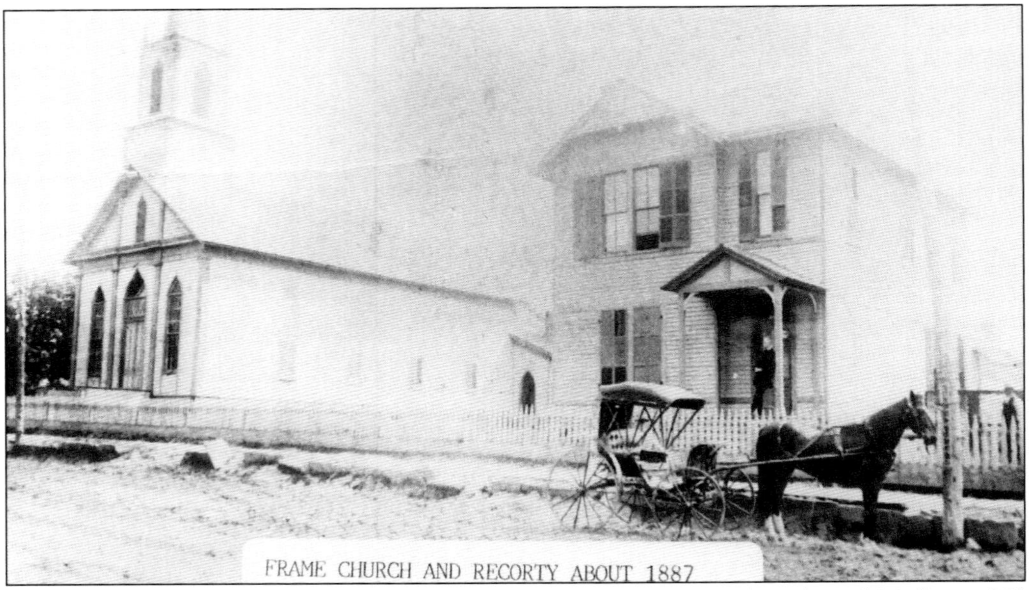

St. John's Episcopal Church was erected 1859–60, on the corner of Sixth and Mulberry (C) Streets. A mission was established there around 1845. The first frame church and rectory are shown here *c.* 1887. In 1997, St. John's Episcopal Church reached its 150-year anniversary. One of St. John's present missions is ministering to, and feeding, the poor and homeless. The first Episcopal services in Fort Smith were held in John Rogers City Hotel. (Fort Smith Public Library.)

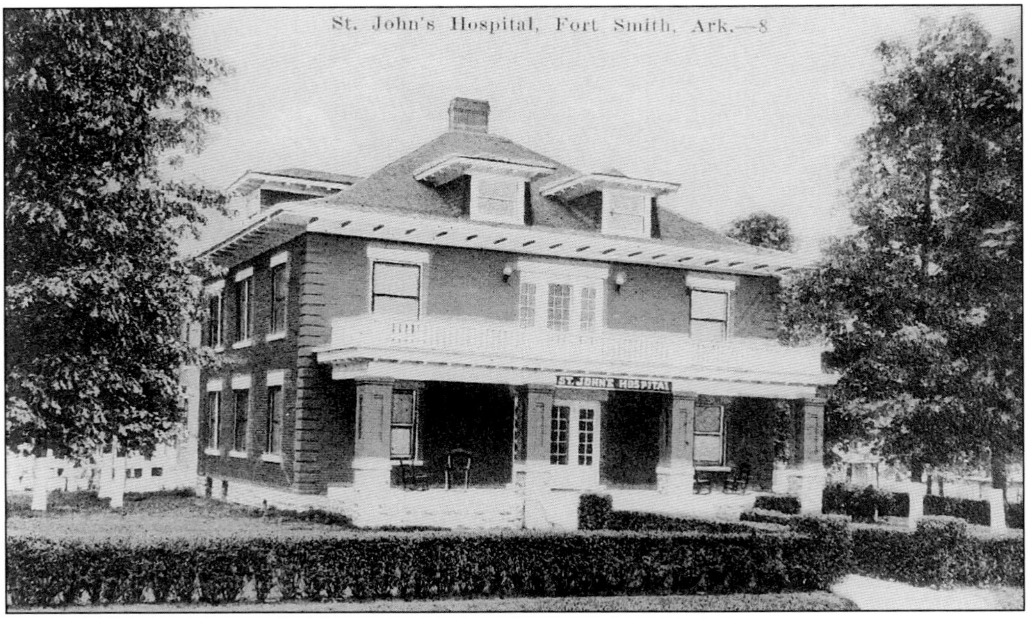

Arkansas's first hospital, St. John's, is shown here in a picture postcard. It is known today as Sparks Regional Medical Center. A railroad worker needed foot surgery here in 1887, and Reverend George F. Degan and his wife raised $500 to pay for the surgery and to rent the Nedry Building at Fourth and G Streets. They named the hospital St. Johns. A year later they moved the hospital to 302 Second Street. In 1899, St. Johns consolidated with Charity Hospital under the name Belle Point Hospital. (Fort Smith Public Library.)

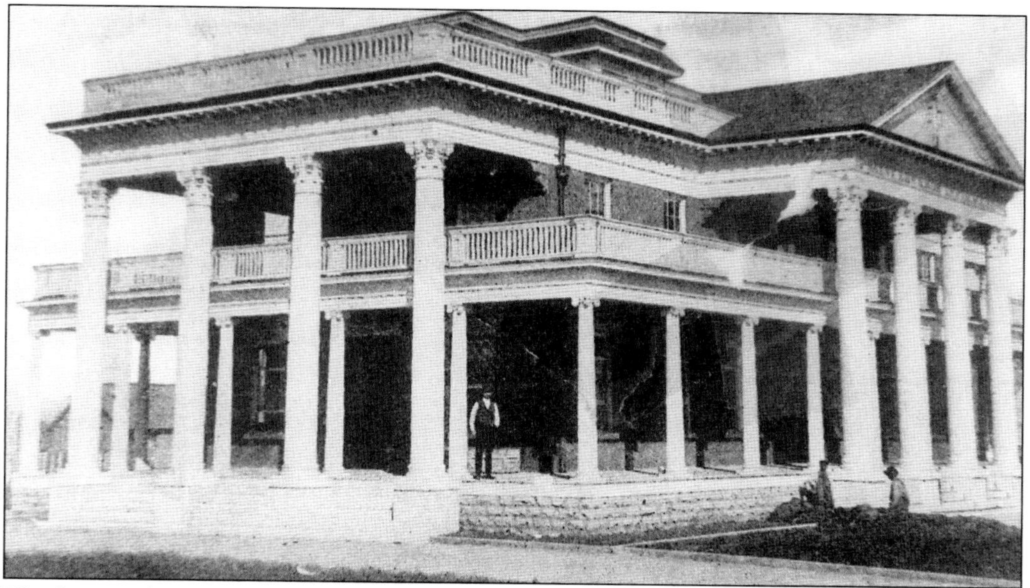

The Sisters of Mercy ministered to the sick, wounded, and dying during the Civil War. In 1869, they erected a two-story frame building on the site later occupied by St. Anne's Academy. They converted their convent into an infirmary, and the frame building was moved to Fifteenth Street. It was remodeled, faced with brick, and enlarged, with wide porches supported by large, white columns. To honor Bishop Edward Fitzgerald, the new hospital was named St. Edward Infirmary. (Fort Smith Public Library.)

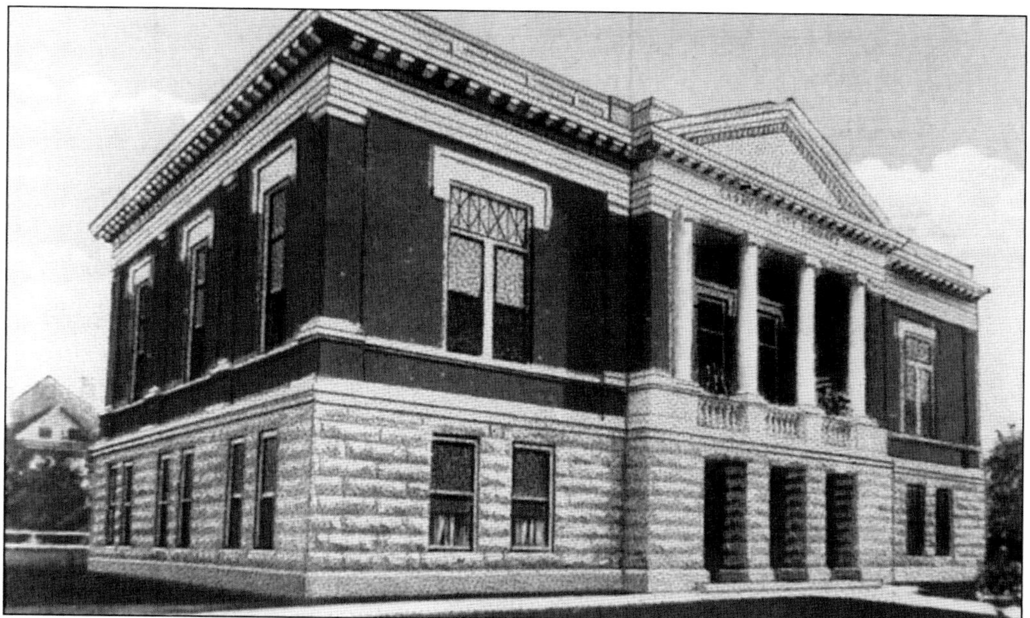

Fort Smith Public Library, shown in this picture postcard, was the first Carnegie Library built in Arkansas. Eight women, with Mary Parker, Judge Parker's wife, as president, organized the Fort Nightly Club in 1888. Years later, the women raised $4,750 to buy the Judge Isaac Parker home site from a now-widowed Mrs. Parker. A cyclone had destroyed the Parker home in 1898. The Carnegie Library cornerstone was laid in 1907. (Wayne Bledsoe.)

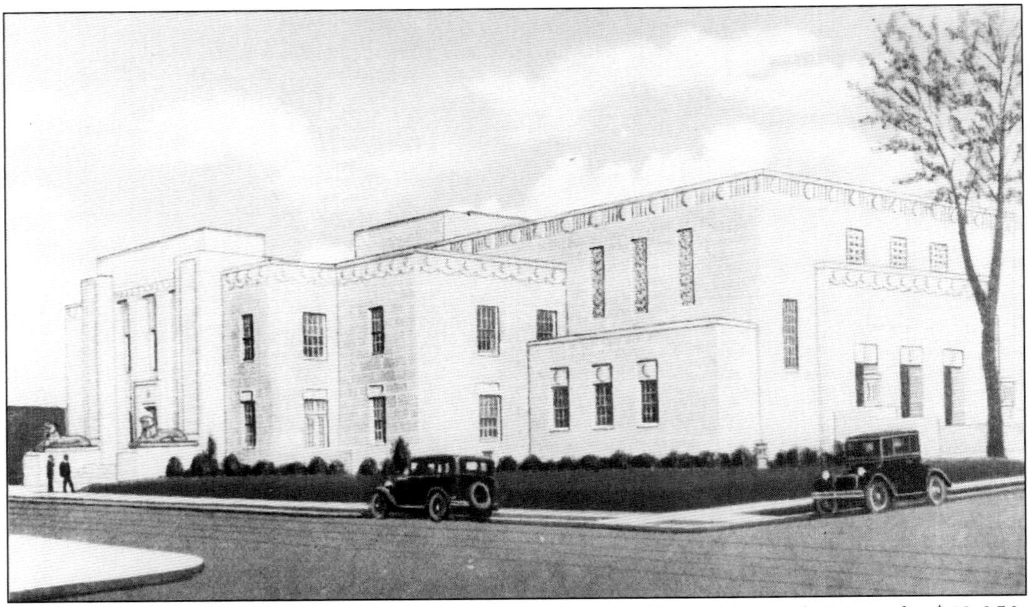

On February 13, 1928, the Masons bought a half block on North Eleventh Street for $49,250. The Masonic Temple, built of Bedford Stone, is shown in this picture postcard taken not long after completion. The building cost approximately $400,000 to construct and furnish. The temple was dedicated by the Grand Lodge of Arkansas on September 9, 1929. It has 50 rooms and compartments, 2 stories, and a basement. The auditorium seats 900, with supplementary chairs for 1,200. (Fort Smith Public Library.)

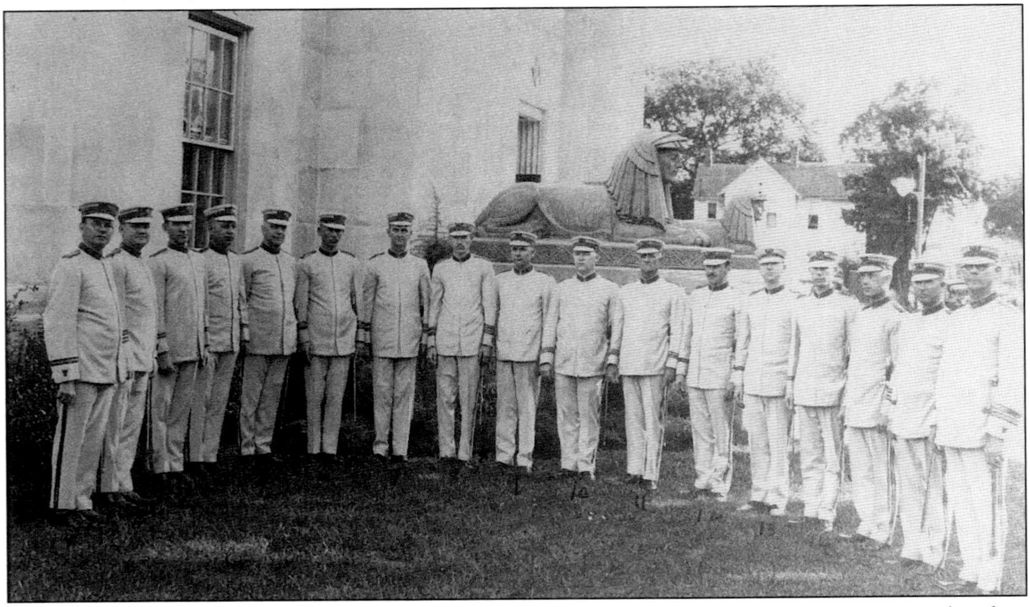

Shown here is a Masonic Temple Consistory Guard, c. 1929. The Masons were the first societies to organize in Sebastian County. Many of the members were prominent early settlers, such as John Rogers. The first Masonic Lodge in Fort Smith was organized in 1817, through the auspices of the Master Masons in the city who met at the home of Dr. Joseph H. Bailey, assistant surgeon of the United States Army. Dr. Bailey lived in the brick quarters at the old military post. (Bracht Collection, Fort Smith Public Library.)

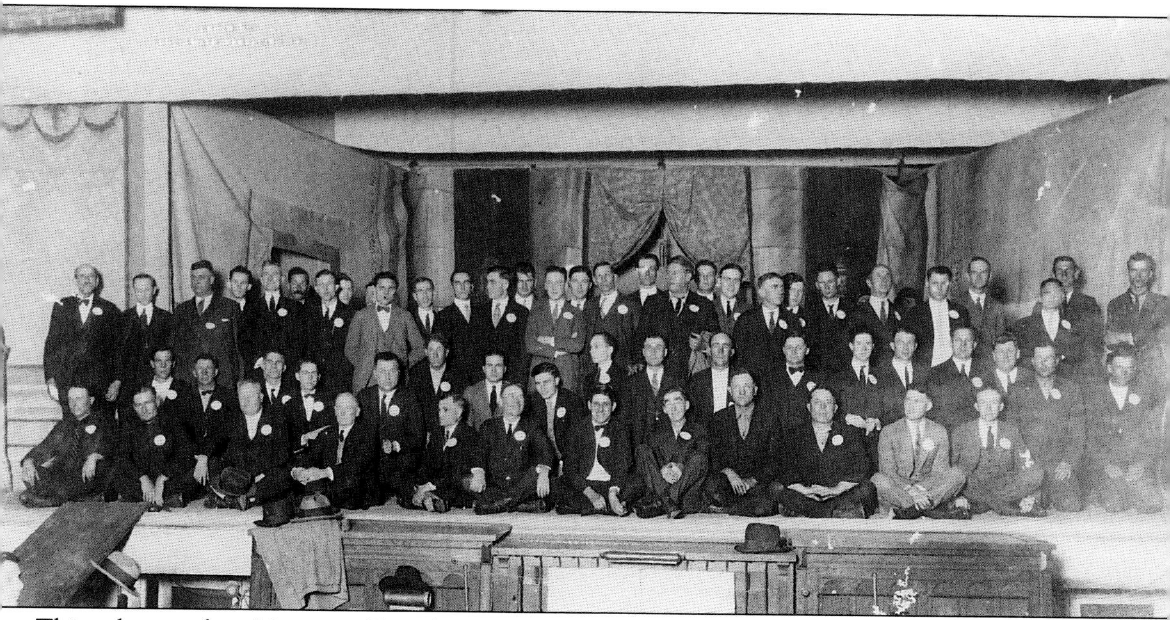

This photo of a Masonic Temple Consistory Class was made prior to the fire of September 4, 1919, in the auditorium of the old Baer Temple on Sixth Street. Baer Masonic Temple was dedicated on December 6, 1889. When the upper two floors of the temple burned, the historic documents and papers inside were also destroyed. The building had been adequate at that time, when only six organizations of masonry existed in Fort Smith. Later more room was needed as the number of organizations increased. The Masonic Temple, still in existence today on 11th Street, was built in 1929. (Bracht Collection, Fort Smith Public Library.)

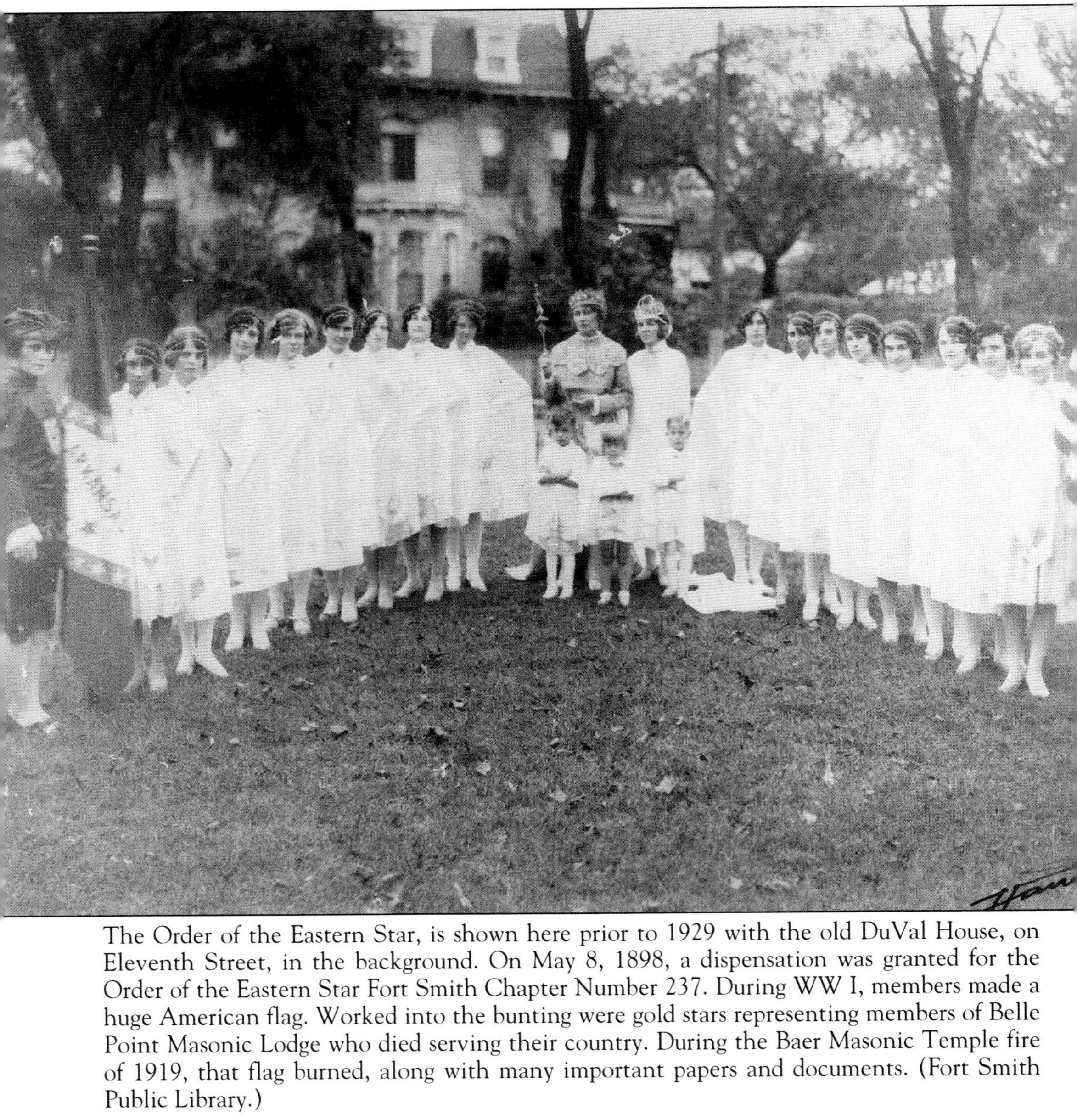

The Order of the Eastern Star, is shown here prior to 1929 with the old DuVal House, on Eleventh Street, in the background. On May 8, 1898, a dispensation was granted for the Order of the Eastern Star Fort Smith Chapter Number 237. During WW I, members made a huge American flag. Worked into the bunting were gold stars representing members of Belle Point Masonic Lodge who died serving their country. During the Baer Masonic Temple fire of 1919, that flag burned, along with many important papers and documents. (Fort Smith Public Library.)

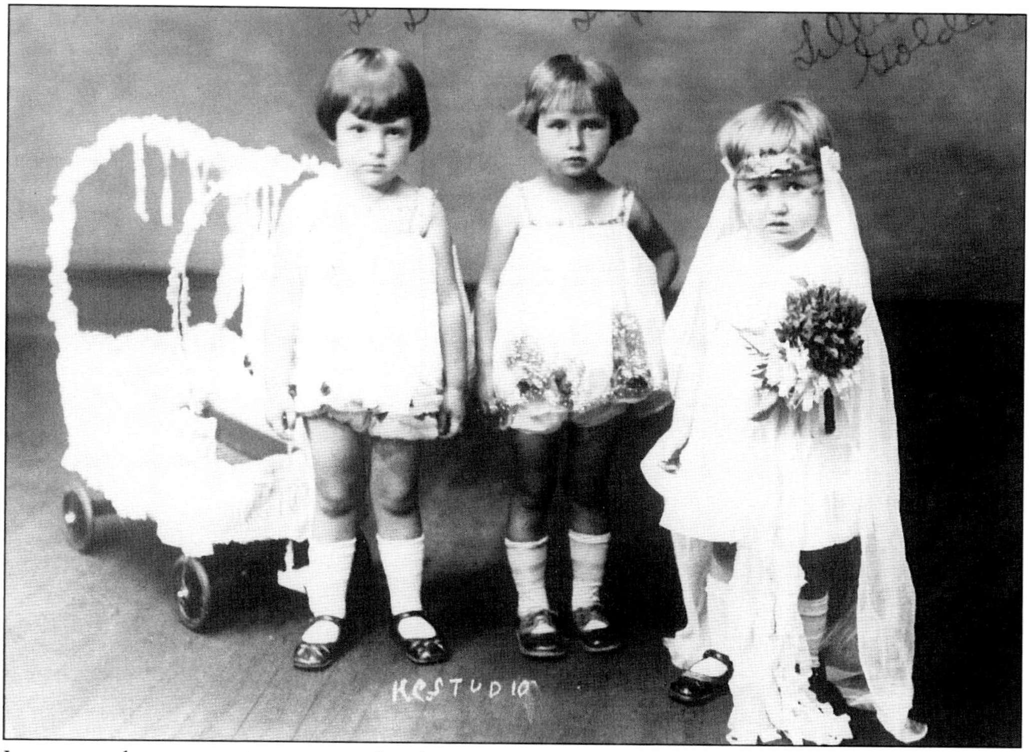

In an era when entertainment was hard to find, each event was a big production, as evidenced by this *c.* 1927 photo. These little girls, all decked out in white, are, from left to right: Lorain Duffine, Lorene Robinson, and Lillian Golden. They participated in a wedding shower, with a cart overflowing with presents. The photographer was K.C. Studio. Lillian Golden's mother, Anna Killion Golden, made use of the newspaper for promotion of her many social activities. (Lillian Golden Hissom.)

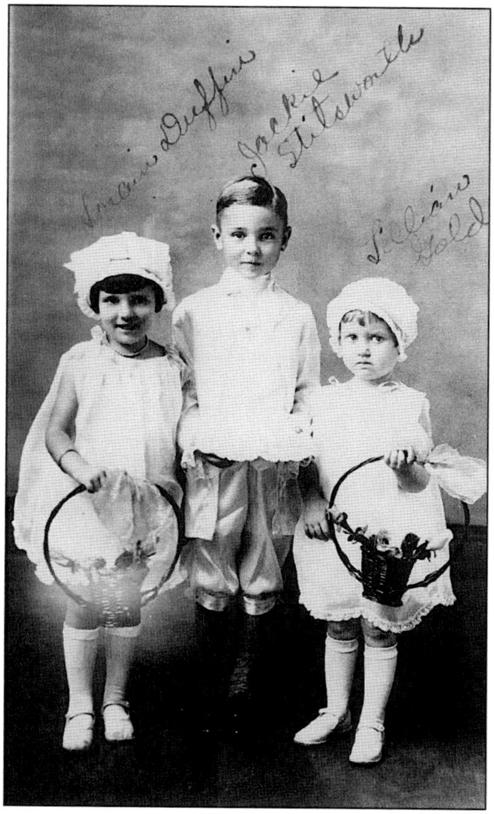

These beautifully attired children were members of a wedding party *c.* 1930. Jackie Stitsworth was the ring-bearer, Lorain Duffine is pictured on the left, and a less-than-happy Lillian Golden is also seen here. Lorain and Lillian were the flower girls. Lillian Golden's grandfather, Henry Killion, worked for the newspaper. (Lillian Golden Hissom.)

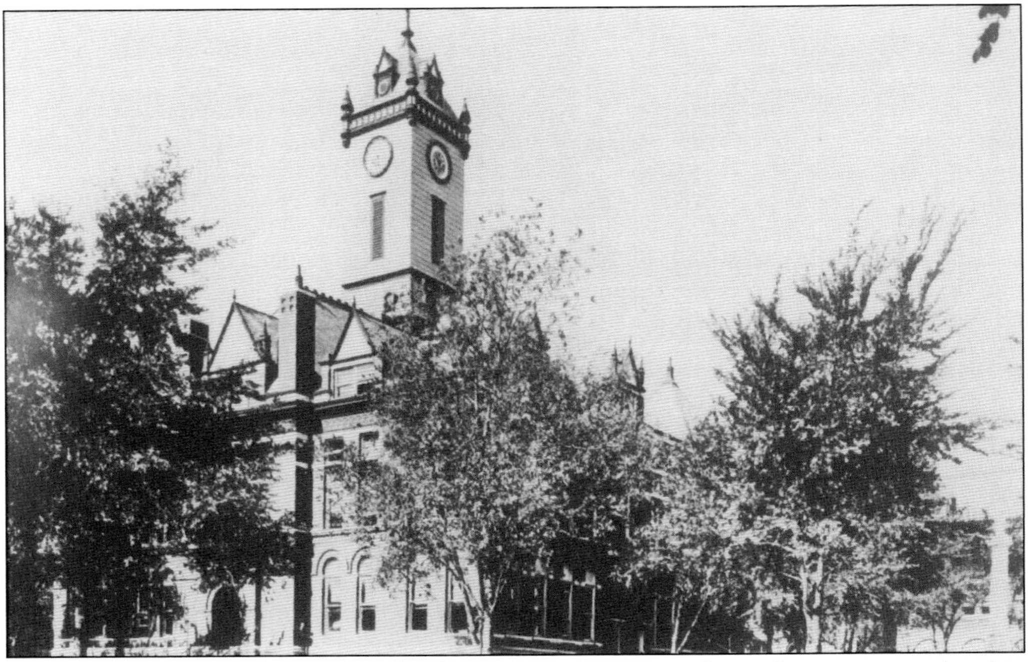

The Sebastian County Courthouse for the Fort Smith District, shown here, was completed in 1889. Years earlier, the staff at the top of the clock tower was splintered by lightning, and in 1910 it was replaced when the vibrations of the clock caused plaster to fall on the second floor. On March 20, 1937, the cornerstone was laid for the present courthouse. (Fort Smith National Historic Site.)

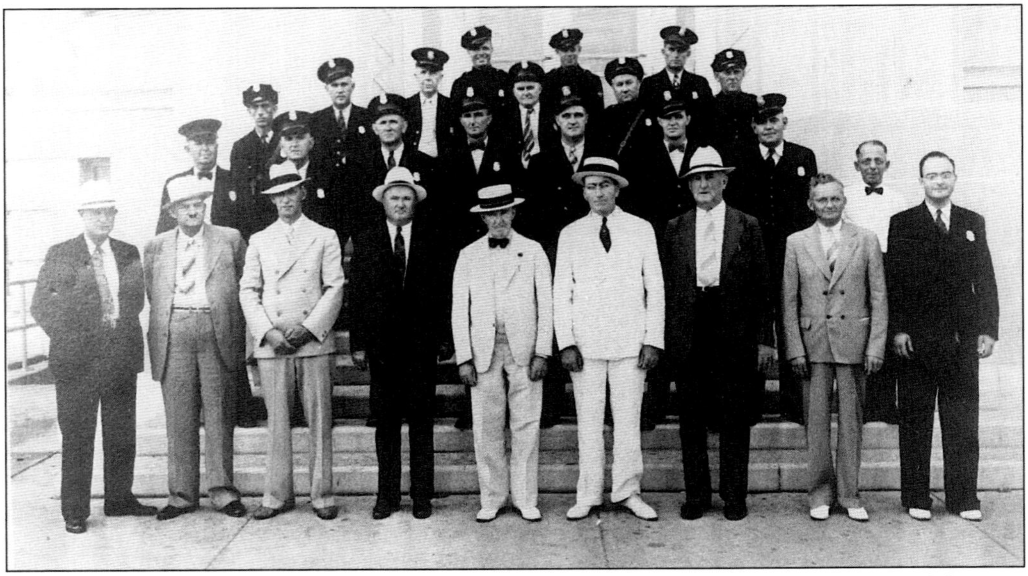

The Fort Smith Police Department, and officials, are shown here in 1938 in front of the new county courthouse. Fagan Bourland, the smaller of the two men in straw hats, was mayor of Fort Smith in 1907. He served periodically until 1933. His tenure as mayor was one of Fort Smith's most controversial ones. According to reports, in true "fatal attraction" tradition, his wife shot and killed Bourland's mistress, who had first threatened to kill her. (Fort Smith Police Department.)

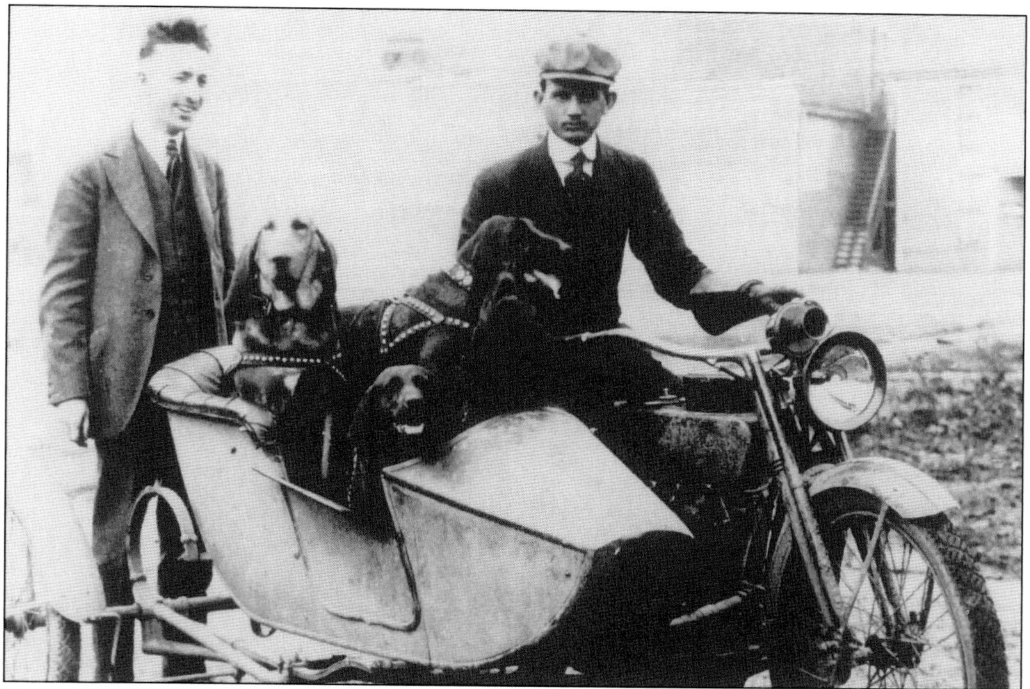

This photo is inscribed "Ben Walker and the City Bloodhounds, phone 3221 Fort Smith, Ark." Four bloodhounds are shown. Bloodhounds tracked burglars, lost persons, etc., as needed. On the evening of May 3, 1923, according to a local newspaper, a streetcar motorman of the Fort Smith Light and Traction Company, H.M. Upchurch, was robbed near the Van Buren smelter stop. The police department's F. Ben Walker brought bloodhounds to track the thief. (Fort Smith Police Department.)

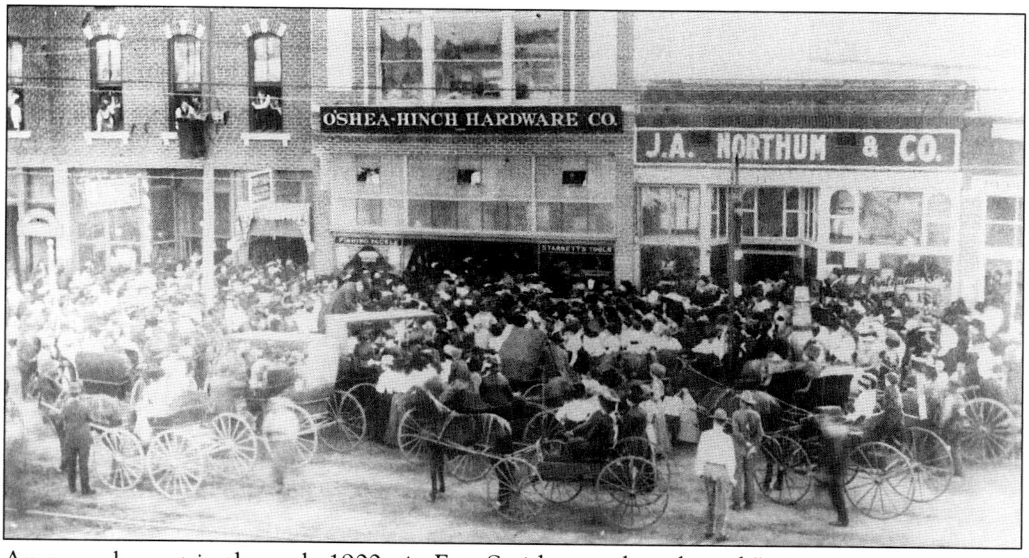

An annual event in the early 1900s, in Fort Smith, was the sale and "prize-give-away," shown in this photo, of the O'Shea-Hinch Hardware Company at Tenth and Garrison. The firm was owned by Pink Shaw, who later became chief of police. It attracted hundreds of people from the surrounding area for the "bargains and prizes." O'Shea-Hinch Hardware was first a train station, then the Missouri Pacific Bus Station. (Fort Smith Police Department.)

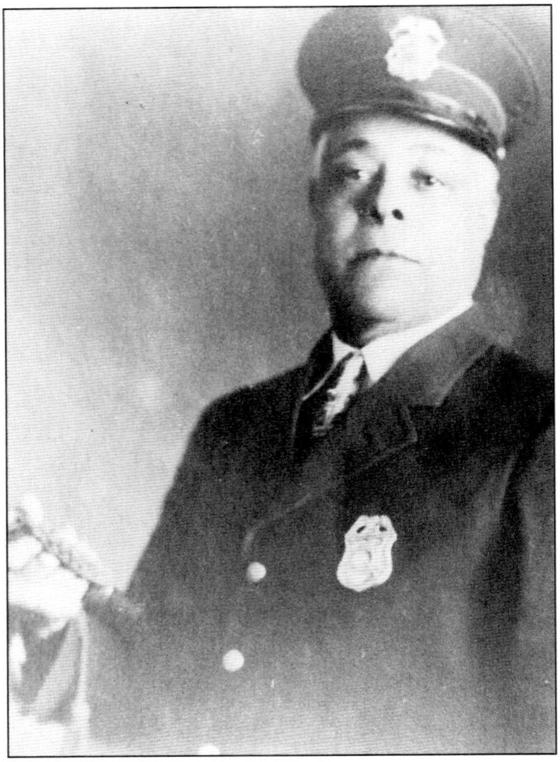

Pictured here is Al Rogers in the late 1920s—believed to be the first African-American Fort Smith police officer after the turn of the century. There had been African-American constables during the late 19th century. Since Al Rogers's day, many fine African-American officers have served law enforcement in the Fort Smith area. Judge Parker, prior to this time, commissioned African-American deputy marshals who served the Federal Court with distinction. (Fort Smith Police Department.)

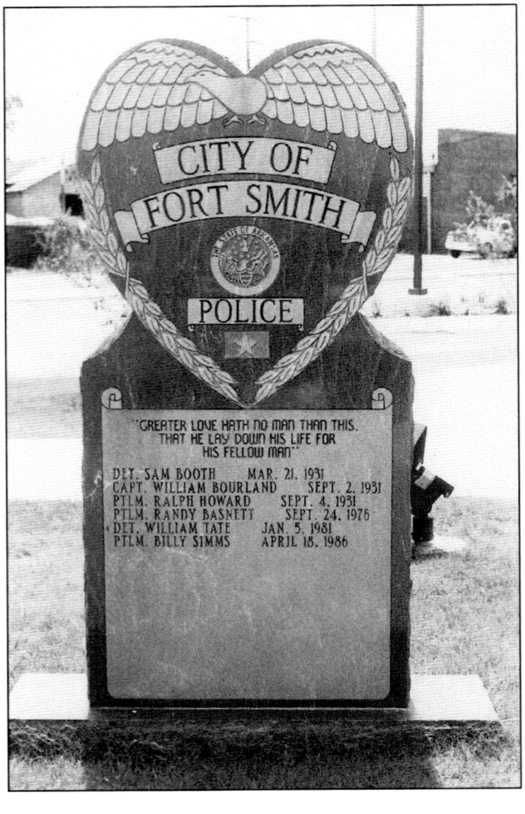

A heart-shaped, red-granite marker, dedicated in 1997, is located at the entrance to the new Fort Smith Police Department. The new facility opened in 1998. The memorial cites officers who have given their lives in the line of duty: Detective Sam Booth, March 21, 1931; Captain William Bourland, September 2, 1931; Patrolman Ralph Howard, September 4, 1931; Patrolman Randy Basnett, September 24, 1976; Detective William Tate, January 5, 1981; and Patrolman Billy Simms, April 18, 1986. (Author.)

Five

Heart of Community

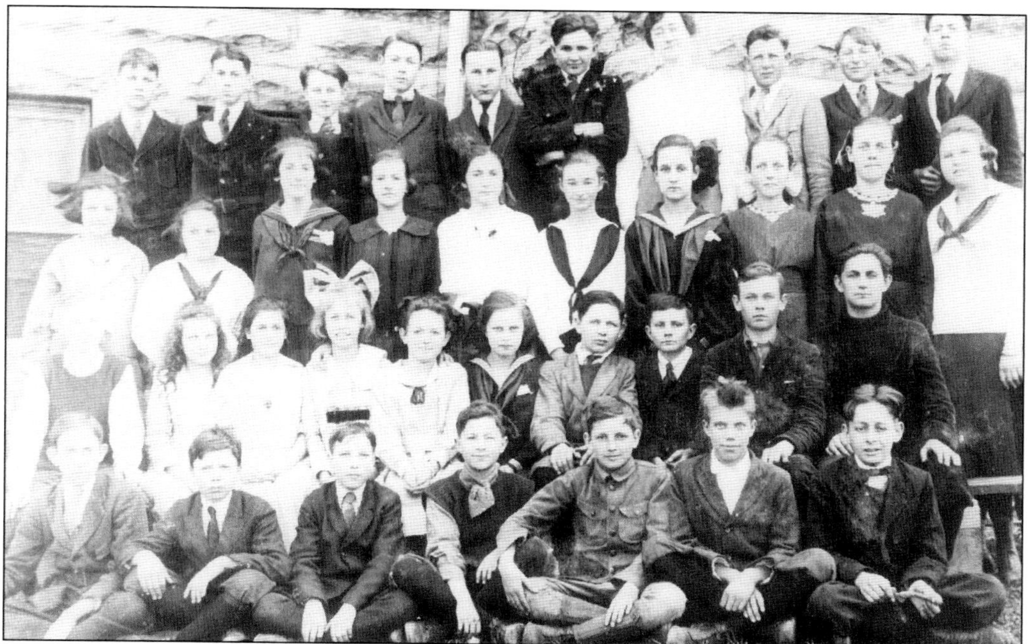

A Fort Smith Junior High School Class is pictured here, *c.* 1916. Note the amazing hair styles, especially among the boys. The sailor-design costume, shown on many of the girls, was a feature that dominated the photo images of numerous young women of the era. In some instances they appear to be a uniform. The boys wore suits, sometimes every day. Early day schools encouraged the study of debate and oratory through such organizations as the Ciceronians and Catalians; literature through the Columbians and the Athenians; and music through glee clubs and operettas held each year. Other clubs and organizations were business, science, voice, writing, drama, chess, high grade achievement through the Beta Club, and languages through the Spanish Club, among others. In athletics the schools had track, basketball, baseball, and football. The girls had basketball and physical education. Each year the Junior and Senior classes presented a play selected from an approved list. With so many organizations each student was allowed to explore the talent that he or she excelled in. (Lillian Golden Hissom.)

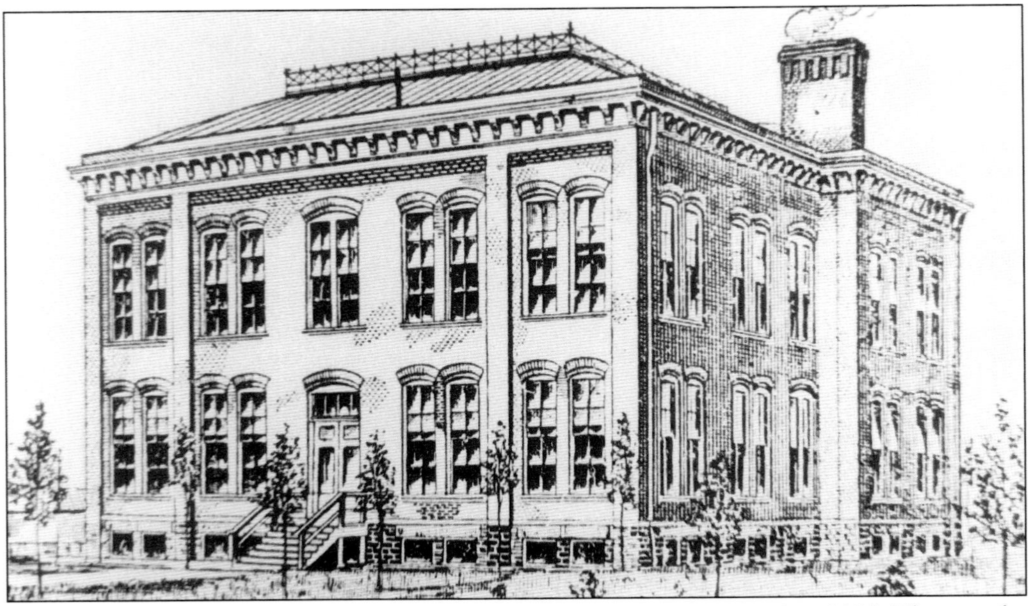

Belle Point School, shown as an etching in this photo, was constructed in 1885. The cost for the two-story, eight-room structure was $18,000. Including the schoolyard, the school occupied a city block at South 9th Street and Wheeler Avenue. Of classic design, it was a plain-square building of red-brick with a basement. Large elm and oak trees shaded the school yard and lined the walks leading to the entrances. A solid wooden fence, rather than the metal fence shown here, enclosed the school yard. (Fort Smith Public Library.)

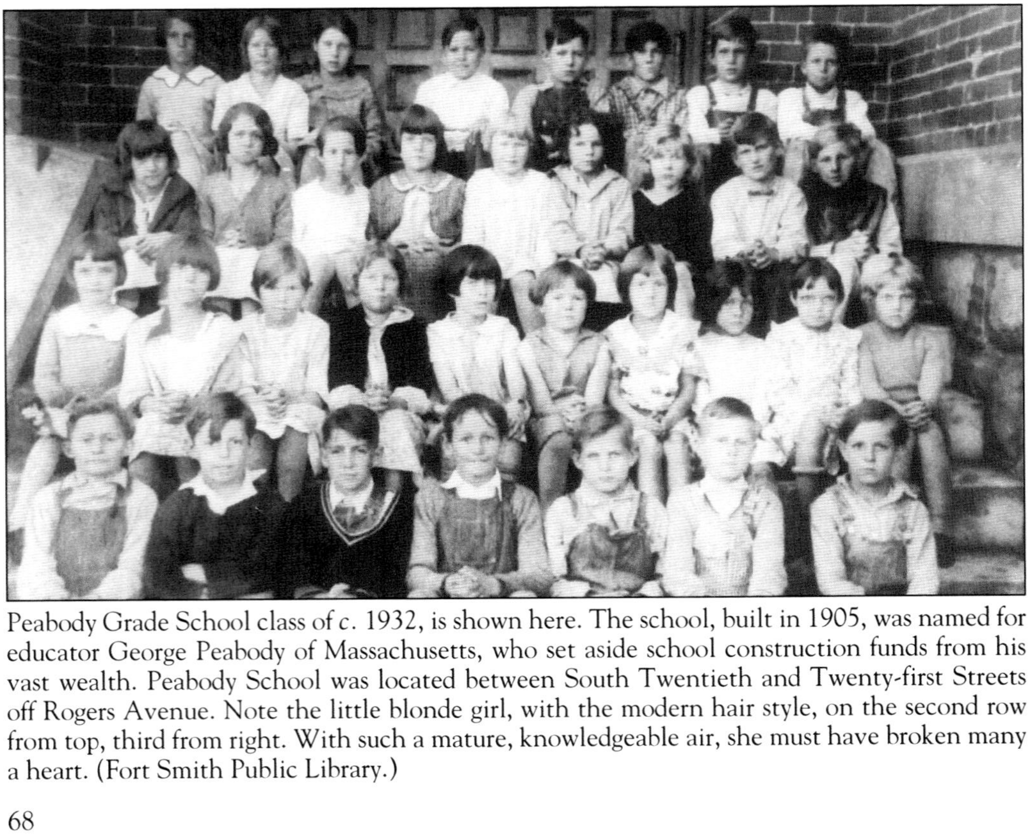

Peabody Grade School class of *c.* 1932, is shown here. The school, built in 1905, was named for educator George Peabody of Massachusetts, who set aside school construction funds from his vast wealth. Peabody School was located between South Twentieth and Twenty-first Streets off Rogers Avenue. Note the little blonde girl, with the modern hair style, on the second row from top, third from right. With such a mature, knowledgeable air, she must have broken many a heart. (Fort Smith Public Library.)

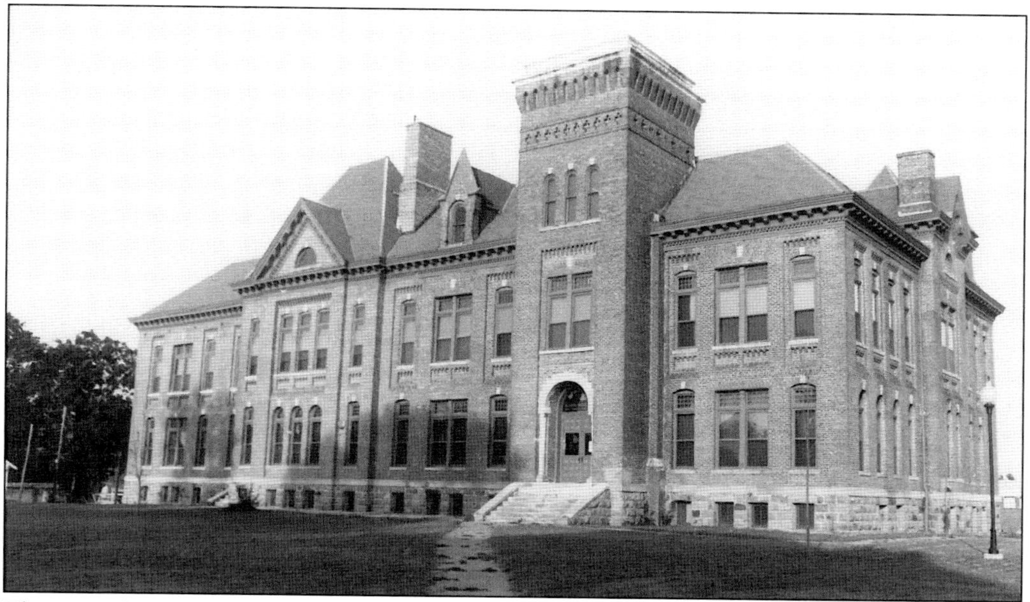

The second Belle Grove School, as shown, was built in 1886. In January 1868, J. Sandels, an Episcopal clergyman, and his wife opened a school for young ladies called Belle Grove Academy. Sandels served as chaplain, and the young ladies were supervised by his wife. Boys under ten were also enrolled. In 1870 the City purchased the Academy and, after a renovation, it became known as the first Belle Grove School. The second Bell Grove School was built on that same site. (Fort Smith Art Center.)

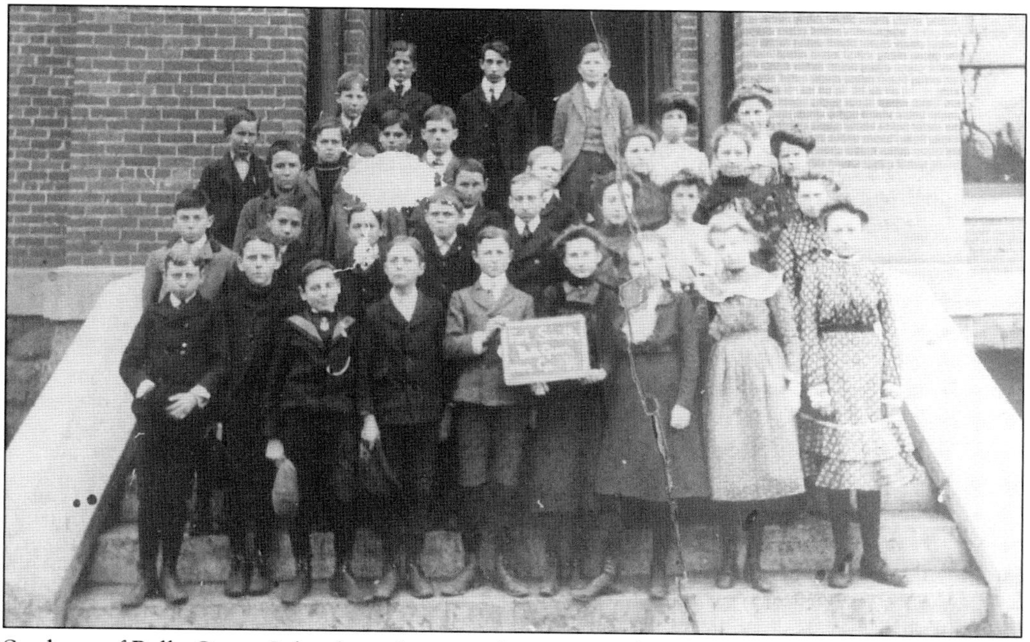

Students of Belle Grove School are shown as they appeared in 1902. When a cyclone damaged the new high school in 1898, the students returned to Belle Grove. Soon, though, they were back at the new high school, which was repaired in a timely manner. (Fort Smith Public Library.)

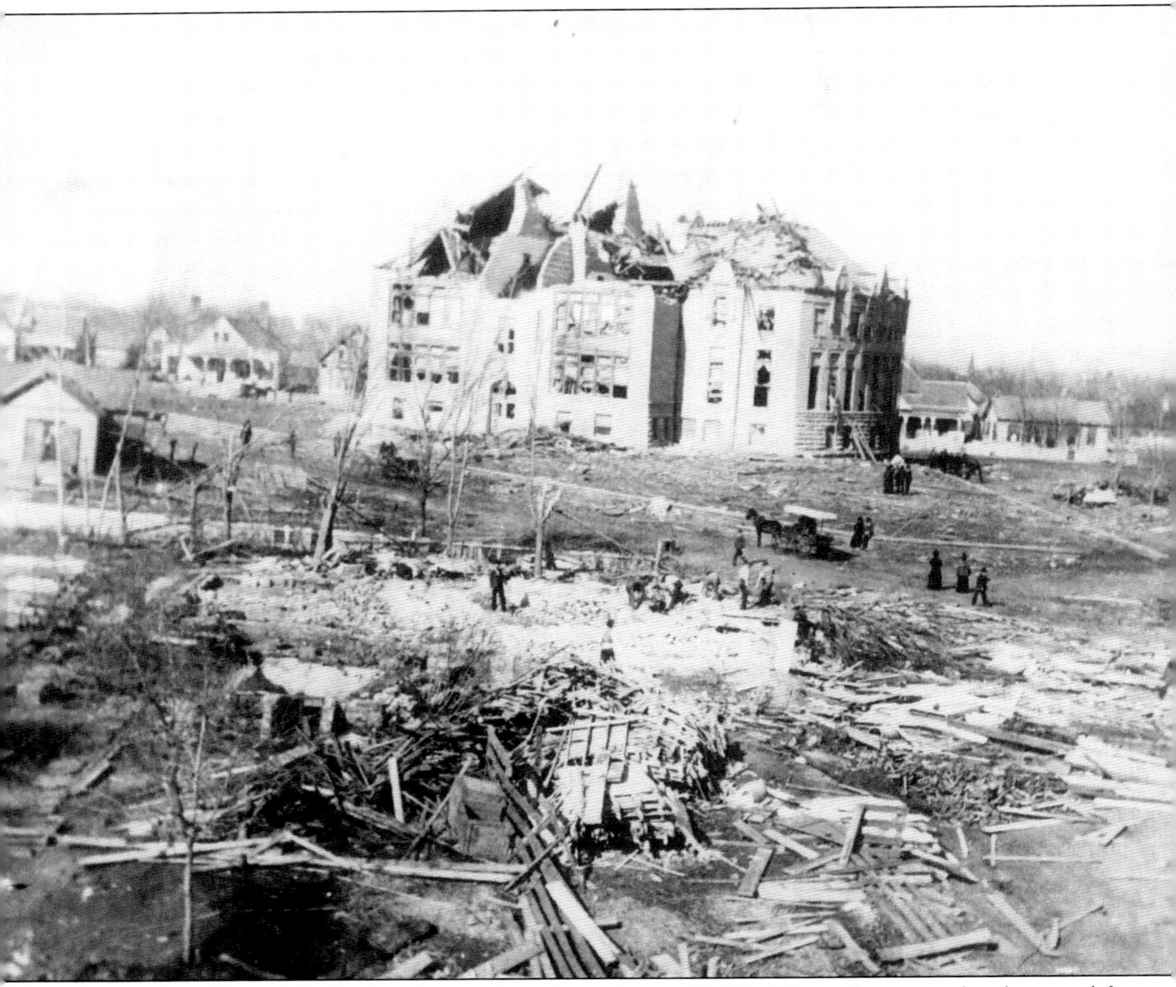

Fort Smith High School is shown after the cyclone of 1898. When the new school opened for the 1897 fall term, it was described as one of the "Seven Wonders of Fort Smith." An English castle-style, buff-brick and grey-stone building, it was lighted with electricity and heated by a combination of steam and hot air. Large ventilating chimneys were located on the roof. The building contained an assembly hall which seated 300 and an even larger auditorium. Three well-equipped science laboratories rivaled any in the state and students traveled great distances to attend the school. Celebrities visited the new school and lectured at length about how impressive it was. Perhaps it was to good to be true. On January 11, 1898, when the school was only three months old, a cyclone almost destroyed it. The roof was blown away and the giant chimneys fell, almost demolishing the building's front exterior. Undaunted, the student body removed, once again, to Belle Grove. Classes at Fort Smith High School resumed, fairly quickly, after the restoration of the building. (Fort Smith Public Library.)

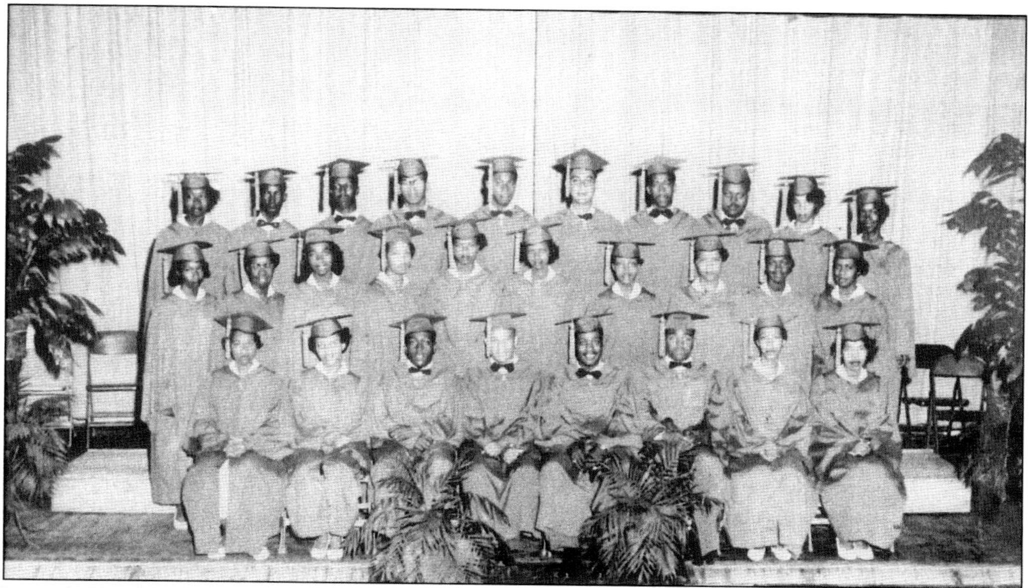

Lincoln High Graduates are shown here. Pictured, from left to right, are: (front row) Alpha Gilliam, June Craig, Felix Driver, Eugene Johnson, Coleman Smith, Ted McGill, Emily Edwards, and Rosie West; (middle row) Evelyn Lincoln, Serrena Adams, Ruth Norwood, Ebbie Sanders, Juanita Christian, Fern Roby, Carolyn Black, Anita Phillips, Audrey Walker, and Bessie Taylor; (back row) Elizabeth Dodson, Billy Perry, Lee Feimster, Melvin Moore, Sullivan Williams, Kenneth Webb, Clifford Straham, Troy Knauls, Jewel Ferguson, and Susie Prince. (Sherry L. Toliver.)

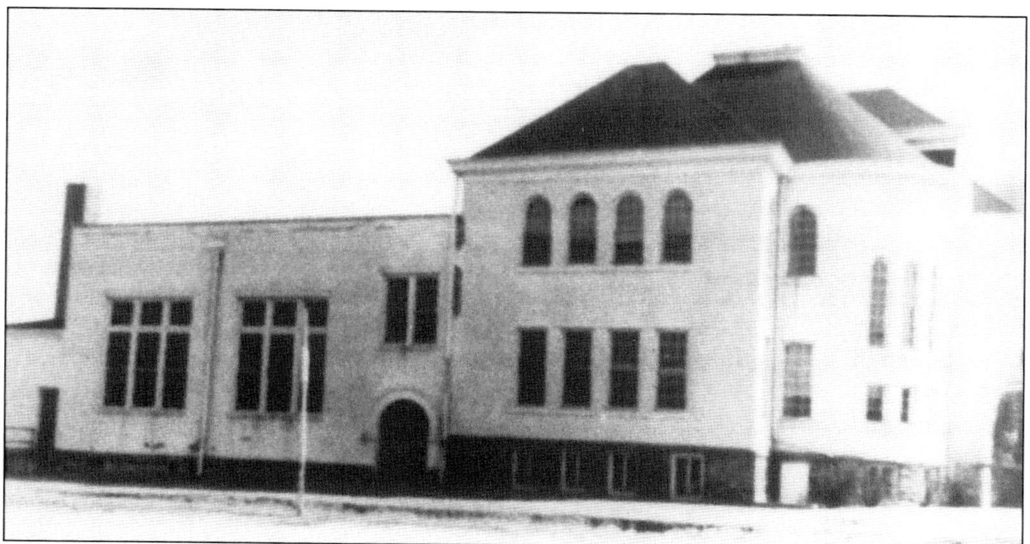

Lincoln High School served the black community from 1892 until 1966. Although Lincoln had fewer activities than the white schools, the students were kept busy, nonetheless. Extracurricular activities included Student Council, Y-Teens, a girls' service club, and Hi-Y, a Christian brotherhood. There was also a glee club and drama club, home economics and a sociology-Negro history discussion group. They also had a basketball program where they competed against other black teams. (Fort Smith Public Library.)

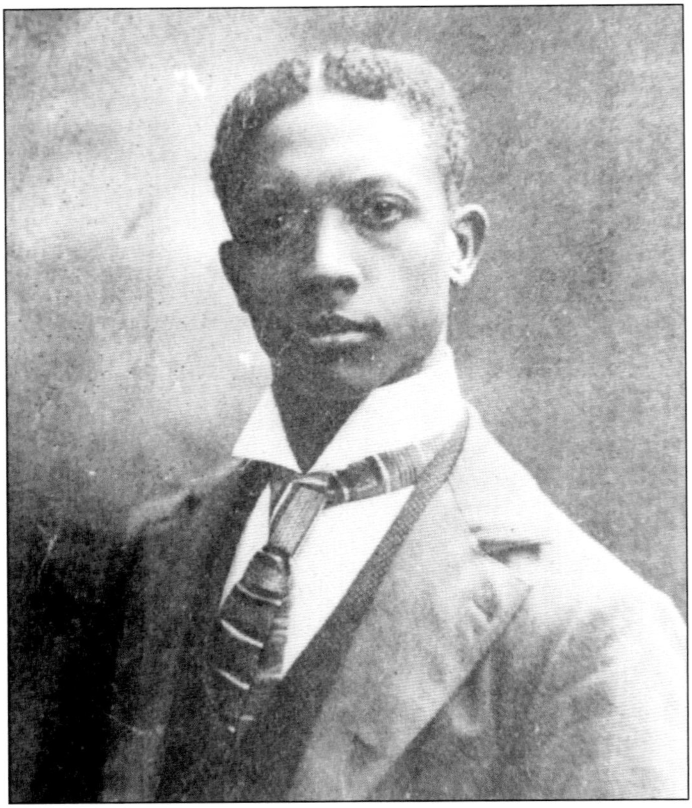

At the turn of the century Professor J. Wilson Pettus, shown here, was a teacher of the Howard High School and the Eighth Grade. E.O. Trent was principal of Howard. Trent was a revered teacher at Howard for many years. Pettus was born in Tennessee in 1872 and moved to Fort Smith in 1897. After seven years of study, he graduated with an A.B. degree from Fisk University in Tennessee. (Cinda Bell.)

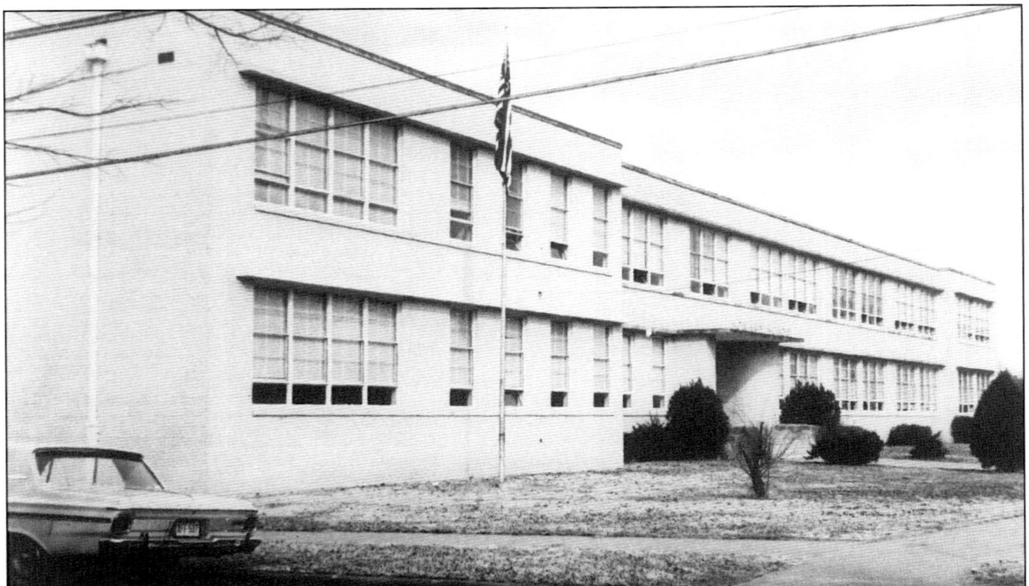

Pictured is Howard School in 1955. On September 5, 1877, the first Howard School opened the term with 72 students. The principal was R.G. Woods and the assistant was Emma Walker. Entering and exiting the building was accomplished through the march drill system. The second Howard School was Fort Smith's first high school built for black students. It was constructed in 1888. (Sherry L. Toliver.)

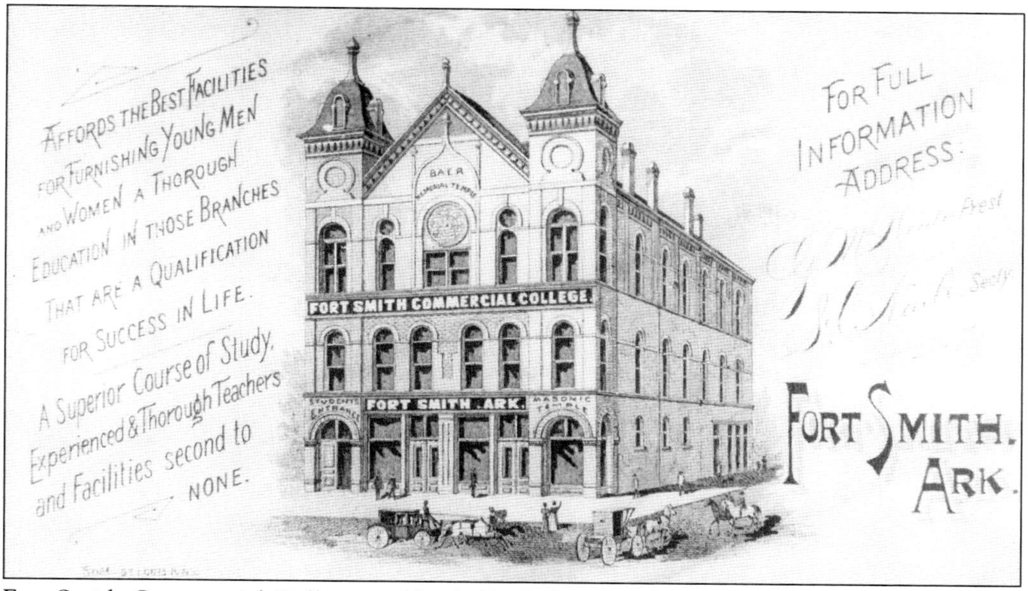

Fort Smith Commercial College on North Sixth Street was established in 1888, in the Baer Memorial Temple. The college occupied the first floor and the Temple was located on the upper two floors. The first year the college had 15 graduates. The fire of September 1919 damaged the Temple and destroyed many of the historic Masonic papers and documents. Now restored, the two-story building, among others, houses the offices of MAHG Architecture, Inc. (Fort Smith Public Library.)

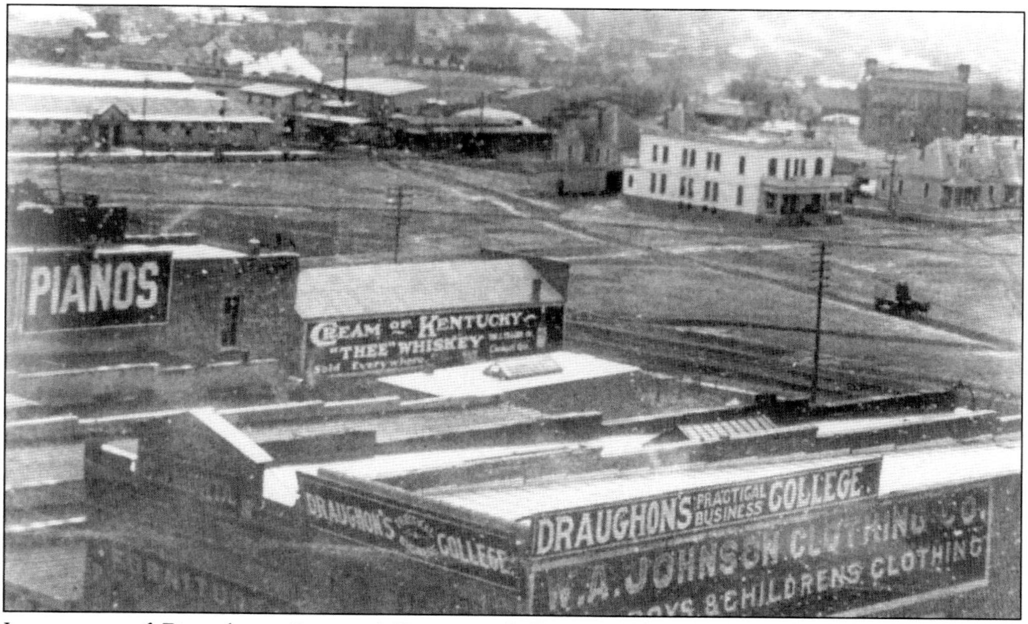

Instructors of Draughons Practical Business College, at the corner of Eighth and Garrison Avenue, Third Floor, taught shorthand and typing, among other subjects, and supplied the business community with skilled workers. Note the carriage moving along Rogers Avenue, a dirt road, in the center of the photo. This winter scene looking toward Towson Avenue has all the appearance of a busy little community. Smoke seems to be billowing up from many factories and businesses. (Fort Smith Public Library.)

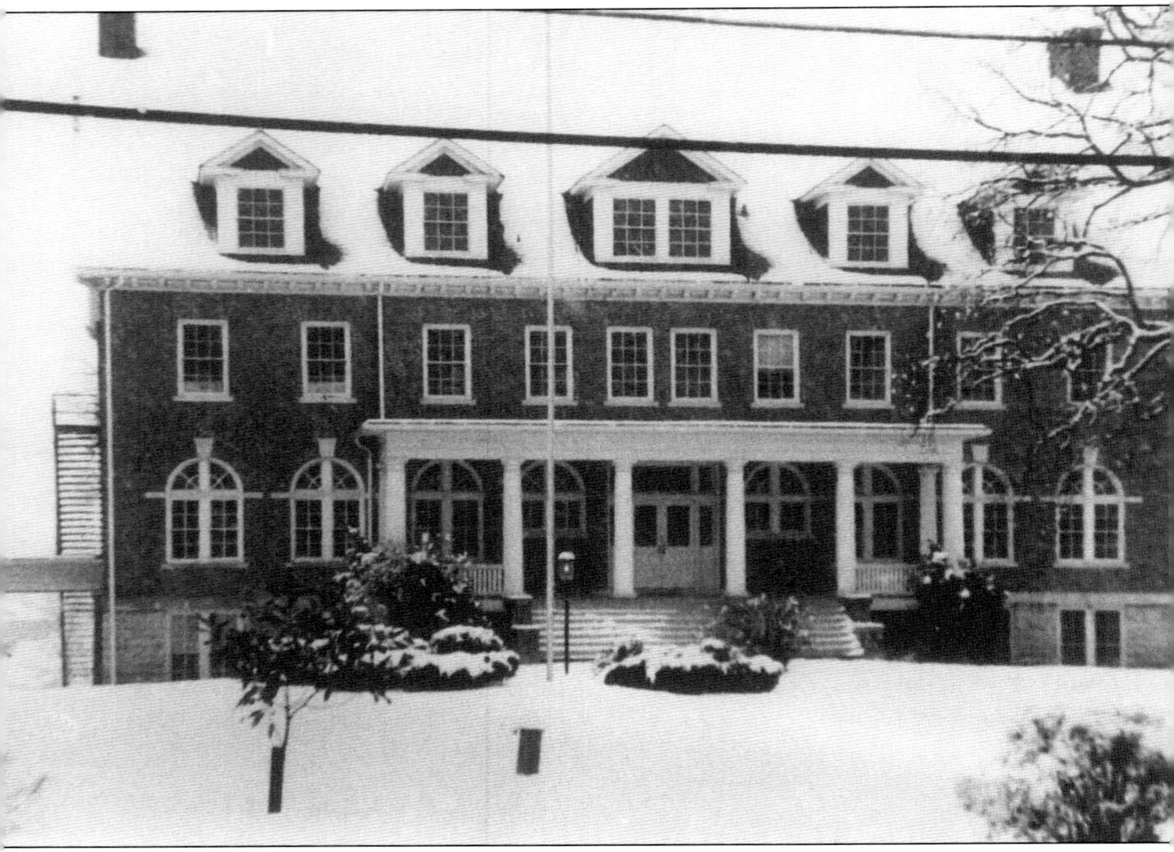

"Old Main," on the campus of what is now Westark College, was part of the old Country Farm for indigent people. Fort Smith Junior College was established in 1928, and located in the basement of the new Fort Smith High School. The superintendent of the school served as its president, and the high school principal was the dean. In September 1952 the college was moved from the high school to the Country Farm site. Two brick buildings were converted into classrooms and offices, and the semester began with 108 students and ten instructors. An innovative vocational-technical division was established to provide local industry with trained personnel. Today, Westark College is one of the leading colleges in the state. The building called Old Main no longer exists. (Wayne Bledsoe.)

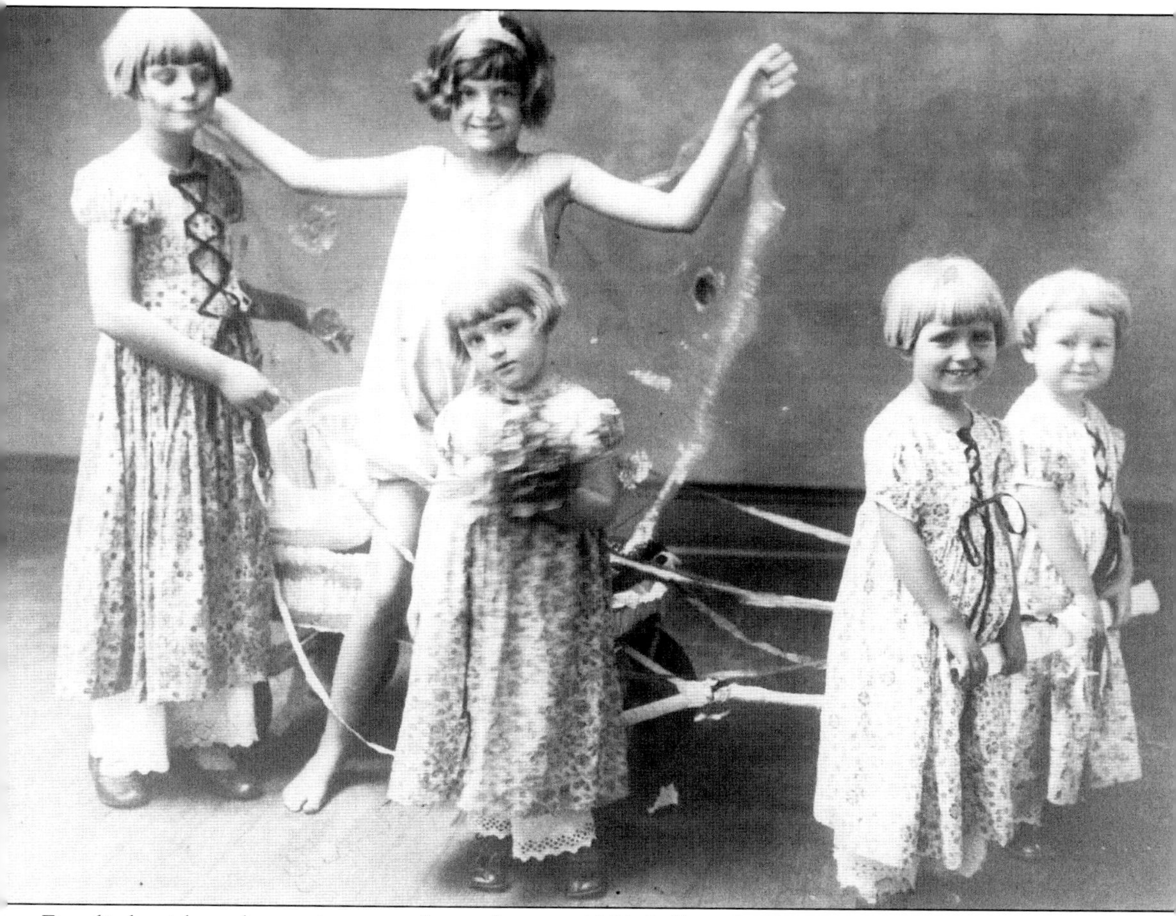

Five little girls and a carriage, are shown here, *c.* 1928. Lillian Golden Hissom is on the front right, along with Lorene Robinson, her cousin, to her right. Lorain Duffine is to the side with head cocked. The butterfly, holding gossamer wings aloft, is Juanita Johnson. The girl to her right is her sister Elma Johnson. The girls pulled the present-filled wagon out, and surprised the bride-to-be, at the beginning of her wedding shower. (Lillian Golden Hissom.)

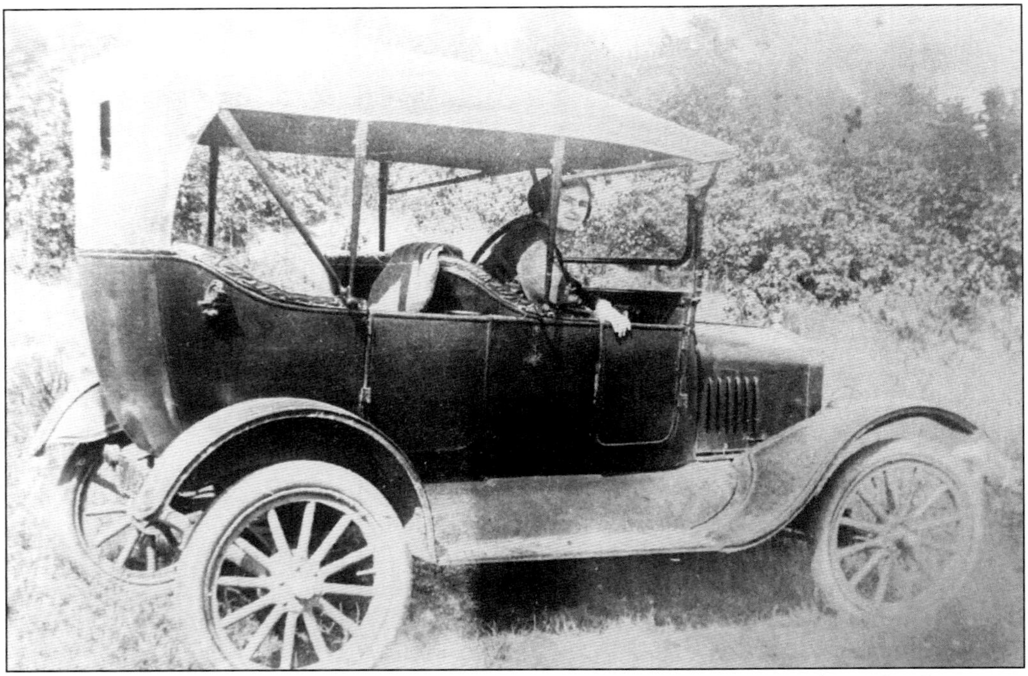

Anna Killion Golden is pictured in a 1923–24 Model T Ford. Anna was the wife of streetcar motorman Frank Golden, and she took photos with her little black Eastman Kodak box camera. In the beginning she just snapped family settings. Later she began to compose what are now considered interesting or novel images. She also began a collection of photos made available by her father, who was an employee of the local newspaper. (Lillian Golden Hissom.)

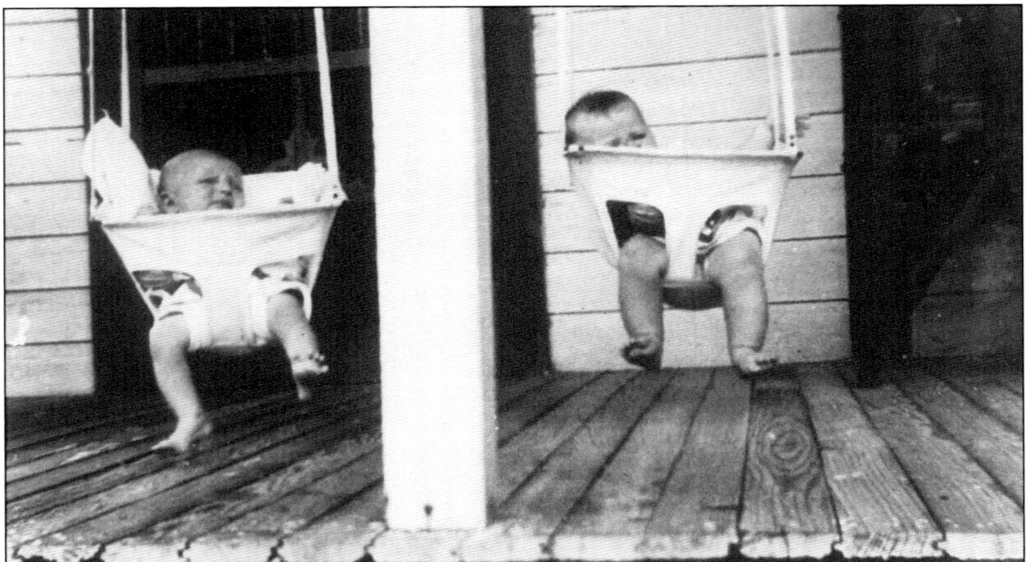

Lillian Golden Hissom, to the right, and her cousin, are shown in baby swings on the front porch of Lillian's home. The photo was snapped by her mother, Anna Killion Golden *c.* 1925. The swings were connected to the ceiling of the porch with elastic-type ropes and they simulated a rocking motion. The babies were thus entertained, although at the moment neither baby looks very happy. (Anna Golden, Lillian Golden Hissom.)

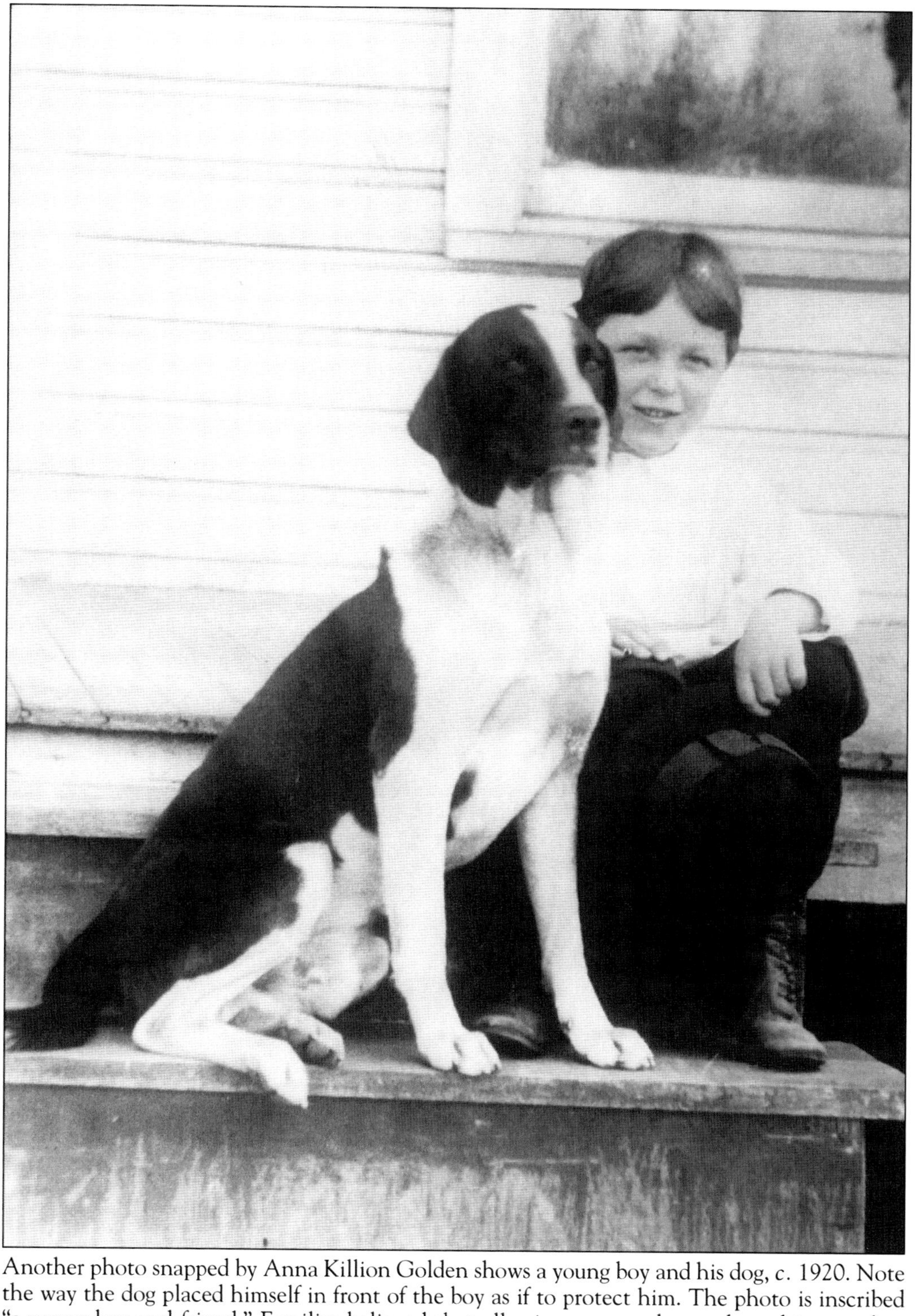

Another photo snapped by Anna Killion Golden shows a young boy and his dog, c. 1920. Note the way the dog placed himself in front of the boy as if to protect him. The photo is inscribed "a young boy and friend." Families believed that allowing a young boy to have his own dog, and to care for it, would teach him invaluable lessons about life. (Anna Killion Golden, Lillian Golden Hissom.)

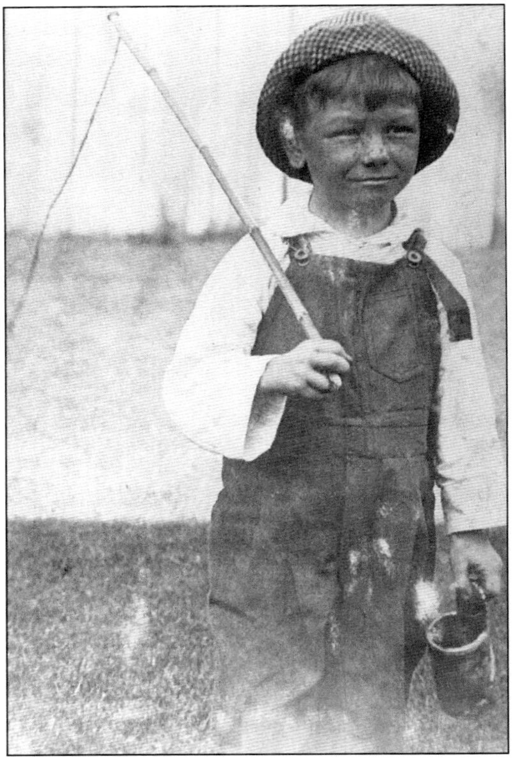

The "Huckleberry Finn" look of this young boy, Gillis Mundell, shown c. 1920 with a fishing pole and can of worms, was not staged. He was actually headed for the fishing hole and the pole and worms were necessary to the venture. However, Anna Killion Golden saw the photo opportunity and captured it for posterity. The location is the vicinity of what is now Kelley Highway and Midland Boulevard. (Anna Killion Golden, Lillian Golden Hissom.)

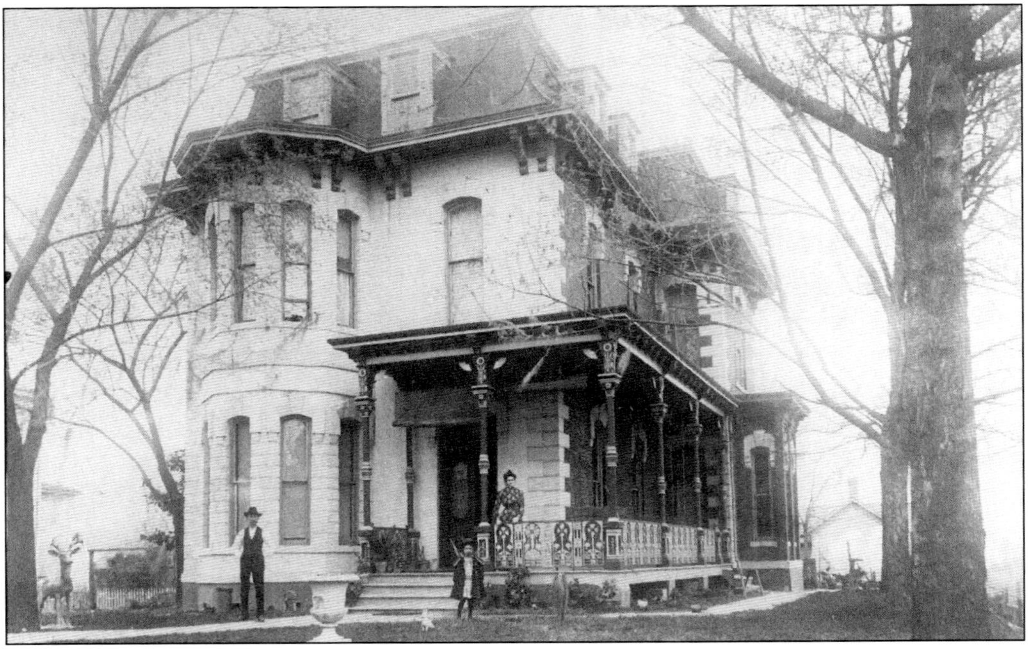

The George Sengel Home was located at Fifth and E Streets. It was a beautiful example of a Victorian Second Empire home with mansard roof. The Sengel family was very popular and well respected in the community. George Sengel owned several businesses, was a state senator, and was a deputy marshal under Judge Parker. The Sengel Home was built c. 1870 and was demolished in 1996. (Fort Smith Public Library.)

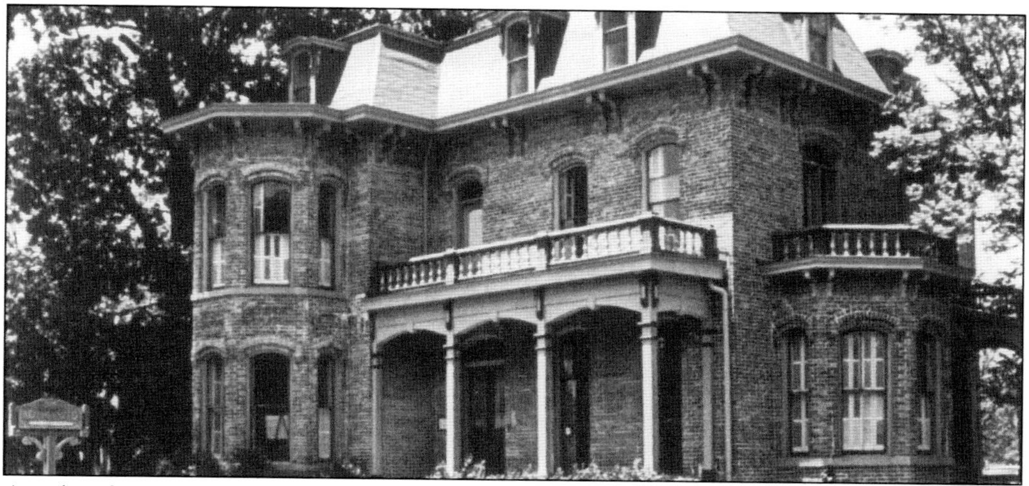

Another fine Victorian Second Empire example, the Vaughn/Schaap House, houses the Fort Smith Art Center and is located in the Belle Grove Historic District on Sixth and E Streets. John Vaughn, an early resident, was an attorney and owner of a hardware business. John Schaap was a wholesale druggist who manufactured many of his own patent medicines. Vaughn/Schaap has been home to the arts in Fort Smith since *c.* 1961, and continues to serve area and regional artists. Annually the Art Center is host to an International Art Competition and Exhibit. A staff of three operates the Art Center five days per week, and a myriad of volunteers assists with fund-raisers and other functions. Director Julie Lind Northrip and Business Manager Tena Coker established the Annual Native American Festival in 1995. During the month of September the Art Center hosts thousands of native peoples and guests from across the country for a month-long art exhibit and one-day festival. Another Art Center affiliate, the Photographic Alliance, meets twice per month. They host an annual international photo competition and exhibit. (Fort Smith Art Center.)

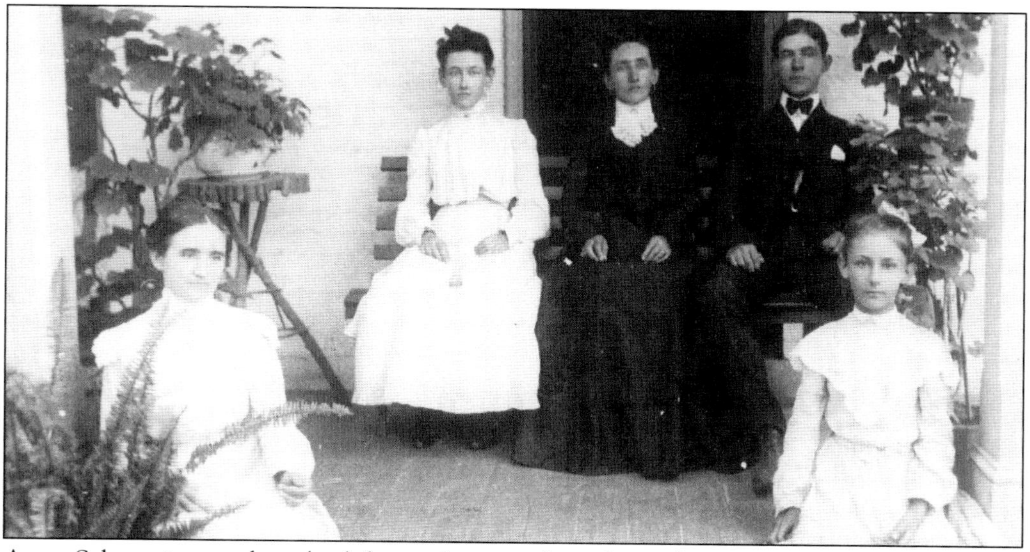

Anna Schaap is seated to the left on what may have been the south porch of the Vaughn/Schaap House. Alma and Amelia Schaap are the young ladies in light color clothing. The couple in black are unknown. Tana Anna, or Anna, was the German maid of the household. When Mary Schaap died John married Tana Anna. The Schaaps lived in the house for over 60 years. Alma was the last Schaap to reside there. (Fort Smith Art Center.)

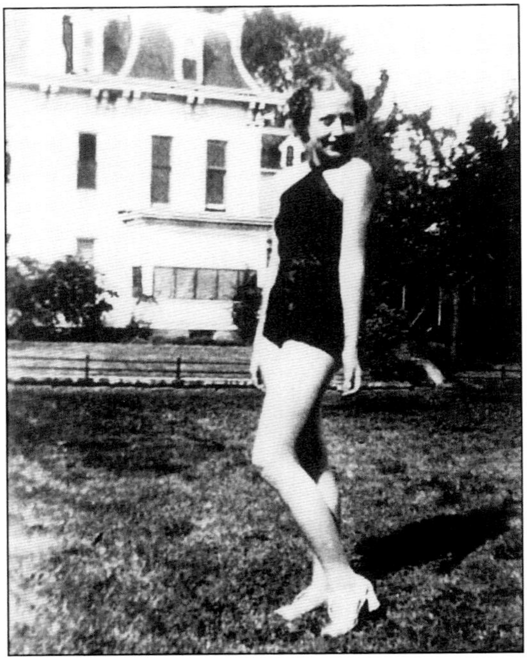

Lois Lester Hobbs is shown in 1937 on the lawn of the Brizzolara Home, modeling the latest in swimwear. The Stephen Wheeler Home, in the background across E Street, was occupied by Dr. Osborne's family. These three massive homes, Sengels, Vaughn/Schaap, and Wheeler, located within a few hundred yards of each other, were all strikingly similar in appearance. The homes were all owned by influential families linked to each other by business or family connections. (Donna Mitchell.)

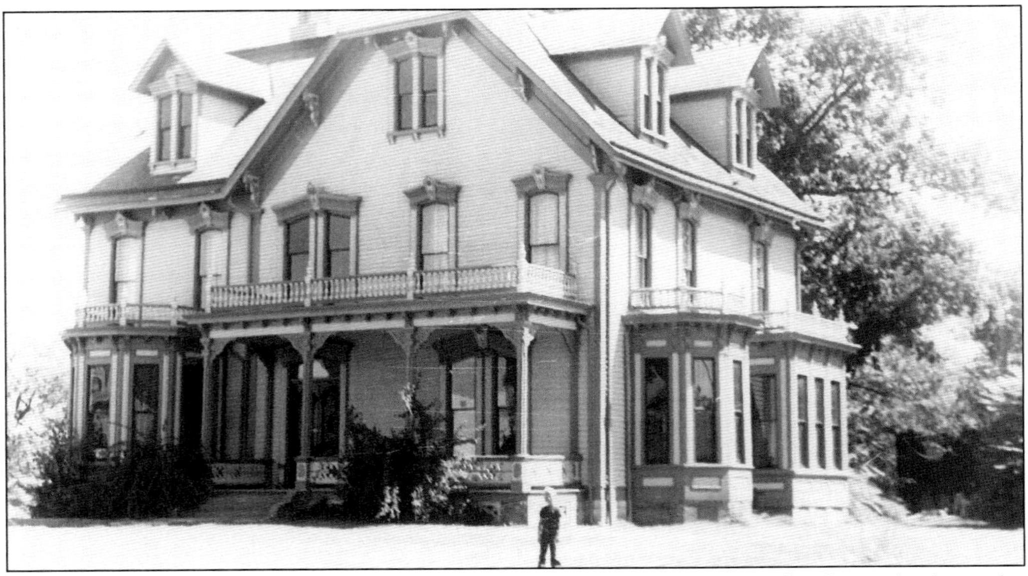

The Clayton House, shown here in 1977, was originally a much smaller home built in the 1850s. The Claytons bought the house in the 1880s and expanded it. The little person shown on the lawn is Brent Shropshire, son of the author. This wood-frame antebellum house, located on North Sixth Street, served for years as the family home of W.H.H. Clayton, the federal prosecutor to the court of the Western District of Arkansas, otherwise known as Judge Parker's prosecutor. The house is an example of total technical restoration. Mott, Mobley, McGowan, and Griffin, local architects, studied old records and photographs, talked to old-timers, and disassembled certain features to arrive at the home's original appearance. Every detail, including paint scheme and landscaping, is loyal to the home's look following the Italianate-Gothic remodeling of the early 1880s. The home, filled with Clayton family furnishings and sporting a beautiful, large plantation-style back porch, is open for tours. (Author.)

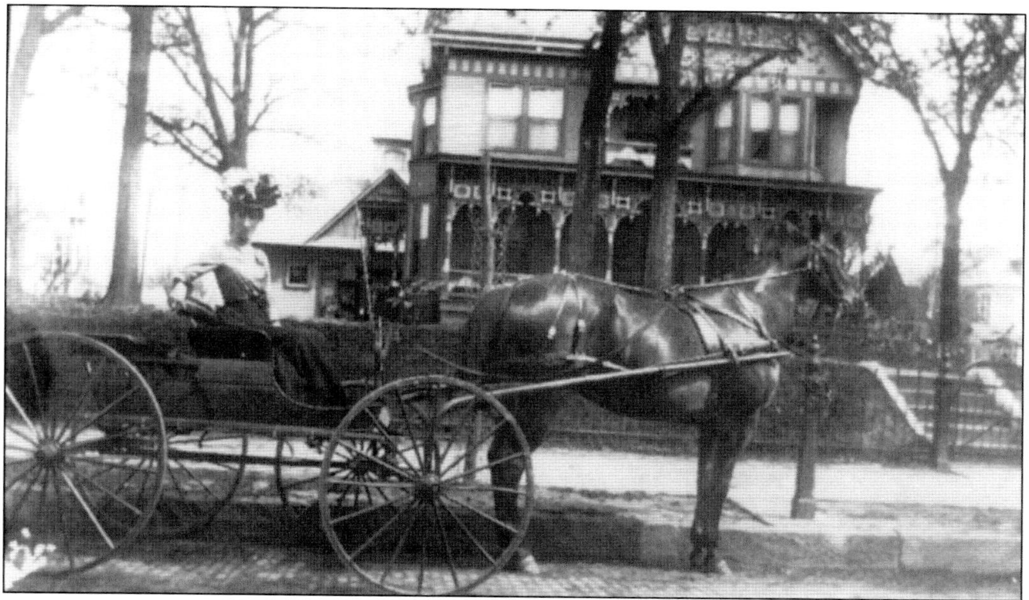

Shown is a relative of Stella Brizzolara, the wife of the Mayor James Brizzolara, at their residence on Sixth and E Streets. She has a beautiful horse, a fine looking carriage, and an exceptional hat. Mr. Brizzolara served as the mayor of Fort Smith from 1878 to 1882. Also an attorney, he was a law-partner of W.H.H. Clayton. The lovely Brizzolara home, with a new look, is still in use as a residence today. (Donna Mitchell.)

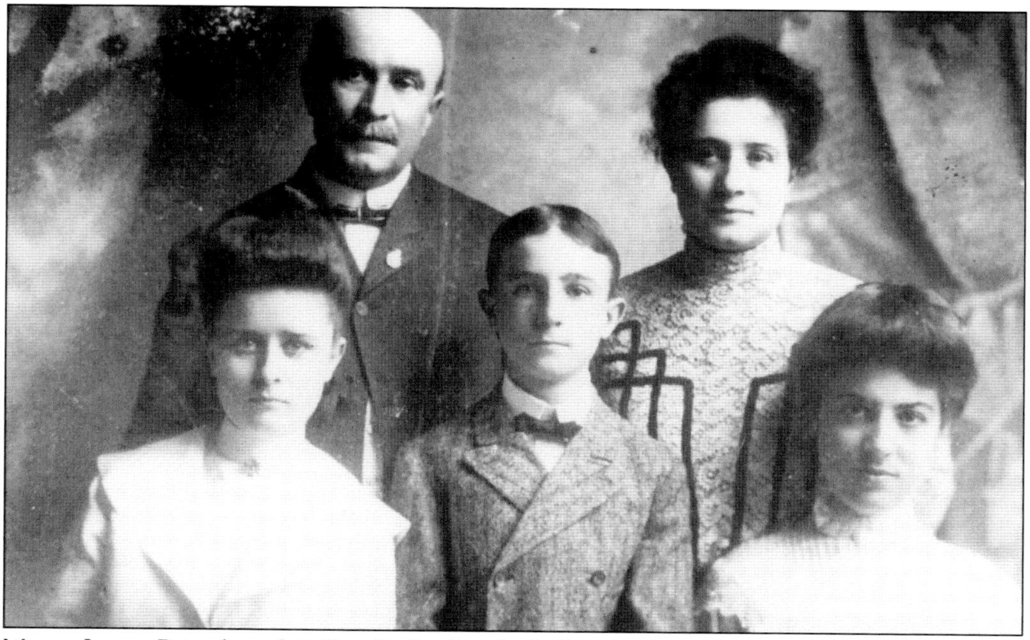

Mayor James Brizzolara, his "legal" third wife Stella, their children, and an unknown lady are shown here. Imagine a surprised, close-knit Fort Smith community in 1877, when friends and neighbors first learned that "Brizz" was married to his niece Jenny, his second "wife." The information became known after she married again without divorcing Brizzolara. When bigamy charges were filed, Jenny responded that her husband was actually her uncle; therefore, her marriage to him was void. (Donna Mitchell.)

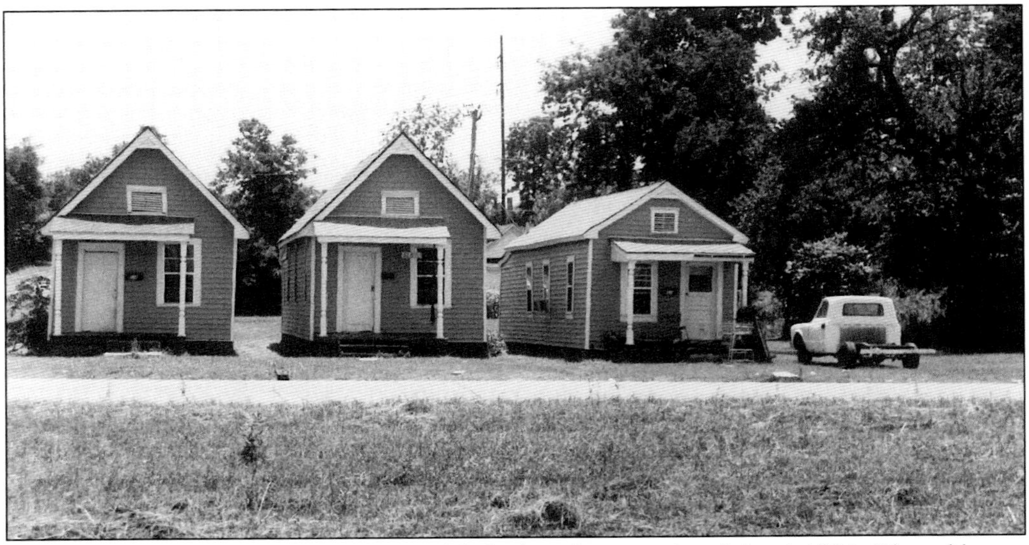

These little shotgun houses were remodeled after the tornado of April 1996. The addresses beginning at left are 112, 110, and 108 North Third Street. Pearl Starr, the notorious "row" madam, and her young daughters once lived at 106 North Third Street. That two-room house no longer exists. These unpretentious little houses can still be found throughout Fort Smith, along with the grand, stylish mansions in the Historic District, and on Free Ferry Road. (Author.)

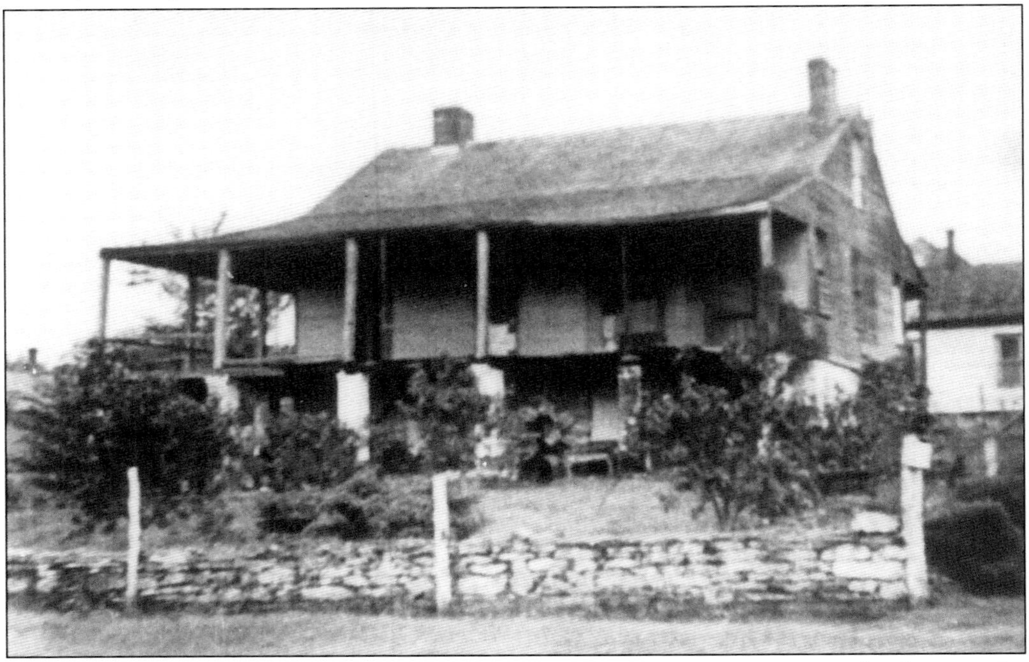

Numerous social events of earlier days, marriages, and other functions took place at the Atkinson home, shown here. It was considered to be quite gracious. The foundation of the old home can still be seen at North Second and C Streets. Second Street and Third and Fourth Streets were, at one time, the most desirable part of town. During the 1950s, when Fort Smith was undergoing a downtown clean-up campaign, many of those historic old homes were razed. (Fort Smith Public Library.)

Six

Our Leisure Time

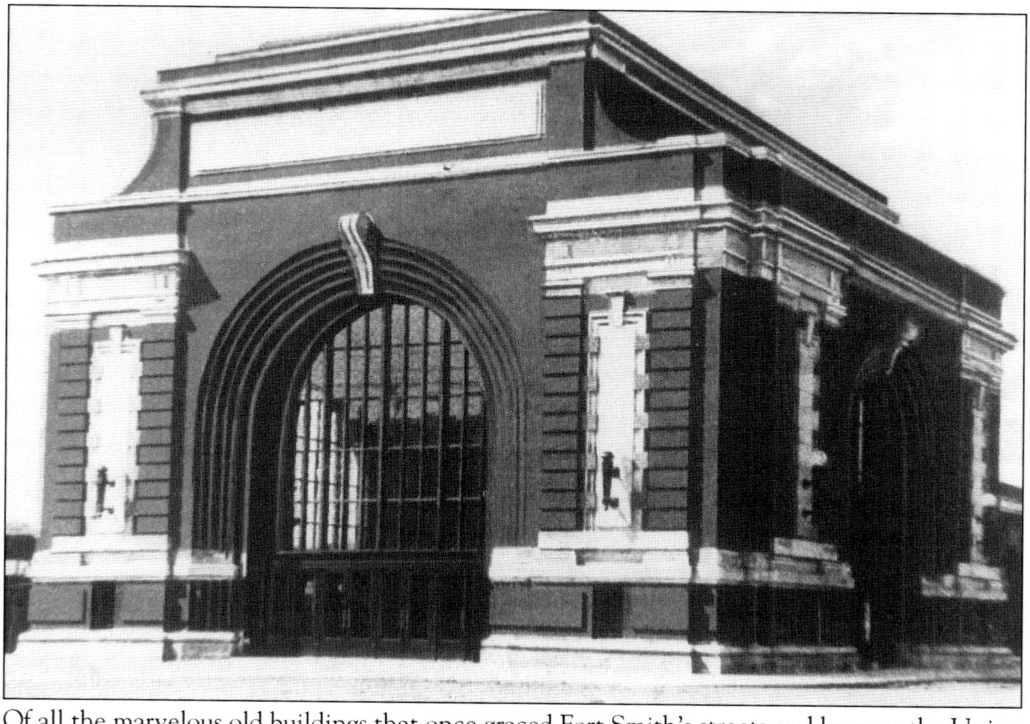

Of all the marvelous old buildings that once graced Fort Smith's streets and byways, the Union Station Train Depot at Seventh and Rogers Avenue, shown in this picture postcard, is the one most highly regarded by old-timers. It is perhaps Fort Smith's Taj Mahal. It seemed an architectural marvel with its immense, multi-storied, glass windows and what appeared to be miles of tunnel and train tracks. The tunnel was filled with the smoky, whoosh and hiss sights and sounds of trains ready to receive passengers. Children were awestruck sensing an enormous power barely contained. It was as though the trains were iron, prehistoric monsters. Also known as the Kansas City Southern Station, this beautiful structure, built in 1913, was demolished in 1960 to make way for the proverbial parking lot. (Wayne Bledsoe.)

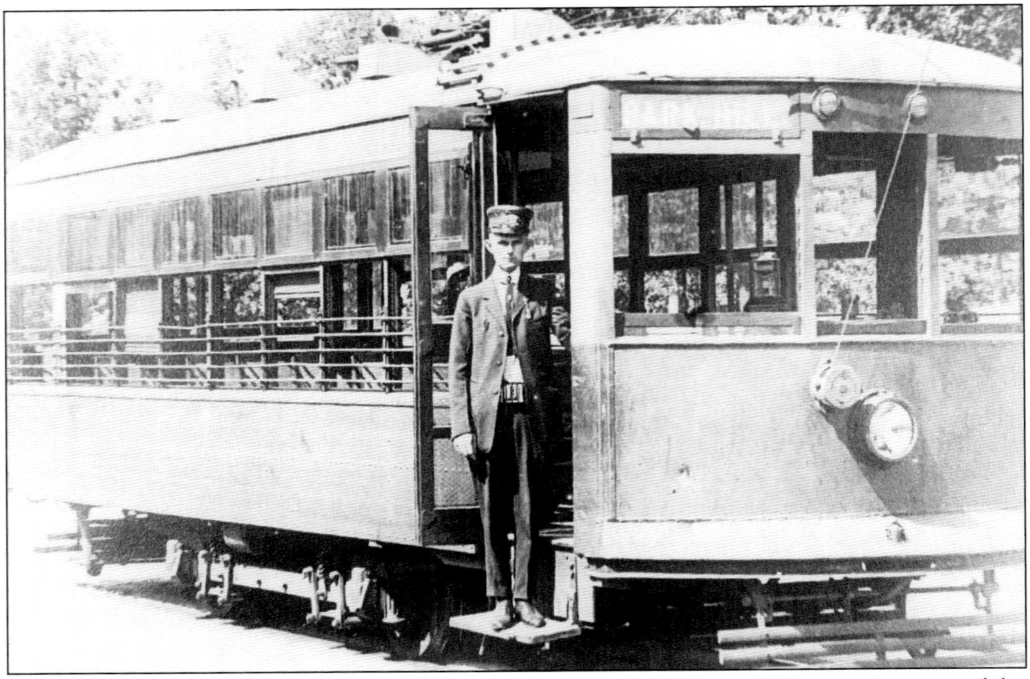

Frank Golden, streetcar motorman, is shown here with a 1919 Birney Safety car, just one of the many streetcars he operated for the Fort Smith Light and Traction Company. The motorman did not have to be a mechanic. When an electrical or mechanical problem arose he had only to call the trolley barn at Kelley Highway and Eleventh Street (now Midland Boulevard) and a mechanic would motor right out on the streetcar line and repair it. (Lillian Golden Hissom, Fort Smith Trolley Museum.)

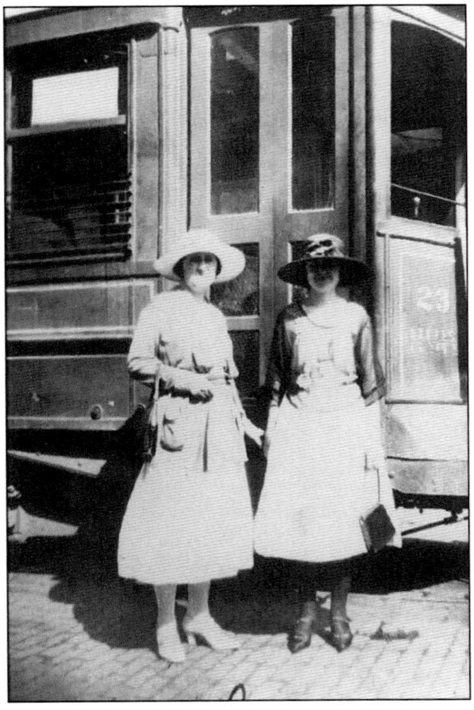

Anna Killion, shown at the right, and a friend are waiting to board a Fort Smith trolley c. 1920. Anna eventually married streetcar motorman Frank Golden. The first streetcars were mule-drawn in 1893. Later, in 1898, electricity became the source of energy to propel the streetcars. (Lillian Golden Hissom.)

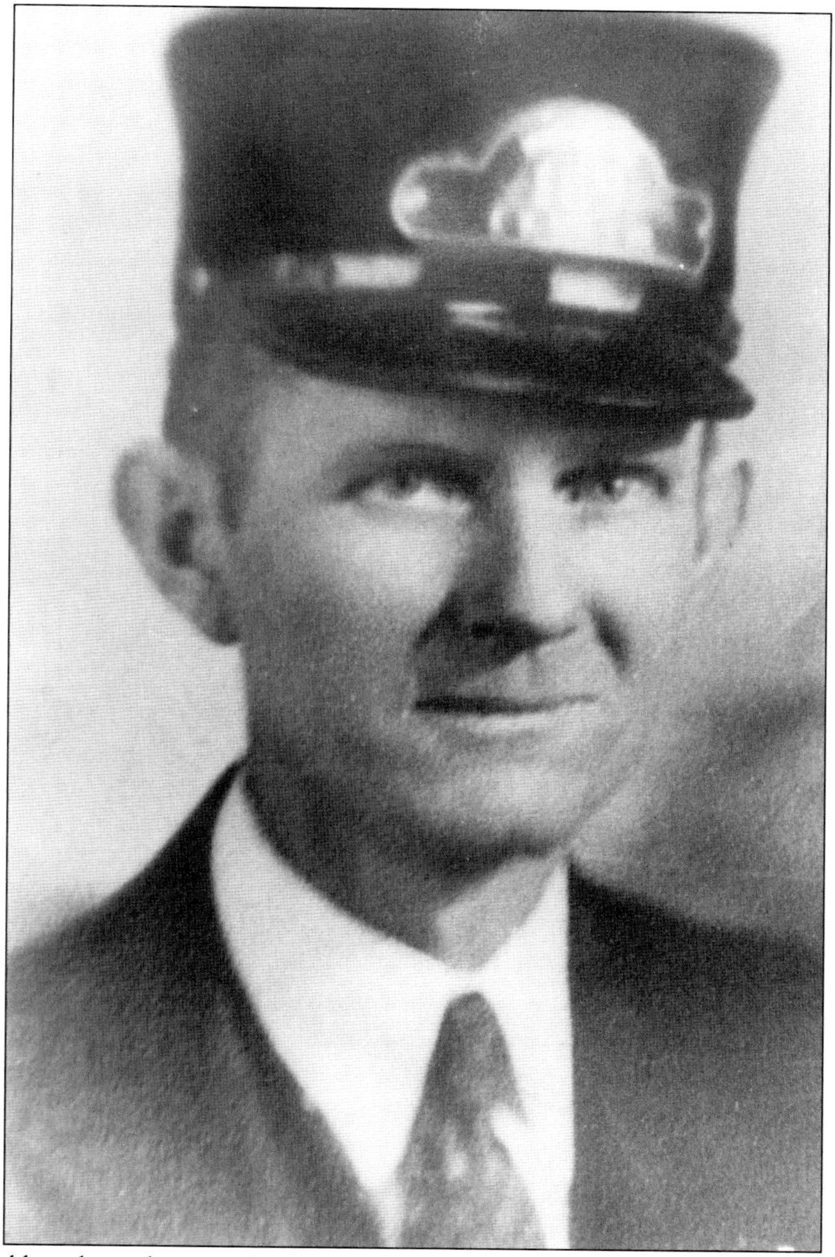

Frank Golden, shown here in a hand-tinted portrait, worked at various jobs such as the South Fort Smith Smelter and Harding Glass Company. He also co-owned Tagolene Gas Station before becoming a streetcar motorman employed by Fort Smith Light and Traction Company. The streetcar barn was located at Kelley Highway and Midland Boulevard where Tommy's Restaurant is today. When the streetcar line was closed, the company parked the cars by the scissors factory and removed the brass from them. Frank and Anna Golden had two seats from an old trolley car on their front porch for years. The seats of the streetcars were cane-bottomed and very heavy. Streetcars ran all the way to Van Buren. Motormen and daily trolley passengers felt a familial connection with one other. For a short time each day they became personally and emotionally involved in each other's lives. (Lillian Golden Hissom Collection.)

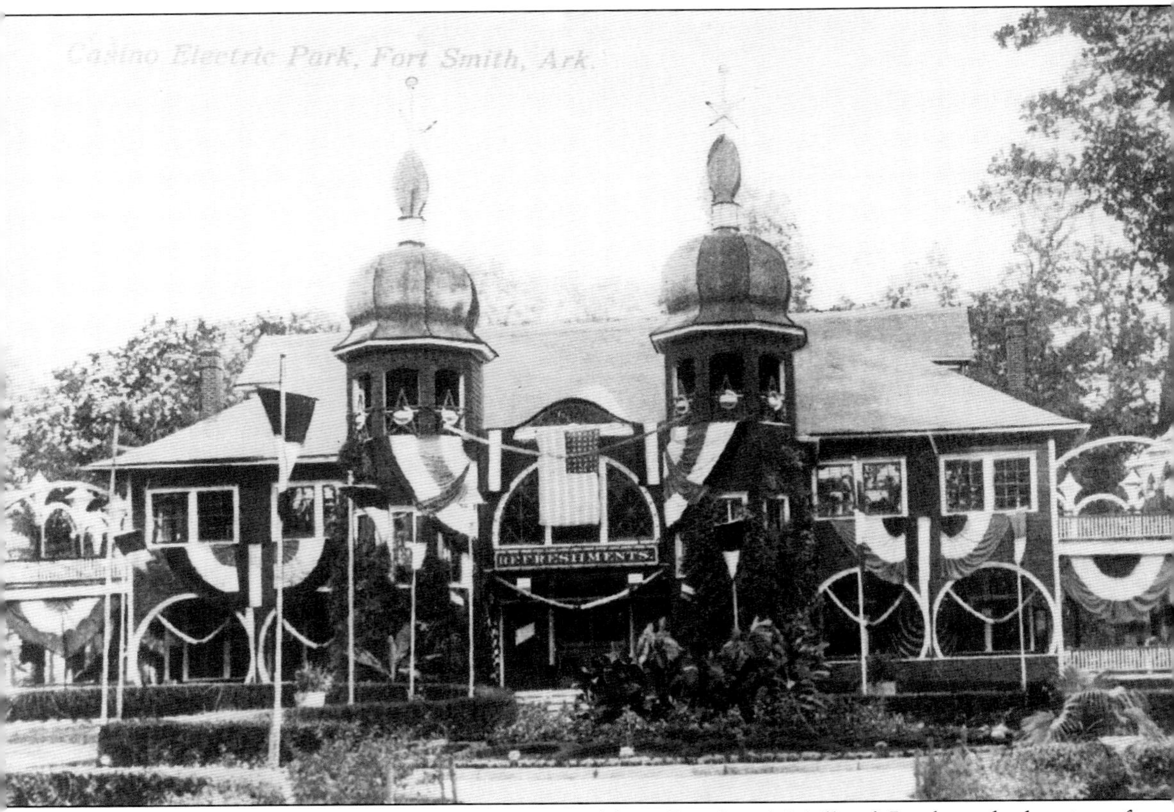

Many people described Electric Park at Waldron Road and Midland Boulevard, the site of present-day Kay Rodgers Park, as an enchanting, light-filled fairyland. The buildings called up images of fairy tales with their somewhat Moorish-style domes and spires. The Casino, shown here, had a grand ballroom on the second floor. Another magnificent building was the auditorium where many popular entertainers of the day performed. Electric Park's shrub- and flower-filled premises were supplied by a greenhouse on the grounds and maintained by a small army of gardeners. Underground generators produced the enormous wattage used to light the park. The streetcar line was built to generate customers. The Park remained a big attraction until the invention of the automobile and the advent of movies. (Fort Smith Public Library.)

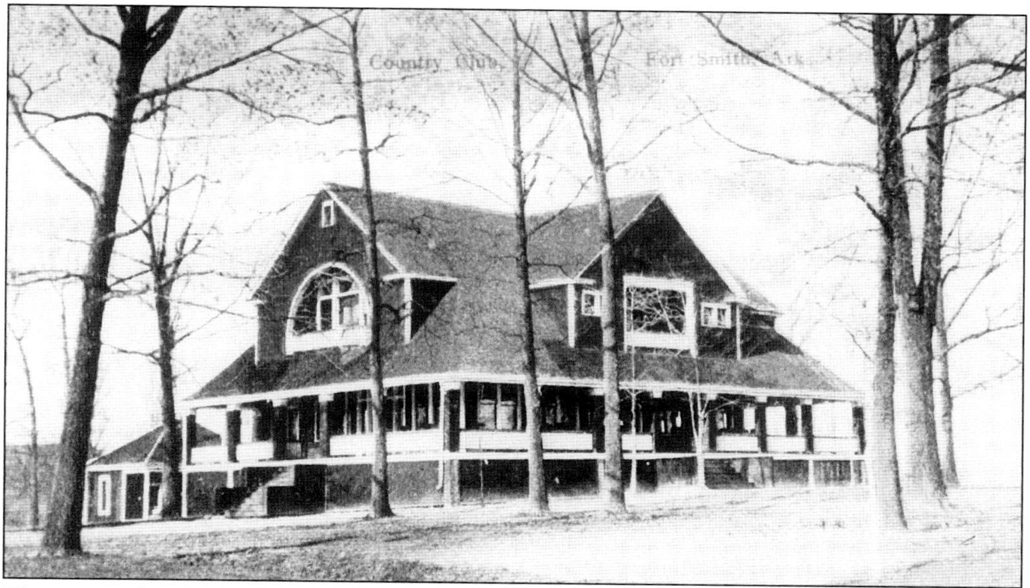

The green-shingle building of United Commercial Travelers Country Club, on Midland Boulevard, as shown in this picture postcard, burned in the early 1940s. That location is today's Forest Lawn Cemetery office. Observers recall golfers playing back and forth across the highway. The club is the second-oldest golf course west of the Mississippi in use at its original location. Pete Parker bought the club in the 1950s and the Parker family continues to operate it today. (Fort Smith Public Library.)

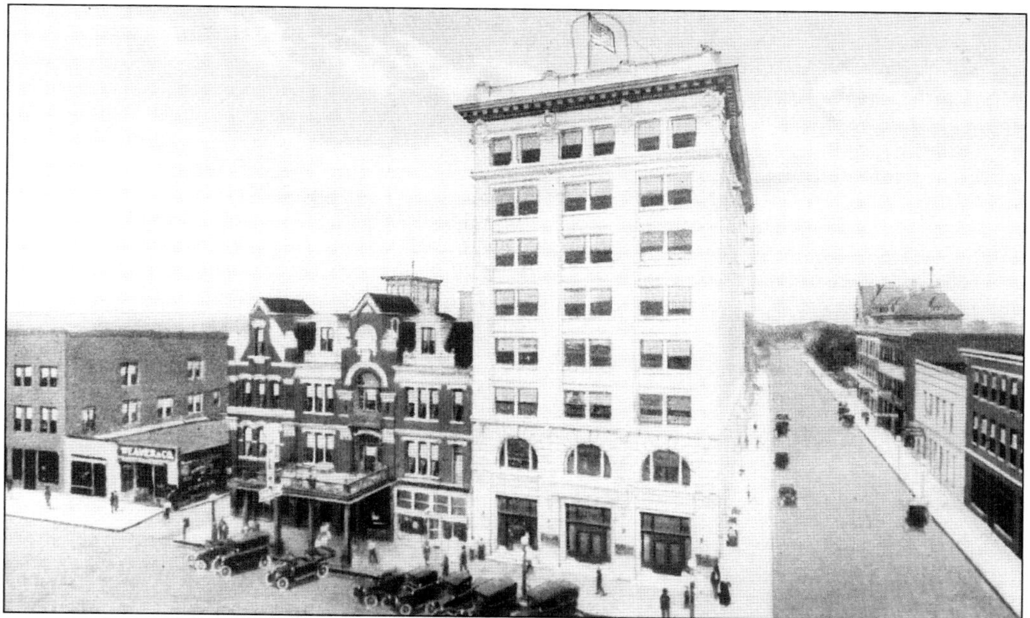

The odd-couple appearance of the Hotel Main to the left, and its Goliath neighbor First National Bank, shown in this picture postcard, have another connection. At one time the First National Bank, established on February 29, 1872, was located inside the Hotel Main. The bank building, still in use today, was constructed in 1909. The Hotel Main burned and the Donoho-Merry Building, now occupied by the Chamber of Commerce, was built adjacent to that site. (Fort Smith Public Library.)

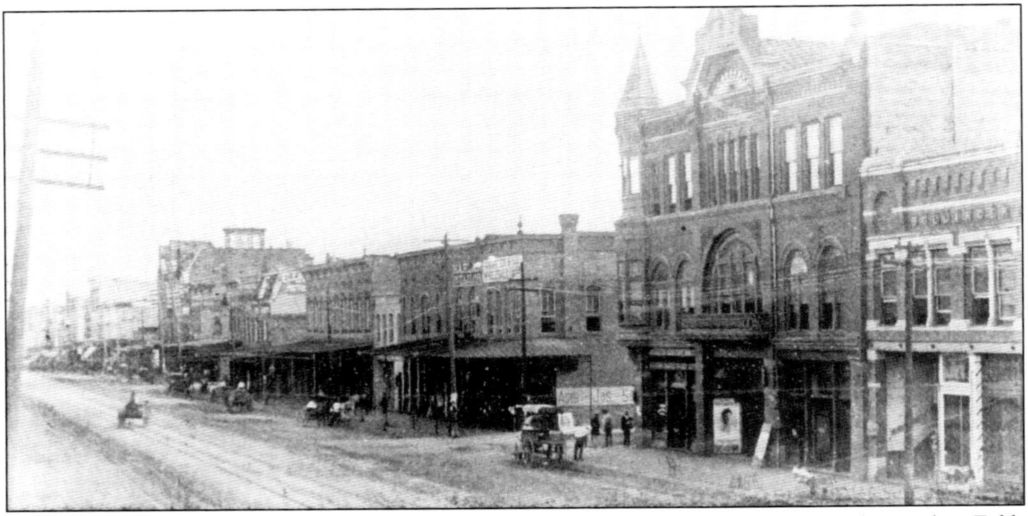

The Grand Opera House, built *c.* 1887, and the Pacific Express Company was located at Fifth and Garrison. The Opera House, also known as the Conservatory, was constructed at a cost of $50,000 and was managed by Chanuncy Lick. Jenny Lind was said to have performed here. The building's use as an opera house was discontinued in 1911, and it became a wholesale grocery house. The Opera House burned on December 5, 1941. (Fort Smith Public Library.)

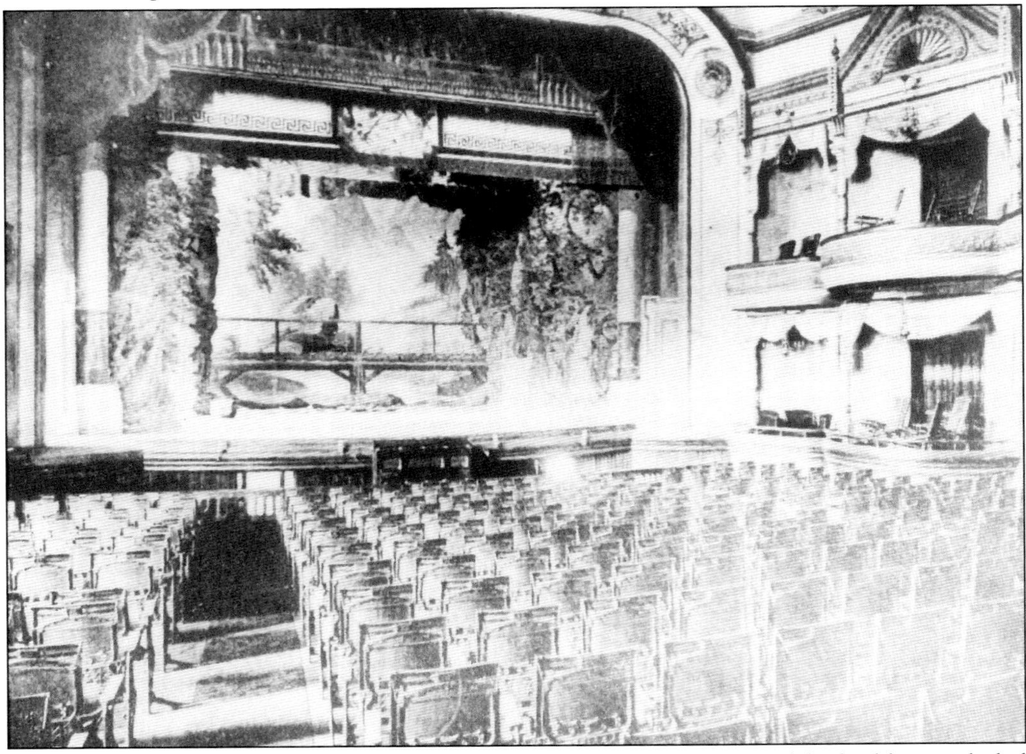

This is the seating inside the opulent Grand Opera House. The interior of the building included a tower which ran up the exterior at the northeast corner of the building. It displayed hand-painted Shakespearean scenes in its rotunda. On the night of the presentations, many young men would hire horse-drawn cabs and take their dates for an oyster dinner at the Mayo Restaurant at Sixth and Garrison Avenue. (Fort Smith Public Library.)

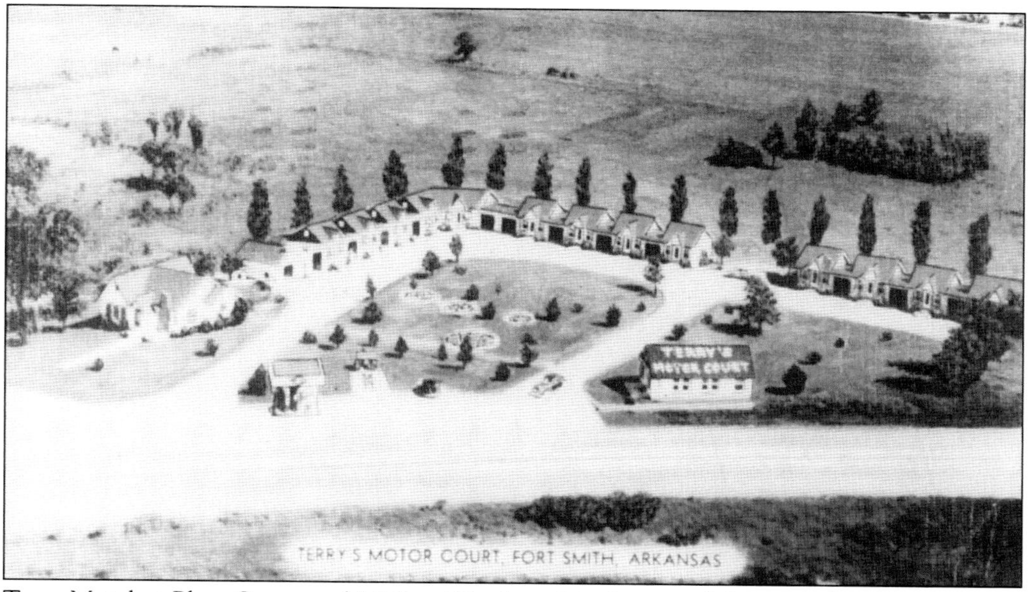

Terry Motel at Plum Street and Midland Boulevard is the site of the second air mail flight in the United States. League Stadium was located at this site and the post office was set up under the stadium bleachers. The mail was picked up by two airplanes and dropped at the Federal Building Post Office downtown. Balloon ascensions took place at this location, also. (Fort Smith Public Library.)

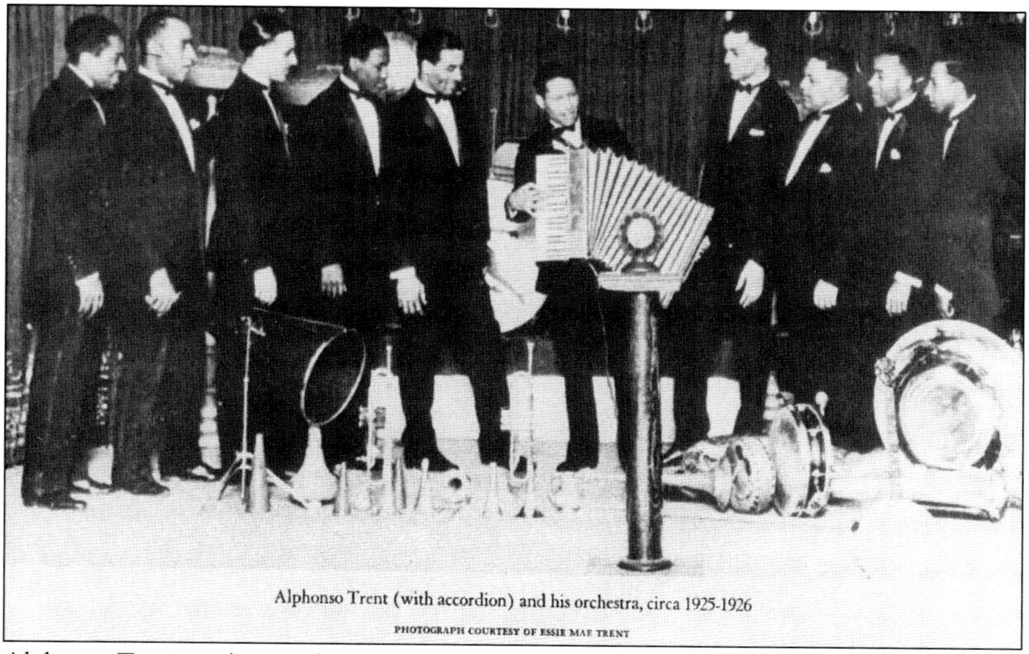

Alphonso Trent, with accordion, and his orchestra are shown here *c.* 1925–1926. During the "Roaring Twenties" Trent and his orchestra broke the color line at the prestigious Adolphus Hotel in Dallas. Their's was the first black band permitted to use the front entrance to clubs and restaurants, instead of the customary entrance for blacks. From 1920 to 1930 Trent's band was the most influential in the Southwest, with a superb brass section and rhythm team, and the finest for over-all performance. (Mrs. Essie Mae Trent.)

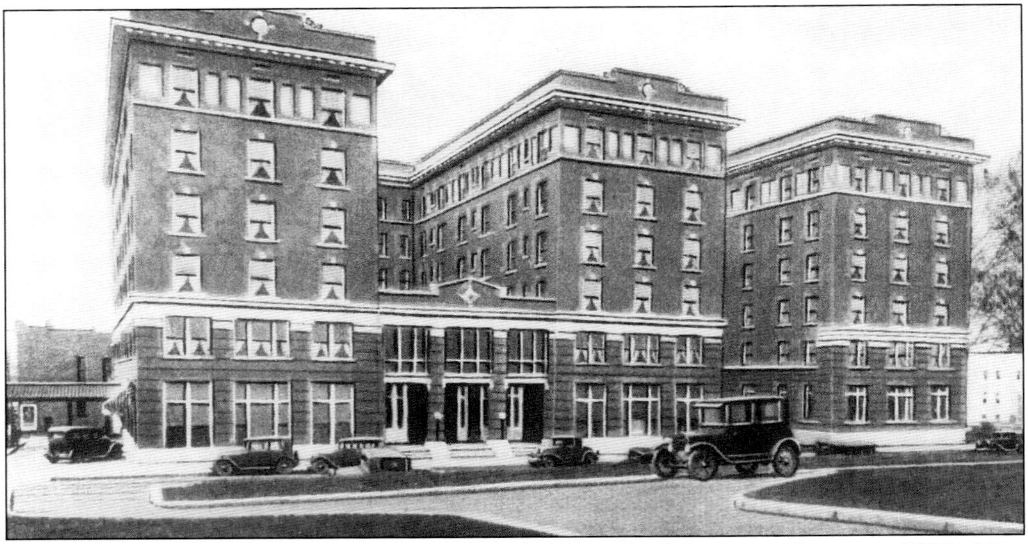

Construction on the Goldman Hotel, by the Sebastian Hotel Company, began in 1908. After only two floors of the six-story building were completed, funds ran out. A new group, the Southwestern Hotel Company, was formed, with seven local residents as board members. They negotiated with Lesser Goldman, a cotton broker in St. Louis, who agreed to supply the needed funds to finish the job, if the hotel would carry his name. The building, fronting on North Thirteenth Street, was completed in 1911. Between 1911 and WW II the Goldman was the focal point of Fort Smith society and one of three top convention centers in Arkansas. Dinner in the glamorous dining hall included tuxedo-clad waiters, candle-lit tables, and ballroom dancing. (Fort Smith Public Library.)

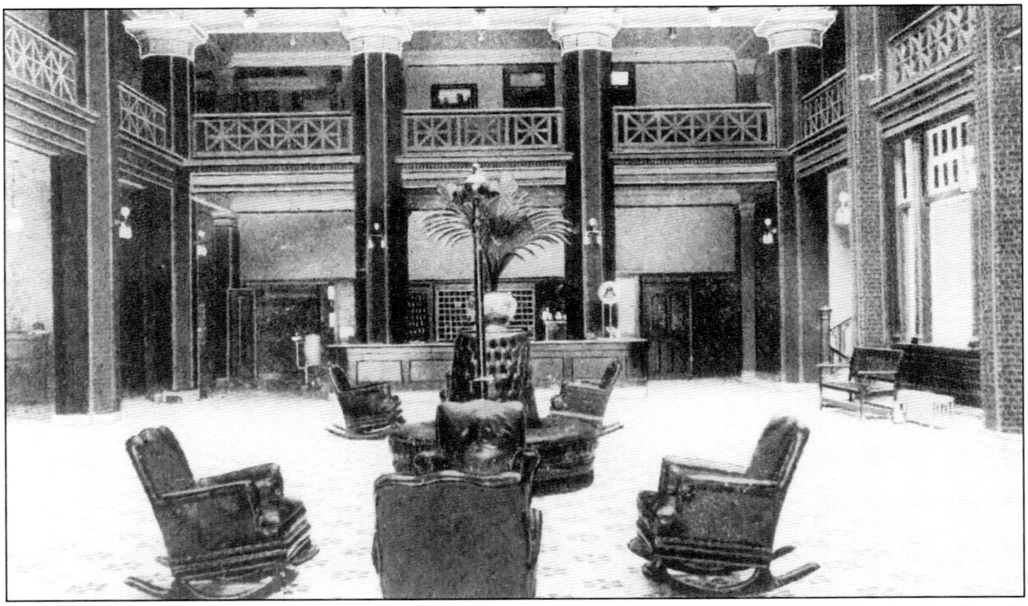

Shown is the lobby of the Goldman, where big-name entertainers checked into the hotel. Among those who stayed at the hotel were Will Rogers, Rosalind Russell, Bob Burns, Susan Hayward, Mickey Mantle, and Dizzy Dean. President and Mrs. Harry Truman were guests several times. Eleanor Roosevelt was honored with a reception here, and KFSA, the first radio station in Fort Smith, broadcast daily from the Goldman. (Fort Smith Public Library.)

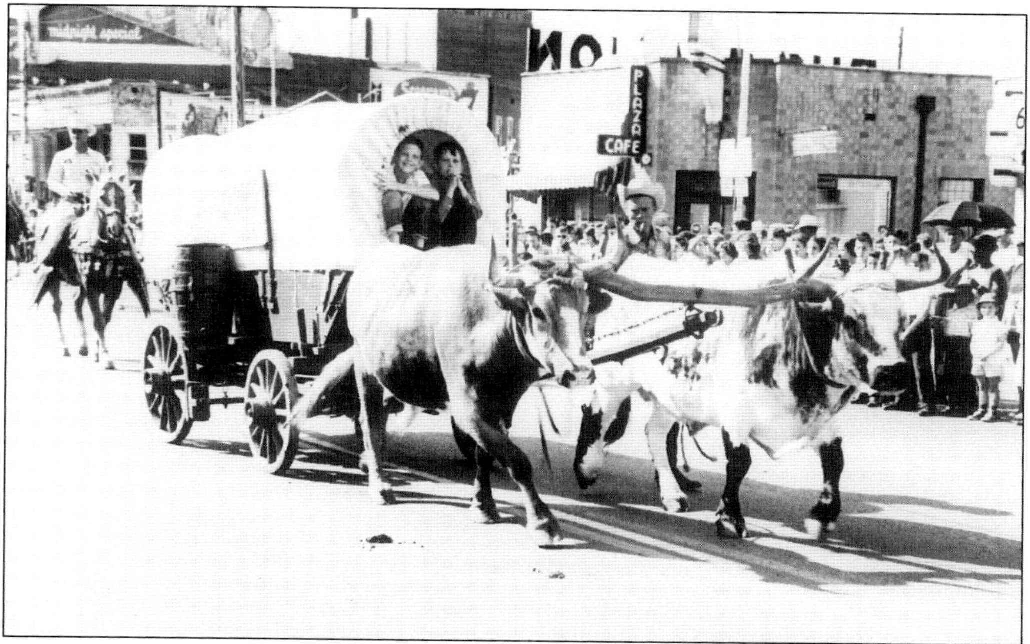

An example of a heavy express wagon drawn by a couple of large bulls is shown in a 1950s Arkansas-Oklahoma Rodeo Parade. The sign on the side of the wagon is promoting the McAlester Prison Rodeo in Oklahoma. The old Plaza Cafe must have done a good business that day, with all the parade folks in town. (Fort Smith Chamber of Commerce.)

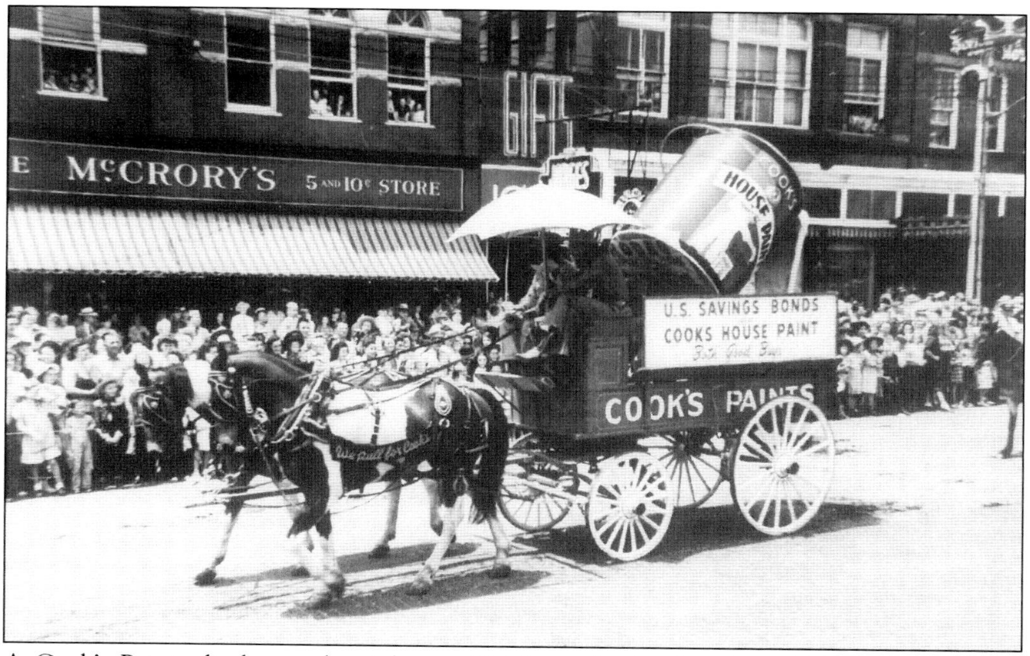

A Cook's Paints display at the Arkansas-Oklahoma Rodeo Parade c. 1950, promoted U.S. Savings Bonds. Note McCrory's five and dime store. Next is Jorgenson's Jewelry Store and Gifts, and the Boston Store. Nearby were Woolworth and Kress, all five and dime stores, and all within two blocks of each other. (Fort Smith Chamber of Commerce.)

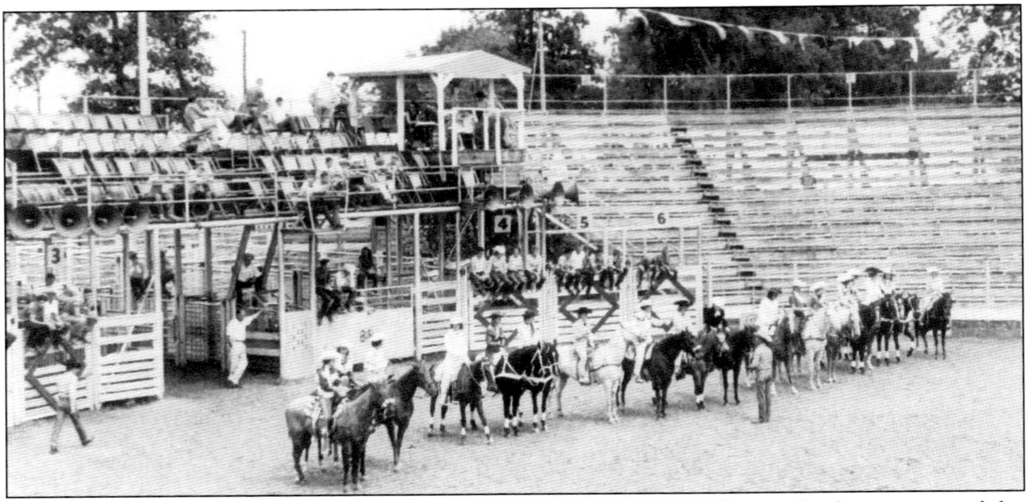

Rodeo Queen contestants lined up on their horses in May 1958. Harper Stadium is one of the oldest facilities of its kind in the United States. The Rodeo Queen contestants would practice for the parade review routine held during the opening minutes of the Arkansas-Oklahoma Rodeo. (Fort Smith Chamber of Commerce.)

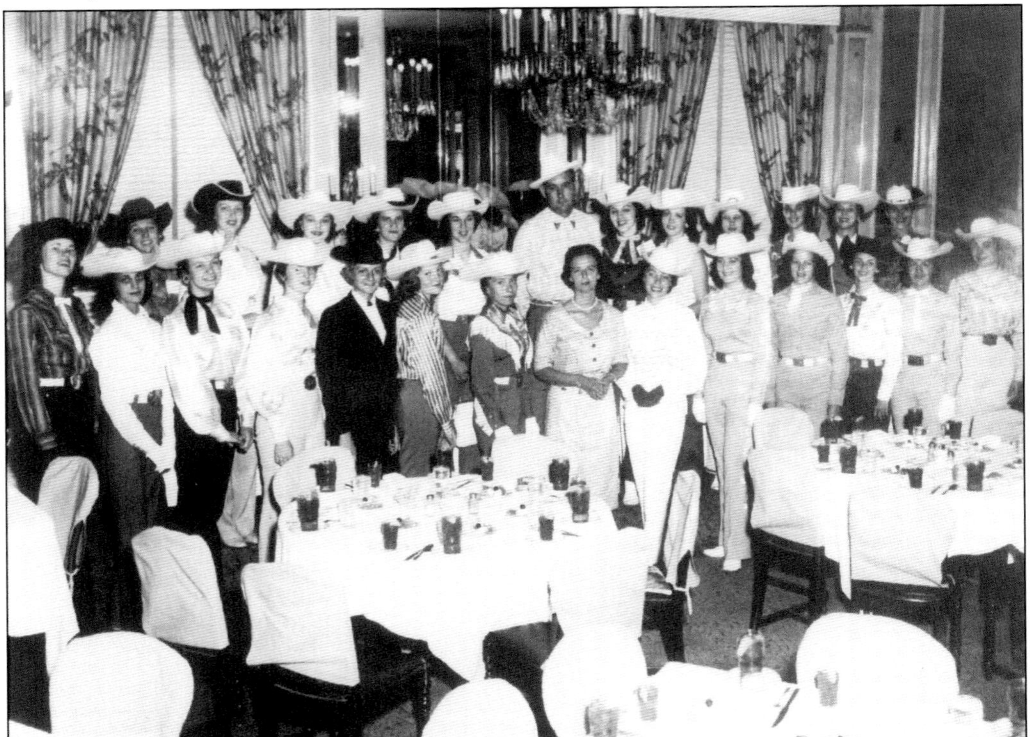

The restaurant of the Ward Hotel is shown here *c.* 1954, with Fort Smith Chamber of Commerce officials and Rodeo Queen contestants. The chamber sponsored the queen contests and the Rodeo Queen winner was determined by who sold the most chuck-wagon dinner tickets. Buddy Smith, the tall man in the white cowboy hat, served as the contest coordinator. A chamber employee recalls that Smith's hat was made of white velvet and had to be cleaned with corn meal. (Fort Smith Chamber of Commerce.)

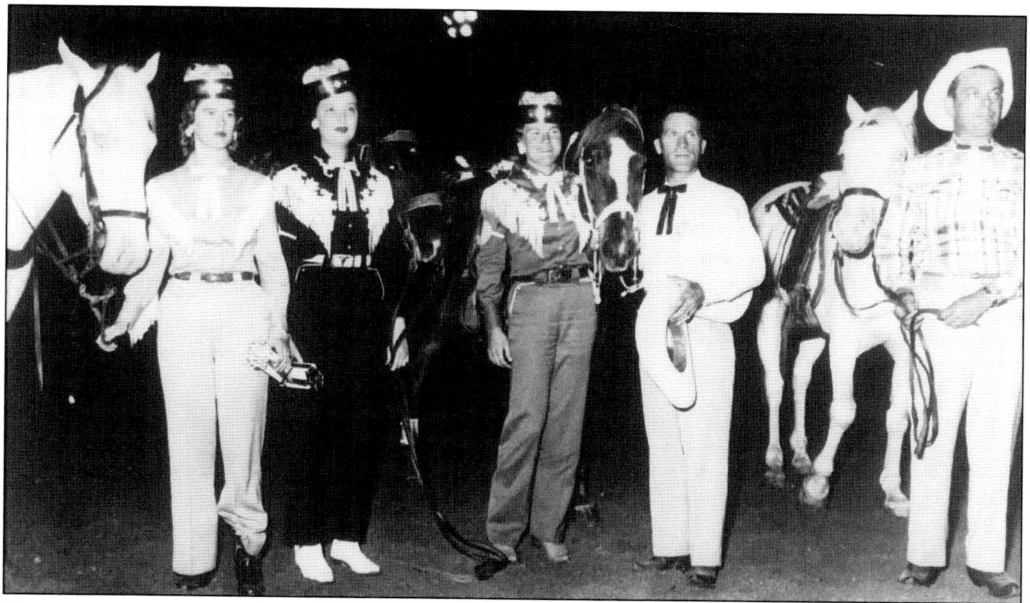

Queen contestants at the Arkansas-Oklahoma Rodeo are pictured in 1955. The winner was Phyllis Jackson from Mulberry, second from left in black. The contestant to her right is Shirley Browning, also from Mulberry. The other contestant is Margaret Bieker. The gentleman to the left is contest coordinator Buddy Smith and then an unknown gentleman. Note the shiny crowns on the heads of the young women. (Fort Smith Chamber of Commerce.)

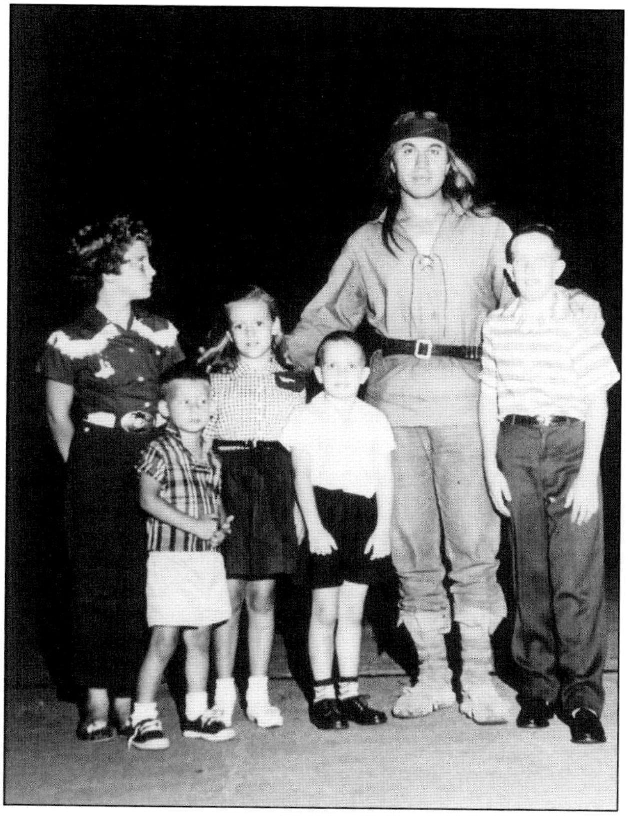

Michael Ansara, is shown here c. 1956, from the ABC-TV series *Broken Arrow*, in which he played Cochise. Ansara was in town promoting the Arkansas-Oklahoma Rodeo. He is shown here with some Fort Smith admirers. Cochise was a Chiricahua-Apache Indian chief who, after being deceived by the white man, becomes a renegade. He waged an incessant war against the white man until he retired to the reservation in 1872. (Fort Smith Chamber of Commerce.)

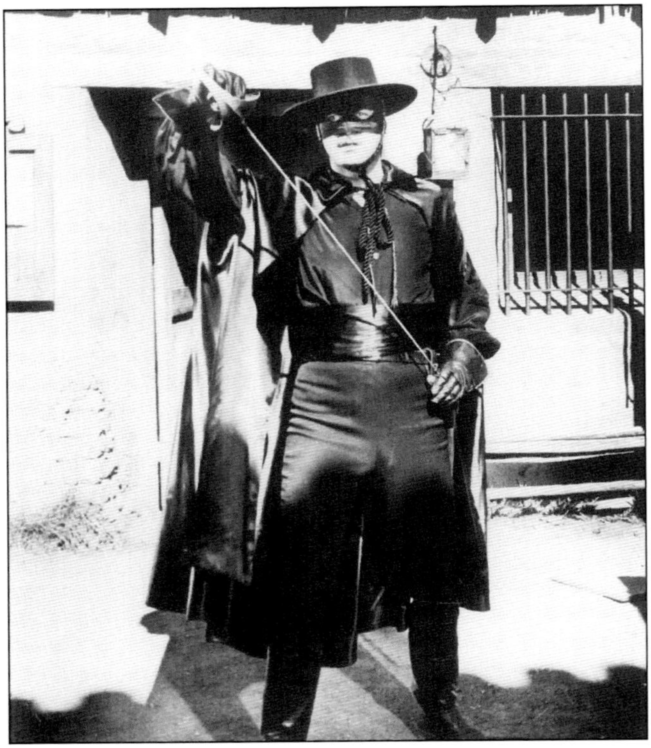

Actor Guy Williams, shown here c. 1958, a handsome 6-foot 3-inch-tall actor, played the leading role in the television show *Zorro*. He portrayed the dual role of Don Diego, a Spanish nobleman's son, and Zorro the masked avenger in the Walt Disney-ABC series. When he arrived in Fort Smith for the Arkansas-Oklahoma Rodeo, Williams brought his wife and child with him. This put a damper on the dreams of many young women. (Walt Disney Studios, Fort Smith Chamber of Commerce.)

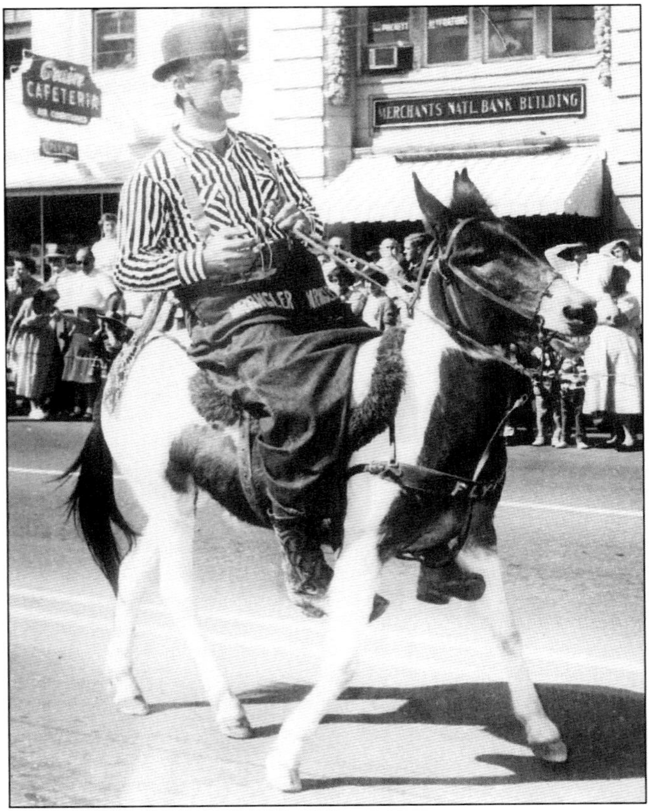

Clown Gene Clark, as shown in the 1950s, is riding a mule during the Arkansas-Oklahoma Rodeo Parade. Clowns are vital to the safety of rodeo performers. As tremendous athletes, they appear fearless, while attracting the bulls away from the downed rider. However, they know their limitations and rarely take chances where they could be seriously injured, unless it's to rescue a cowboy. In the background, note the Crain Cafeteria, where many downtown workers paused to have lunch. (Fort Smith Chamber of Commerce.)

Champion Rodeo Performers of the Arkansas-Oklahoma Rodeo c. 1950 are, from left to right: Ross Dollarhide, Casey Tibbs, and Bill Linderman. Promoters of the day claimed these cowboys could ride anything on four legs. Rodeo performers, especially those who ride broncs and bulls, tend to acquire injuries throughout the rodeo season, but claim that they heal very quickly. (Rodeo Information Commission, Fort Smith Chamber of Commerce.)

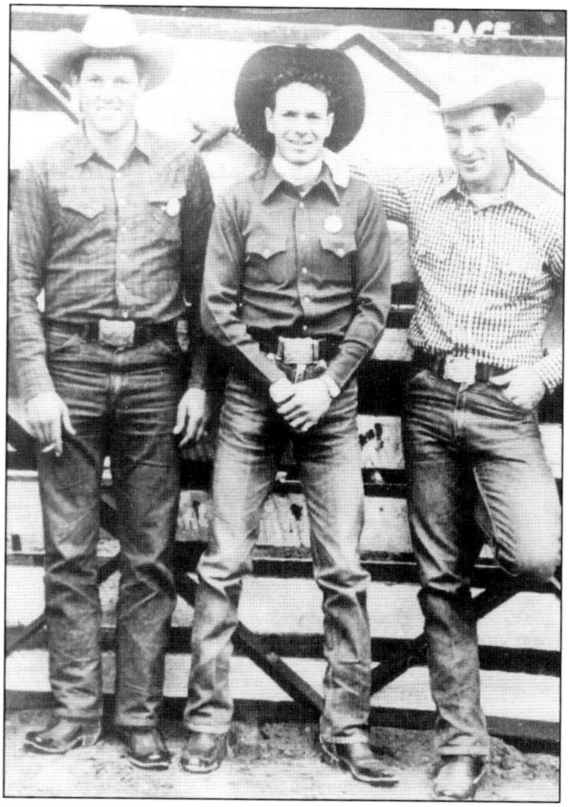

A cowboy is shown in the 1950s riding a four-footed fury during the bareback contest at the Arkansas-Oklahoma Rodeo. The bronc, so far, has failed to unseat the well-balanced rider. To stay aboard, the rider has a simple rigging to hang onto, a plain band with a leather handhold. The ride must last for eight seconds, an eternity on this kind of hot seat. The horse has almost bent himself double trying to unseat his rider. (Fort Smith Chamber of Commerce.)

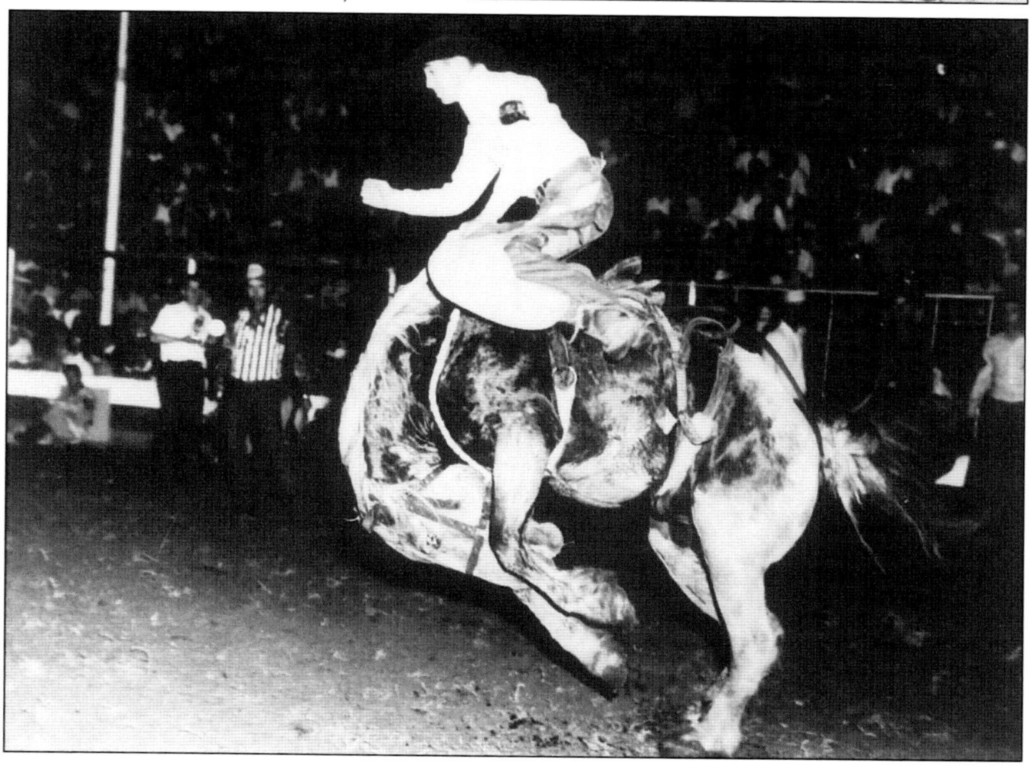

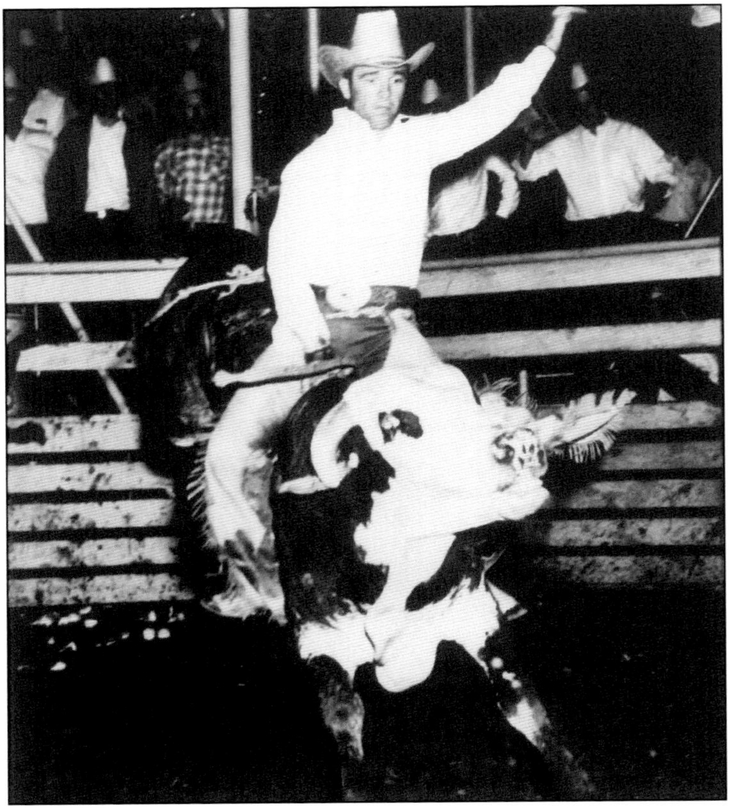

Larry Mahan, All Around Champion Cowboy, is shown here riding a bull in the 1967 Arkansas-Oklahoma Rodeo. Mahan, a wonderful athlete, was adept at bronc and bull riding, and roping, among other talents. He captured all-around rodeo honors for many years. The annual Rodeo at Kay Rodgers Park, Harper Stadium in Fort Smith, is one of the oldest rodeos of its kind in the United States. (Fort Smith Chamber of Commerce.)

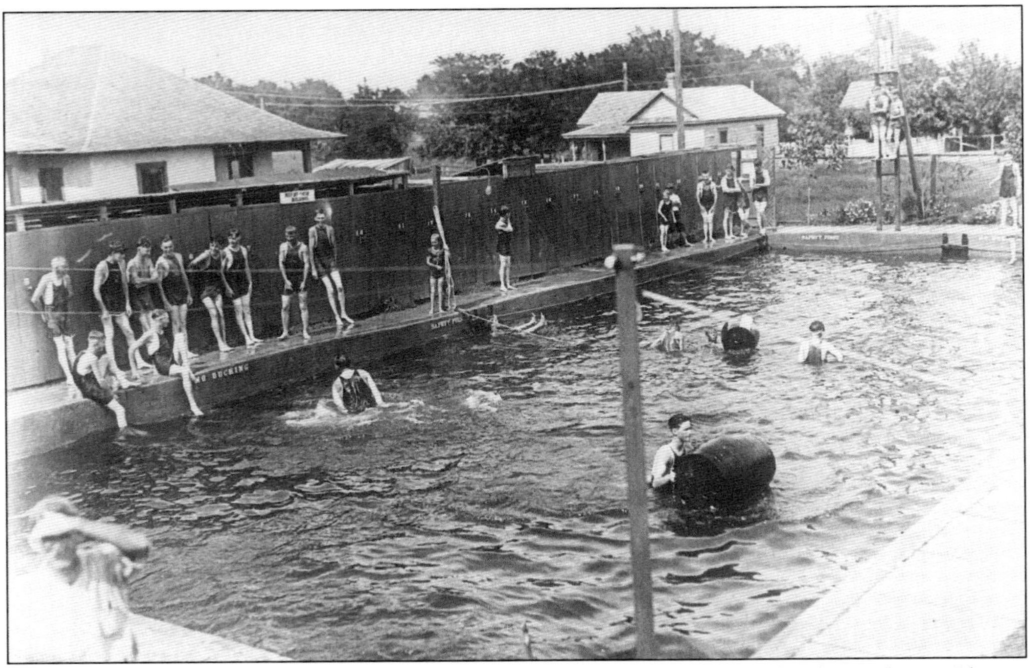

Whittaker's Swimming Pool at North 32nd and Kelley Highway *c.* 1925 is shown here. Almost everyone in Fort Smith would go to the pool on those hot summer afternoons. It stayed open until 10 p.m., and the fee for swimming all day was 5¢. (Lillian Golden Hissom.)

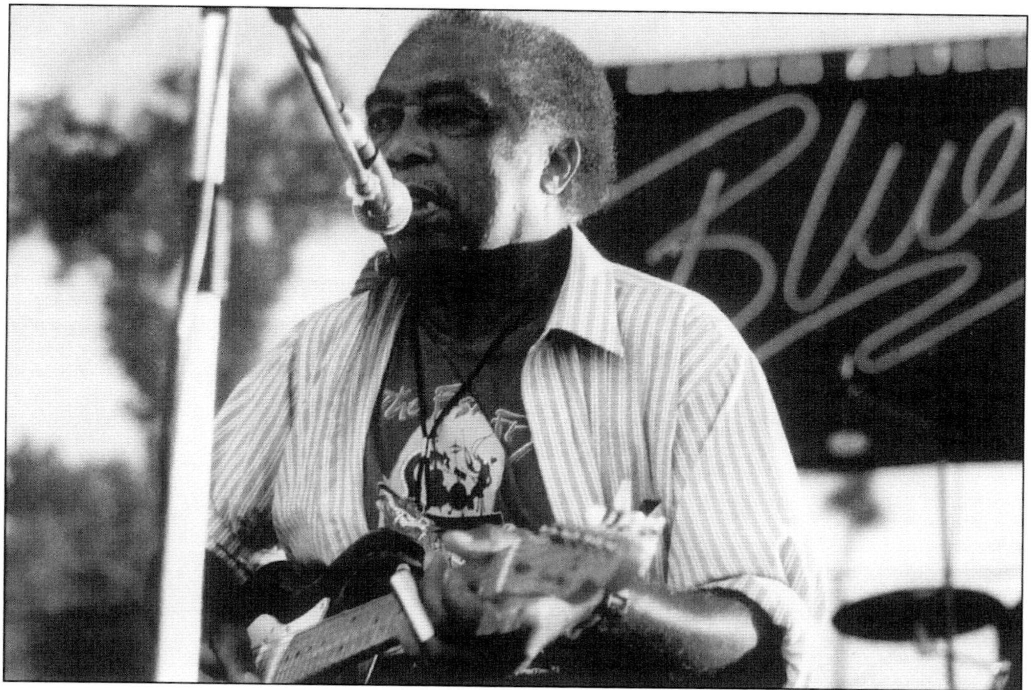

In 1997 the Riverfront Blues Festival featured veteran Bluesman R.C. Barnside, among others. The Riverfront Blues Society is a local nonprofit organization with a membership of about 700 local residents. The Society is dedicated to presenting an affordable annual Blues Festival, preserving and promoting the blues, and supporting the preservation and development of downtown Fort Smith. (Linda Seubold.)

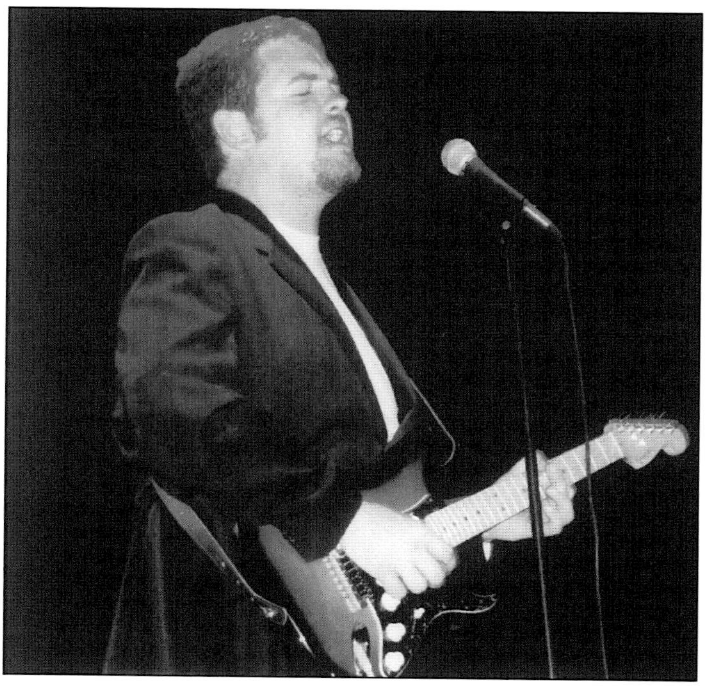

The Fort Smith Riverfront Blues Festival of 1998 presented Chris Cameron and the Chris Cameron Band. Nineteen-year-old Cameron won the 1997 International Blues Talent Competition, exhibiting the stage presence of a well-seasoned professional. In the past the Blues Society has scheduled performances by prominent bluesmen Jimmie Vaughan, W.C. Clark, Tommy Castro, and others. The Society's successful, highly-charged productions are performed to sell-out crowds. (Linda Seubold.)

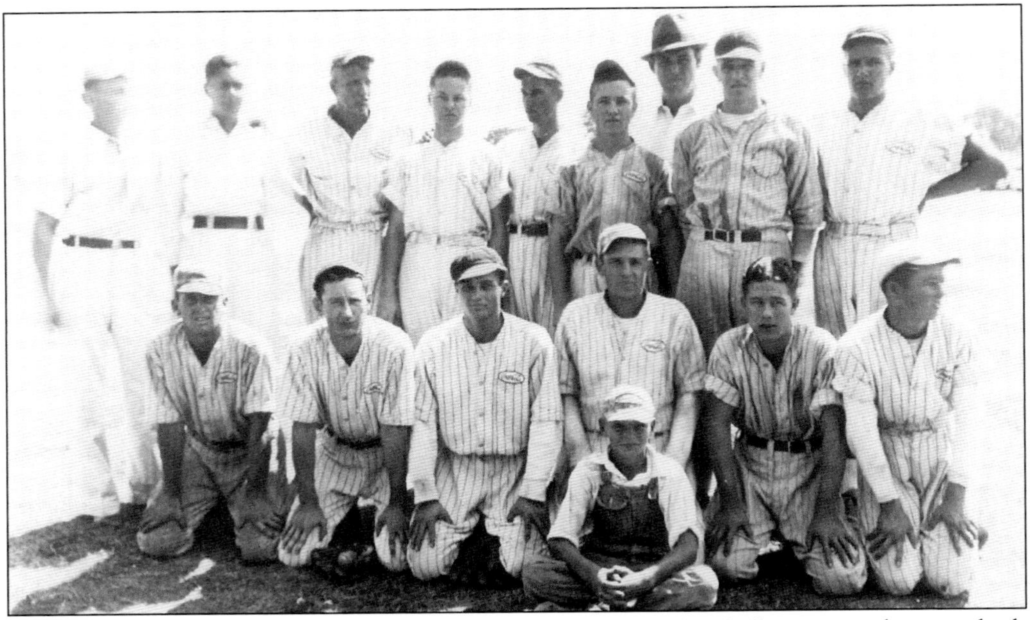

In the 1940s the Coca-Cola Bottling Company sponsored a baseball team, as shown, which played other amateur teams at Andrews Field, located between South Fifth and Seventh Streets. In 1919 John M. Andrews Sr. first began raising funds to build a baseball field. When the field was dedicated in May 1921 it was named in his honor. Fort Smith became a farm club of the St. Louis Cardinals in 1923 and later served as a farm club for the Detroit Tigers. (Coca-Cola Bottling Co.)

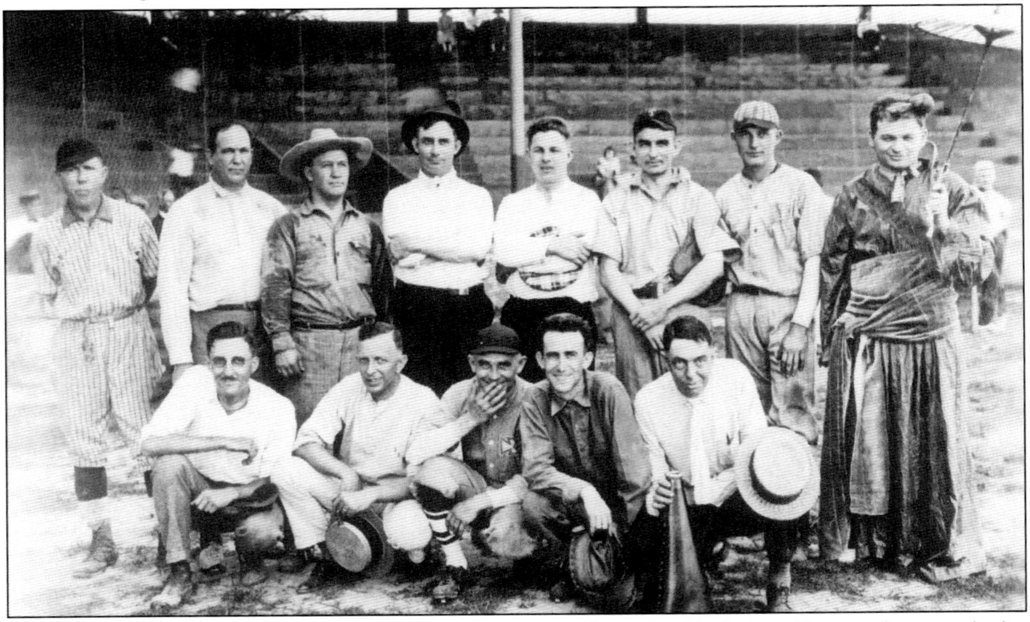

An amateur baseball team is shown in the 1920s at Andrews Field. George Rye, in front with the megaphone and straw hat, was the announcer. Rye also owned a flower shop. His slogan "some florist" was one of the most successful in Fort Smith. A lot seems to be going on here. There's a fellow to the right in a dress holding an umbrella, and a gentleman center-front attempts to hide his humor. (Lillian Golden Hissom.)

Seven

SEBASTIAN COUNTY

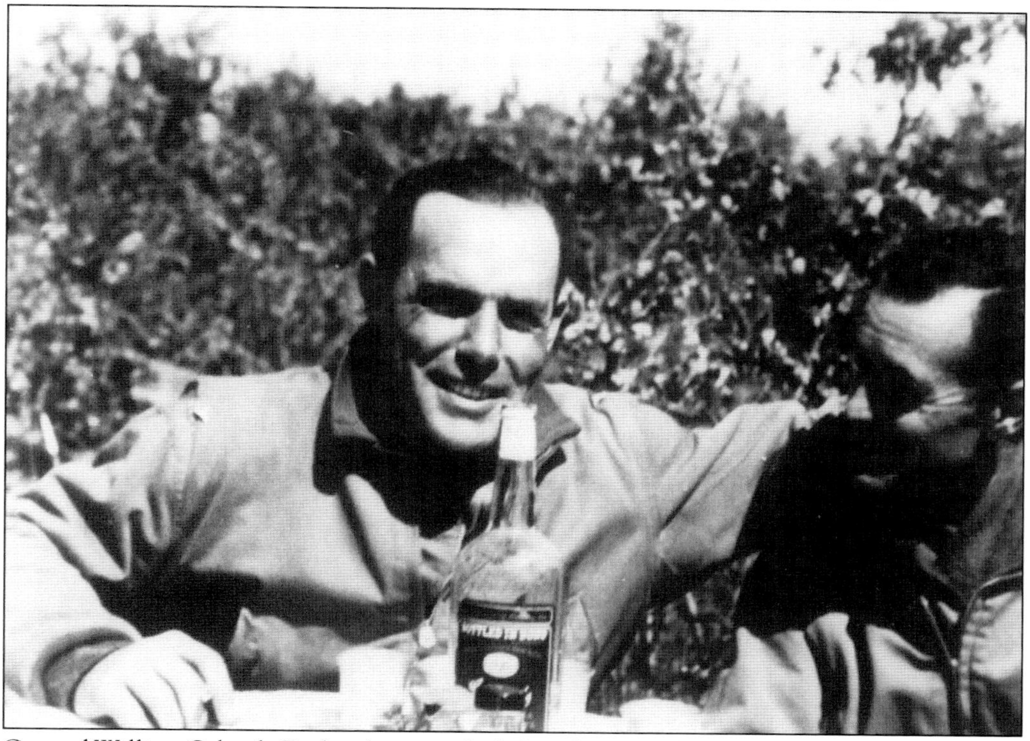

General William Orlando Darby, shown to the left in this 1944 photo, and his best friend Captain Roy Murray, were photographed in Anzio, Italy. Captain Murray was returning to the United States and never saw Bill Darby alive again. Darby, born in Fort Smith on February 8, 1911, was founder and leader of the American Rangers of WW II fame. After two of his three Ranger Battalions were destroyed, he commanded the 179th Infantry, 45th Division until April 1944. Afterward he spent 11 months in Washington before returning to Italy as assistant commander of the 10th Mountain Division. He was killed in action by artillery fire in Po Valley, Italy, on April 30, 1945. Darby was wounded three times and was awarded numerous decorations. He was only 34 years old when he died. (The Darby Foundation.)

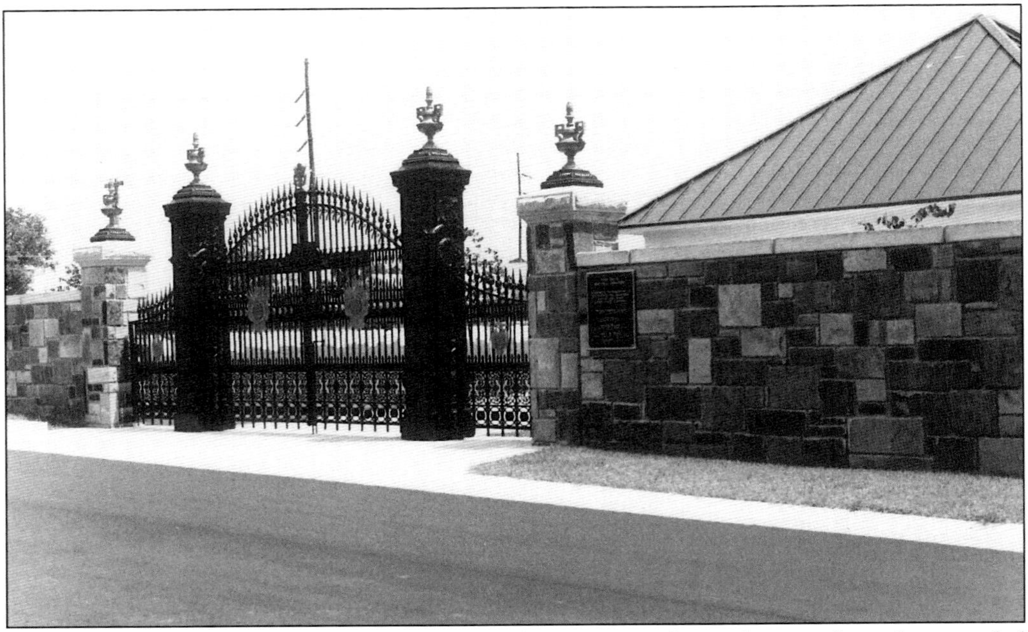

The gates to the new section of the National Cemetery, shown here, reflect the crowded conditions in the old cemetery. The first internment of the Fort Smith National Cemetery dates back to Surgeon Thomas Russell, in 1819, who accompanied Major William C. Bradford in establishment of the first fort and was a veteran of the War of 1812. The National Cemetery is an enlargement of the post cemeteries of the first and second Fort Smiths, established in 1817 and 1838. Among those buried in the 15.8 acre cemetery are 473 Confederates and 1,464 unknown soldiers. The occupants include soldiers from all wars, except the American Revolution. (Author.)

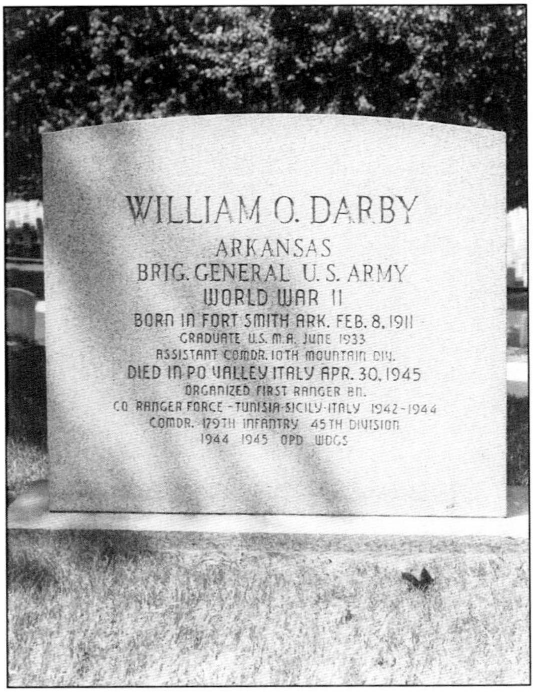

This is the tombstone of Brigadier General William O. Darby, U.S. Army. Darby's final resting place at the Fort Smith National Cemetery is a quiet tree-shaded haven located along a pleasant slope of land. An occasional songbird trills its note on a gentle breeze. This is a peaceful place, a far cry from the circumstances under which many of its occupants died. Visitors are requested to please be respectful of this hallowed ground. (Author.)

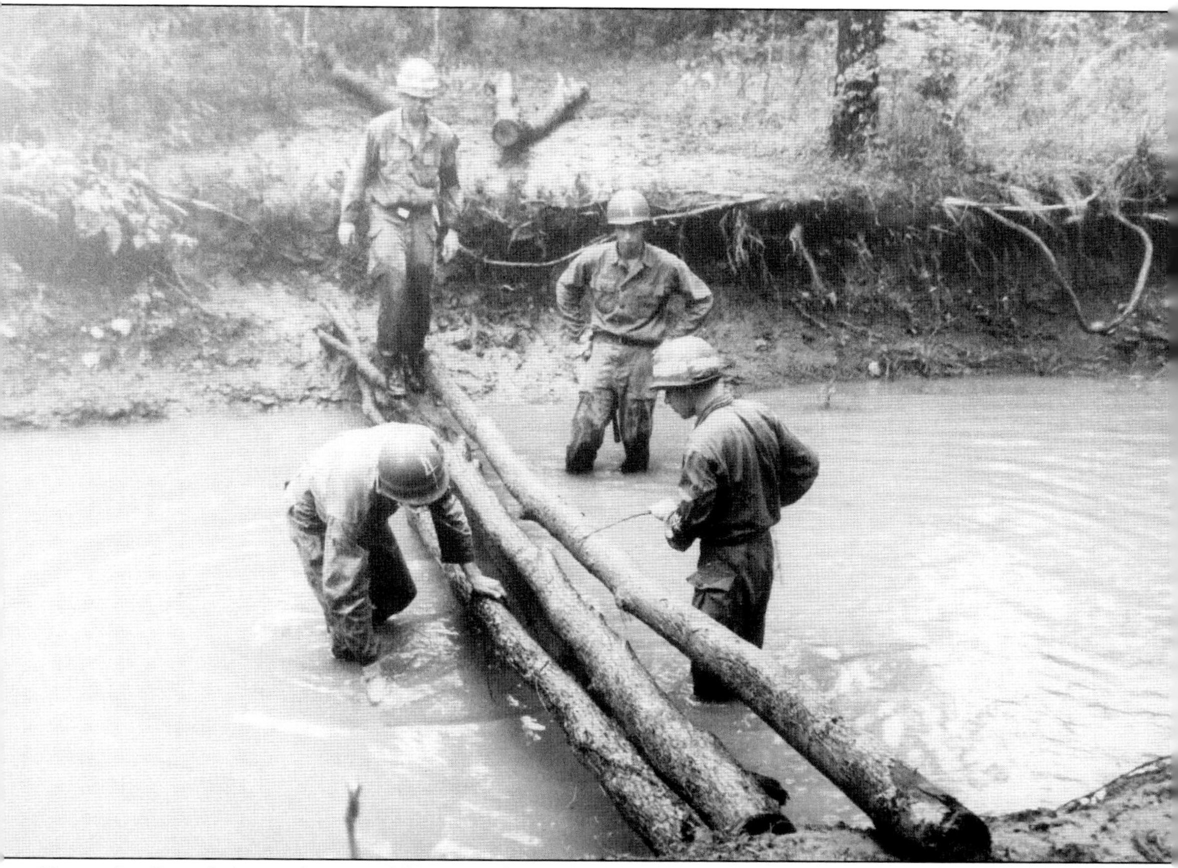

Here, the Signal Army Corps soldiers are shown in training at Camp Chaffee. Camp Chaffee, later renamed Fort Chaffee, was constructed in September 1941, in Barling, Arkansas. It was named in memory of Major General Adna R. Chaffee, first chief of the armored forces, who died that same year. The camp served as a training ground for the 6th, 14th, and 16th Armored Divisions, each of which saw combat in WW II. The 44th Infantry Division occupied the west camp area of Camp Chaffee late in the summer of 1945. Combat training was also given to an infantry regiment, several field artillery groups, a combat engineer unit, and several ordnance and quartermaster battalions. The reservation was also home to three Women's Army Corps detachments during the war. (Fort Smith Chamber of Commerce.)

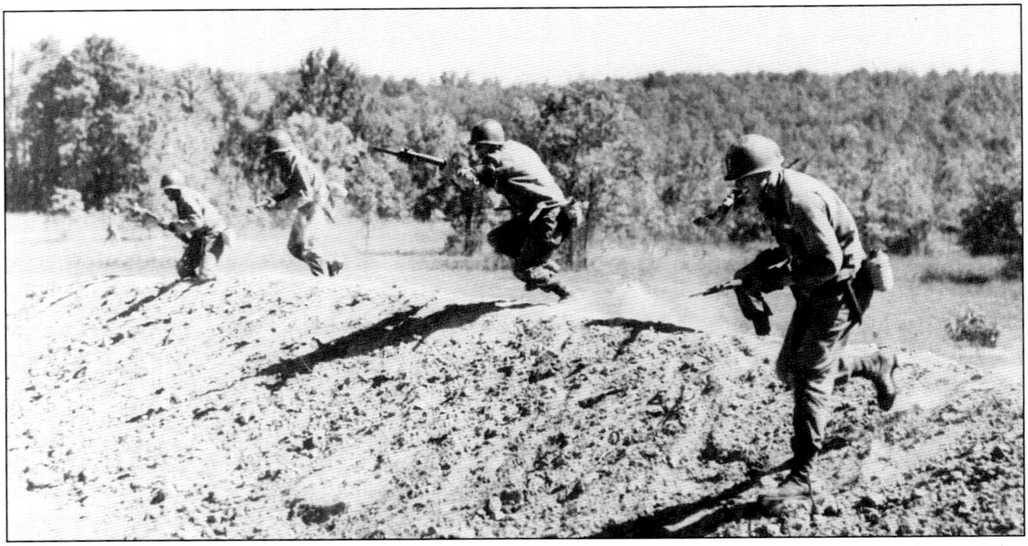

Soldiers taking part in combat training at Camp Chaffee in 1955 are shown here. The training given the soldier at Camp Chaffee included marching in squad, platoon, and company formation; battalion and combat command parades and reviews; military courtesy and discipline; personal hygiene and sanitation under garrison and field conditions; first aid; defense against chemical attack; physical training; hot and cold weather indoctrination; interior guard duty; character guidance; inspections; and care of clothing and equipment. (Fort Smith Chamber of Commerce.)

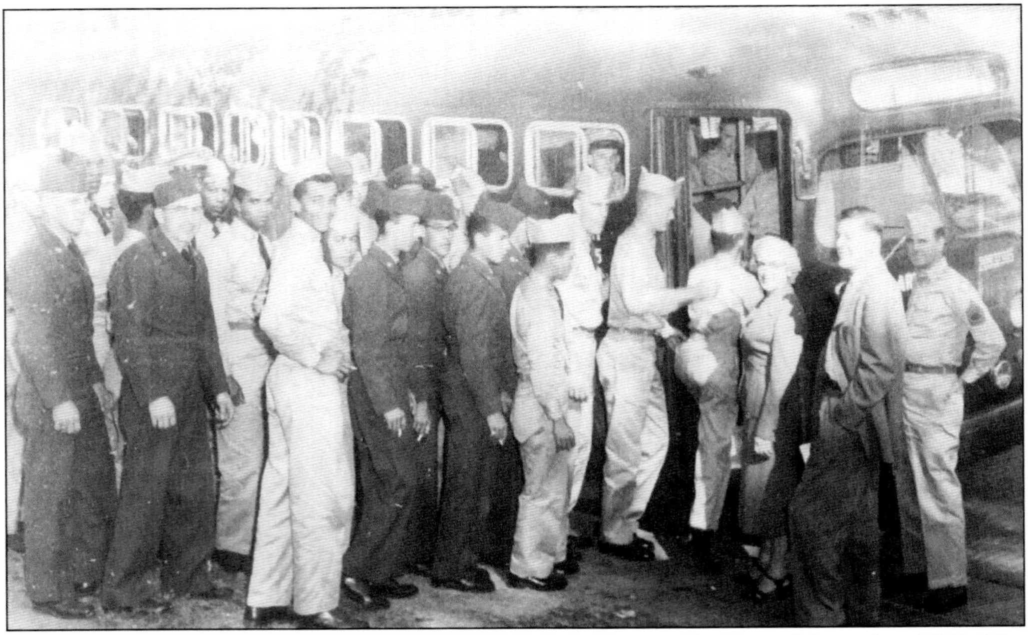

Here, soldiers prepare to board a bus for the last tour of Camp Chaffee in November 1956. The continual opening and closing of Camp Chaffee caused a see-saw economy in the Fort Smith business community. In 1950 Camp Chaffee was closed and then opened again preparatory to the United States entering the Korean Conflict. In 1956 the camp was made a field artillery training center. However, a delegation from Fort Smith to Washington requested that Fort Chaffee be closed permanently. (Fort Smith Chamber of Commerce.)

Morton B. Marks was born September 20, 1916. When he entered the military in 1942 he was 26 years old. Although he was from Fort Smith, near Camp Chaffee, Marks took his basic training at Fort Sill Army Base in Lawton, Oklahoma. This photo was made when he was on leave. He trained in artillery but became an administrative clerk after the Army found he had done clerical work in his father's store. (Morton B. Marks.)

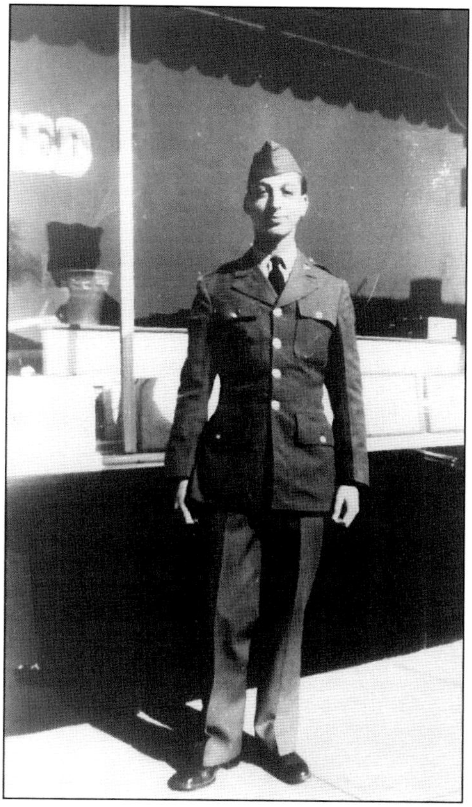

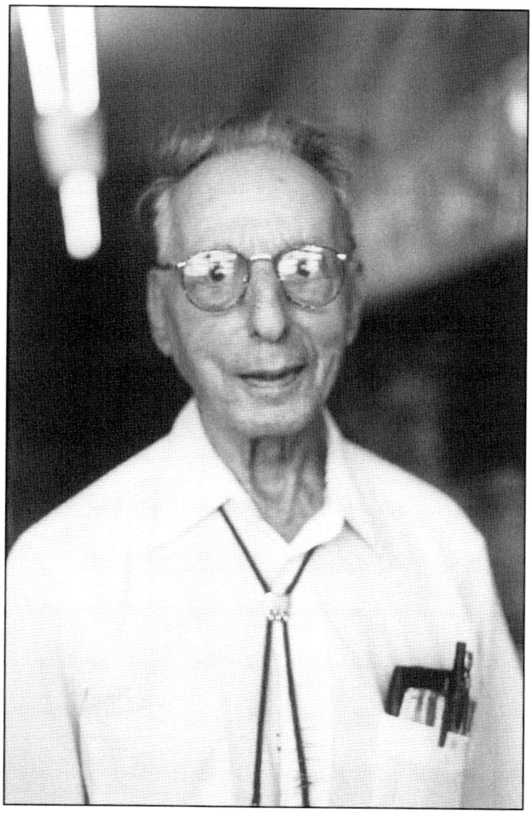

Morton B. Marks, pictured here at 81 years old, closed Mr. Vic's Men's Store at 908 Garrison Avenue, in June 1998, after 60 years in the retail clothing business. After graduating from high school in 1934 he first worked in his father's business, Leader Department Store. His father began operating the Leader *c.* 1907. When the younger Marks came back from WW II, in 1946, he opened Mr. Vic's Men's Store at 1002 Garrison. He made that name up because he thought it had a modern sound. (Morton B. Marks.)

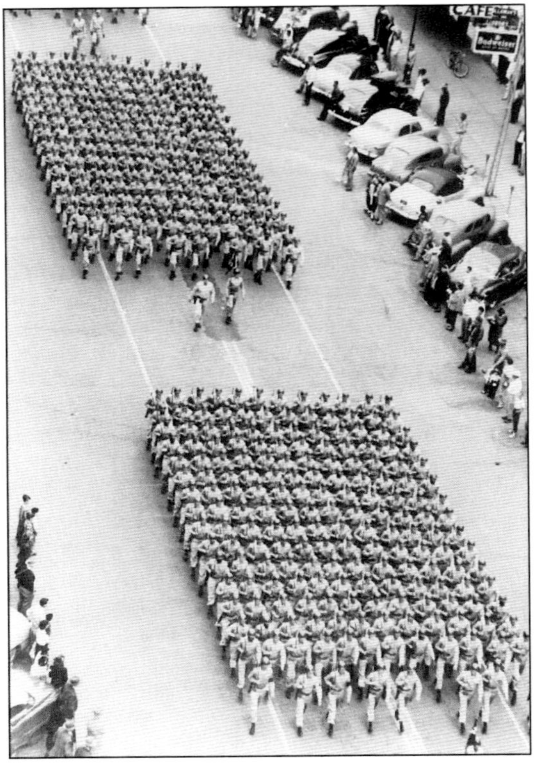

Units of the 5th Armored Division at Fort Chaffee march through downtown Fort Smith during a May 1953 Armed Forces Day Parade. After the war, the base was made inactive, but was reopened for the 5th Armored Division two years later. The camp's designation was changed to Fort Chaffee on March 21, 1956 by the Secretary of the Army, the Honorable Wilber M. Brucker. In 1956 the camp was made a field artillery training center, but three years later, was placed in a caretaker status. (Fort Smith Public Library.)

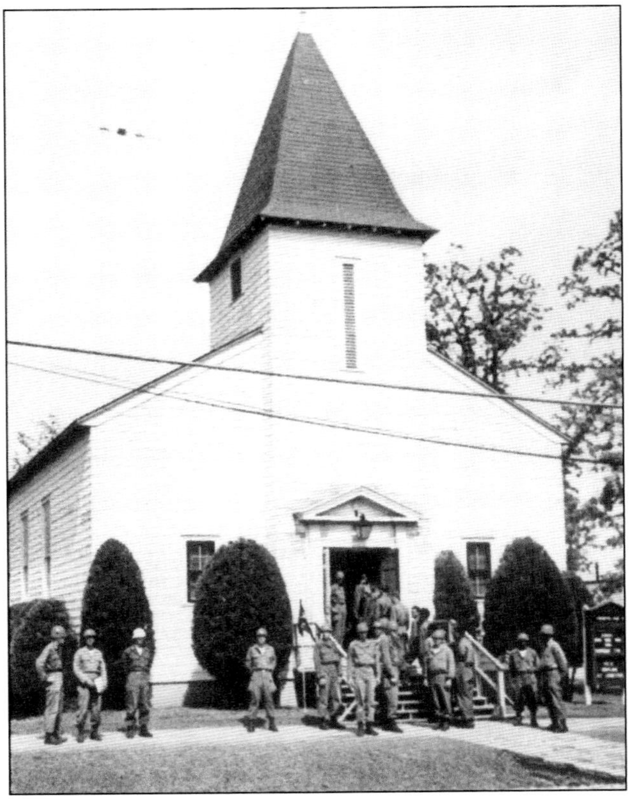

Pictured is Chapel Number 5 at Camp Chaffee. The difficult basic training took care of the physical needs, but many of the spiritual needs of soldiers stationed here during WW II were met in this chapel. Many a young man prayed that he would one day return and see his family again. Things are very quiet around the little chapel now. People do not seek out the spiritual needs of the soul as they once did. (Fort Smith Public Library.)

The largest weapon at Camp Chaffee, the 155 millimeter gun, was displayed at the 1955 Arkansas-Oklahoma Exposition and Fair. Besides working with basic weapons the new soldiers were trained to understand the mechanical functioning capabilities and actually fired .30 caliber machine guns, rocket launchers, and both hand and rifle grenades. Advanced individual training at Camp Chaffee included firing the 105 mm howitzer. This rugged schedule of training was designed to increase the Victory Division's striking power. (Chamber of Commerce.)

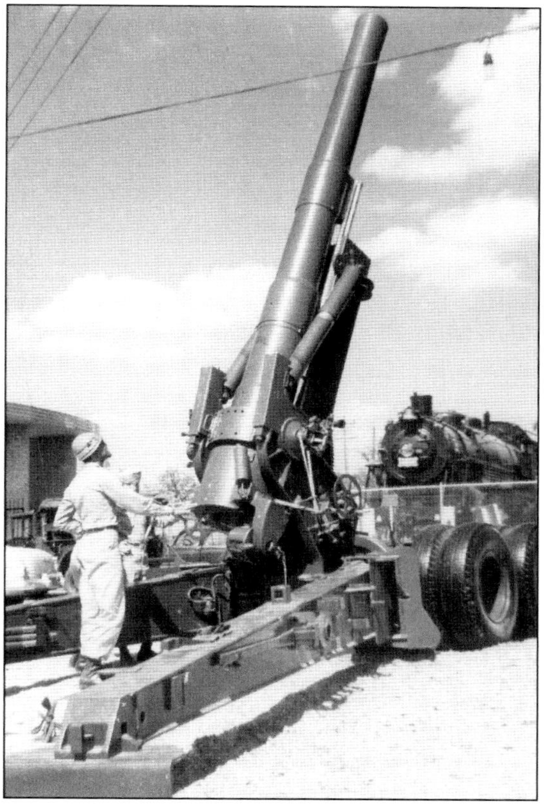

During WW II, Company C of the 10th Medium Tank Battalion members shown here were stationed at Camp Chaffee, where they engaged in basic training prior to being shipped out to Europe to fight the German scourge. In addition each soldier was taught the care, function, and use of weapons. Each soldier in the Army had what was called his basic weapon, a .30 caliber M-1 rifle. (U.S. Army Photo, Fort Smith Public Library.)

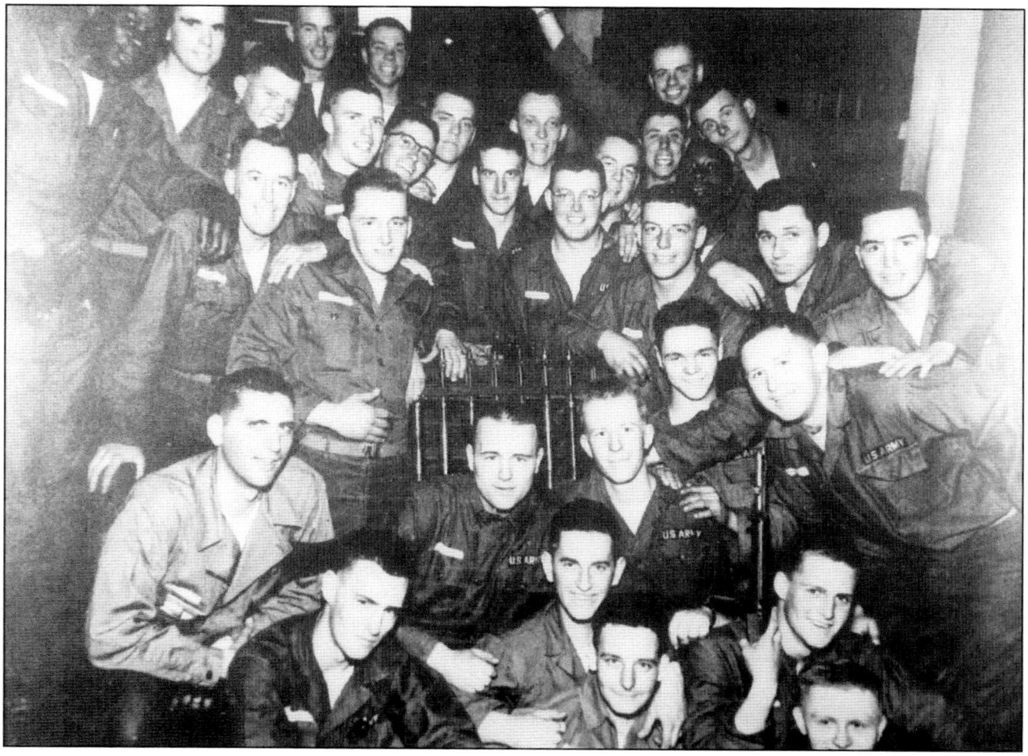

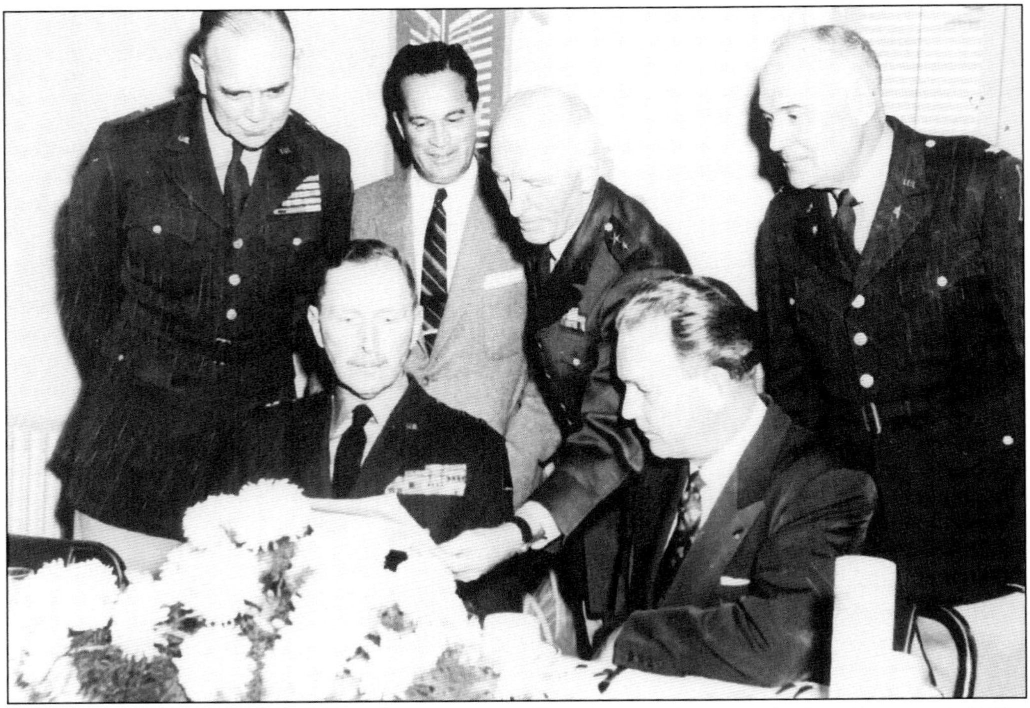

Military personnel and Chamber of Commerce officials were photographed on January 4, 1956. From left to right they are: Brigadier General William H. Barnes, General William H. Calbern, C.T. Hubbard, Major General John J. Binns, James E. Clendening, and Colonel Carleton E. Merritt. (Fort Smith Chamber of Commerce.)

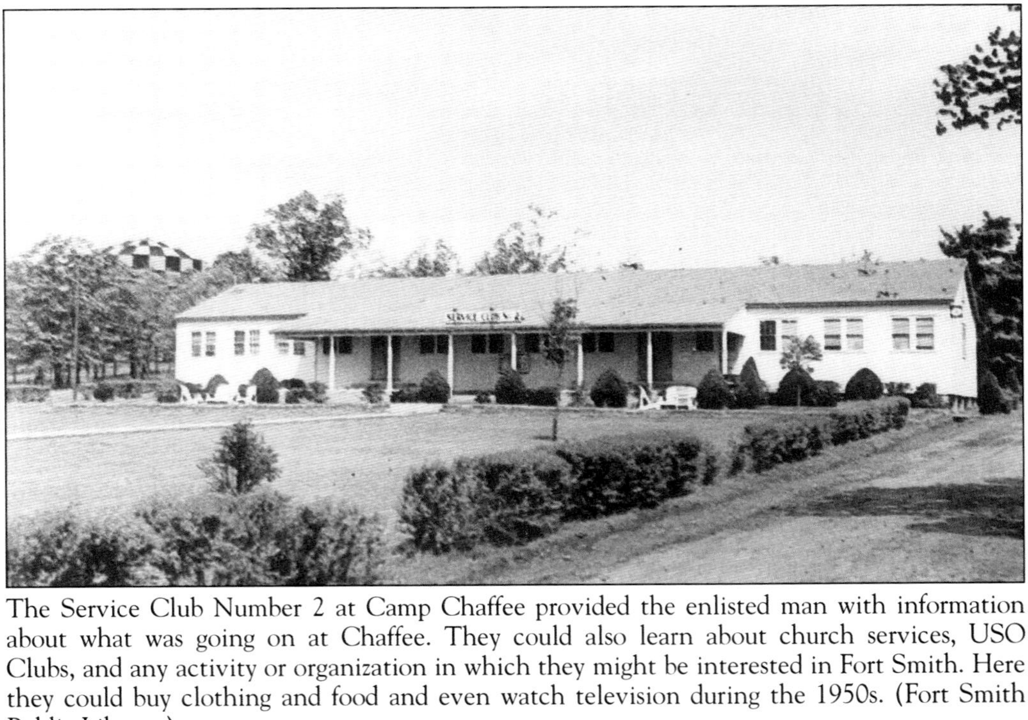

The Service Club Number 2 at Camp Chaffee provided the enlisted man with information about what was going on at Chaffee. They could also learn about church services, USO Clubs, and any activity or organization in which they might be interested in Fort Smith. Here they could buy clothing and food and even watch television during the 1950s. (Fort Smith Public Library.)

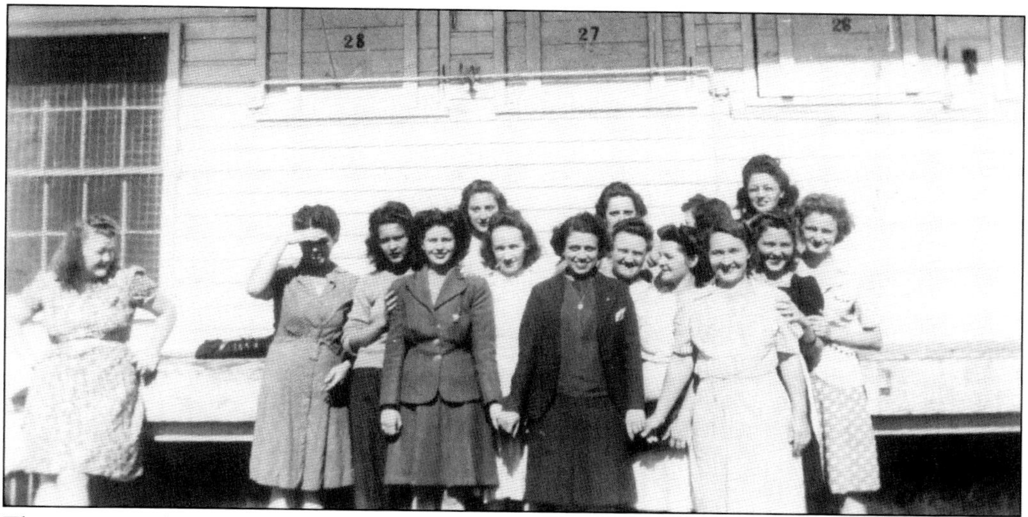

This c. 1943 photo shows "Markers" at Camp Chaffee Laundry during WW II. These young women were a small part of the civilian work force at Camp Chaffee during WW II. Note the numbered doors above the heads of the women. The soldiers would toss laundry bundles into those numbered doors once they were let down. The laundry was taken from the bins and marked by the women to keep it from being lost. Then it was put into large washing machines. The women also sorted the laundry when it was finished. The young woman with glasses is Edith Page Brewer-Wright, shown right rear, mother of the author and now 82 years old. The women were not allowed to work with German prisoners-of-war, but saw them each day. (Edith Page Brewer Wright.)

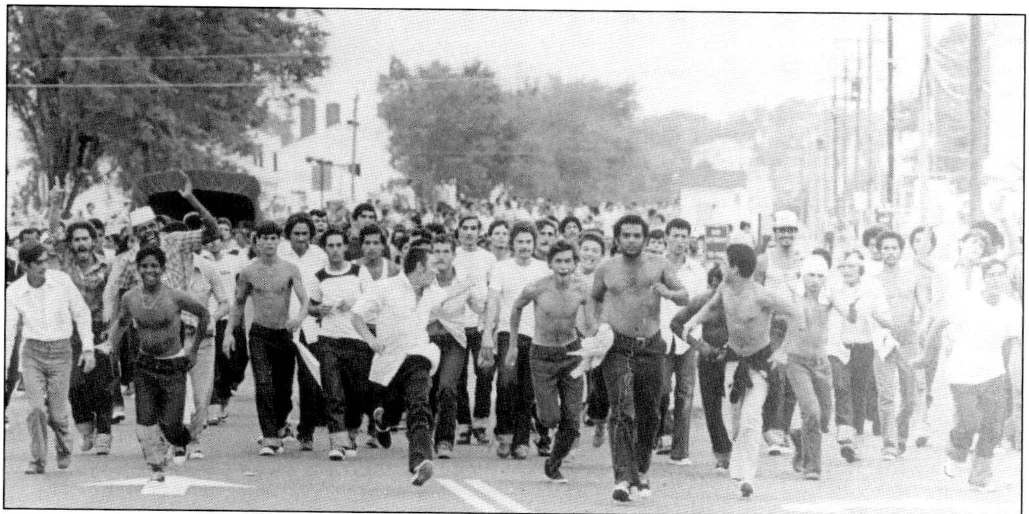

During the presidency of Jimmy Carter the unpopular Cuban boatlift people were accepted for relocation at Fort Chaffee. This was a trying time for Fort Smith, and Barling, where Fort Chaffee is located. The immigrants, most of them men, became angry due to delays in the system. They began rioting and burned five buildings in two days. In this photo they are headed directly for the *Southwest Times Record* cameraman. Several policemen were injured in the riots. The police feared more trouble in the nearby city of Barling if the Cubans were allowed to remain unchecked, so they were forced to fire upon them. Several were injured before the rioting was halted. The cameraman was unharmed. (Zac Coker, James Groves, *Southwest Times Record*.)

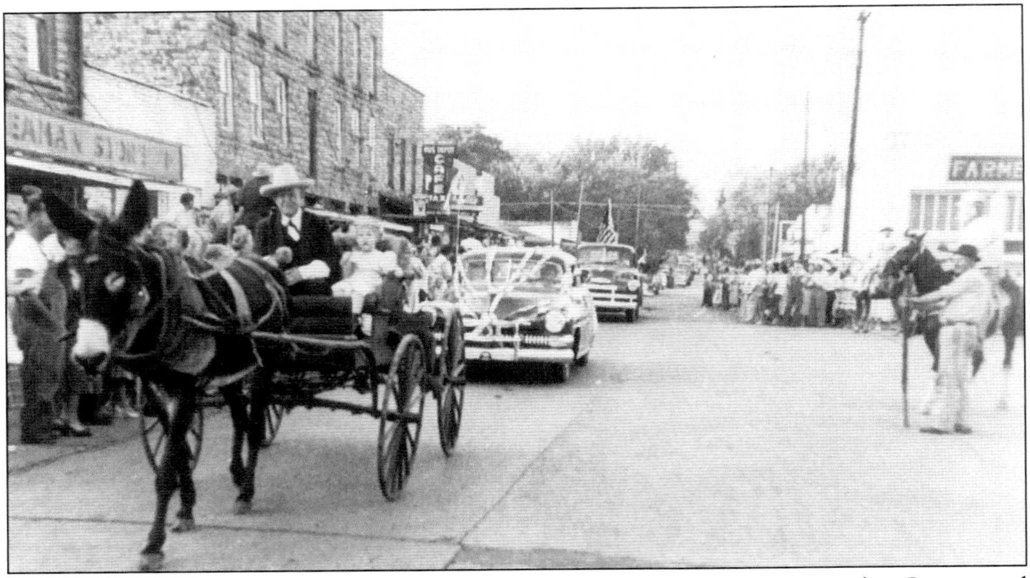

Cinda Bell and her grandfather, Henry Bell, are pictured in a buggy at the Greenwood Centennial celebration parade in 1951. The mule's name was Peanut. The location is the old square in Greenwood. Cinda Bell is a descendant of the Osborn family and now runs the insurance agency, which has been in the family for five generations on the Greenwood square. (Cinda Bell.)

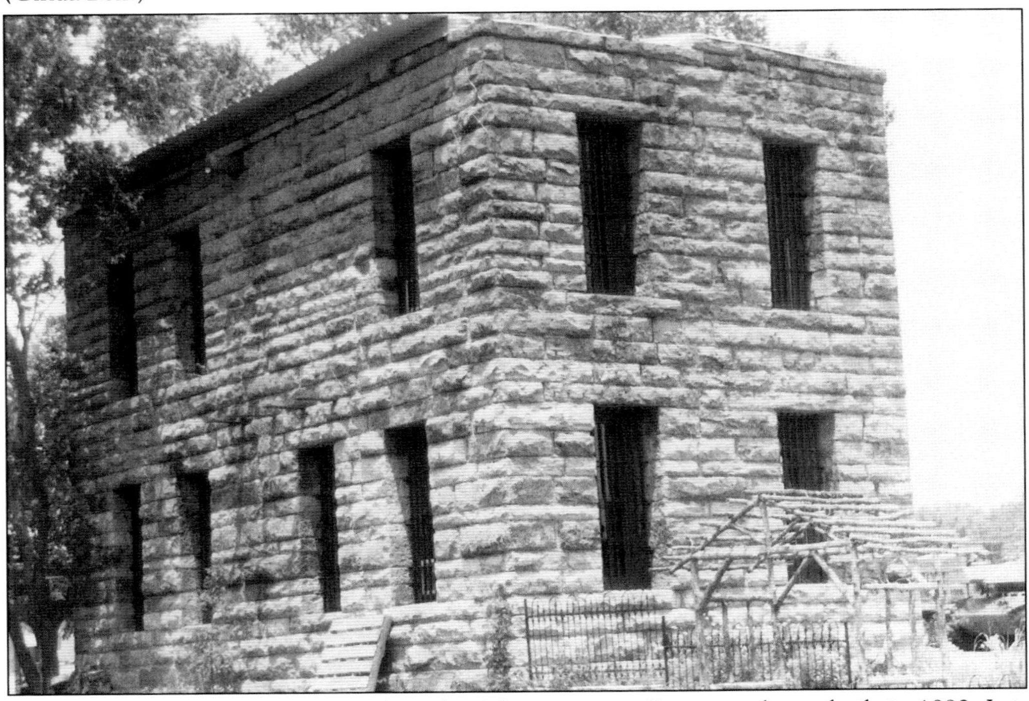

The Sebastian County Jail, located south of the square in Greenwood, was built in 1892. It is one of the oldest buildings in downtown and is on the National Register of Historic Places. Stone for the building was quarried on Backbone Mountain. Holes were drilled into a larger stone which was then left overnight to freeze and then was split into manageable sizes. The jail, now a museum, is open one or two days per week. (Author.)

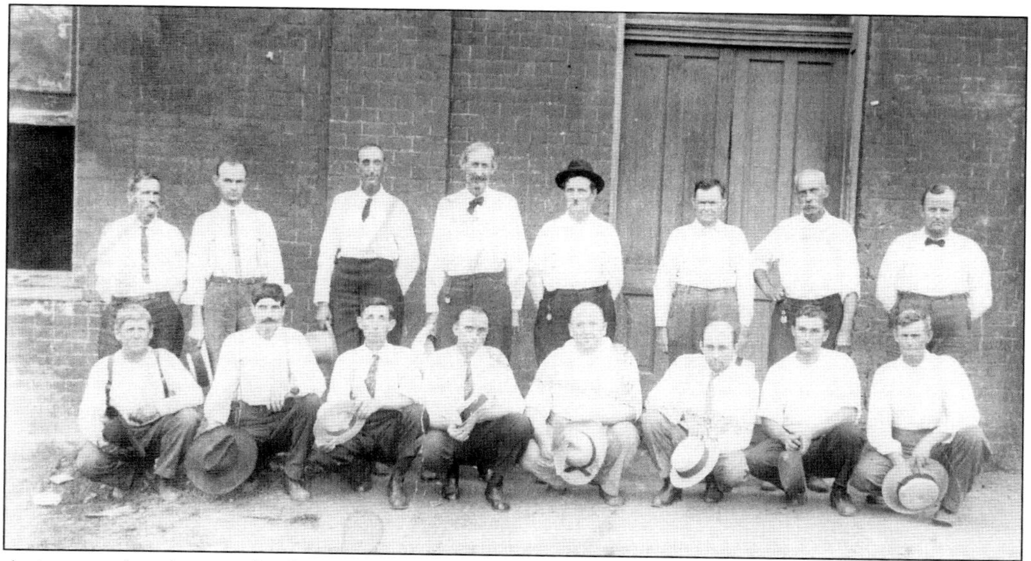

A jury on break outside the Greenwood Courthouse is shown here, sometime before 1916. From left to right are: (front row)Willie Southard, J.F. Martin, Nath Raney, unknown, Fred McCord, unknown, A.W. Tomlin, and unknown; (back row) unknown and Jess Coleman. The rest are unknown. In 1860 the General Assembly of Arkansas established two circuit courts in Sebastian County, one to be held at Greenwood, the county seat, and the other at Fort Smith. (Cinda Bell.)

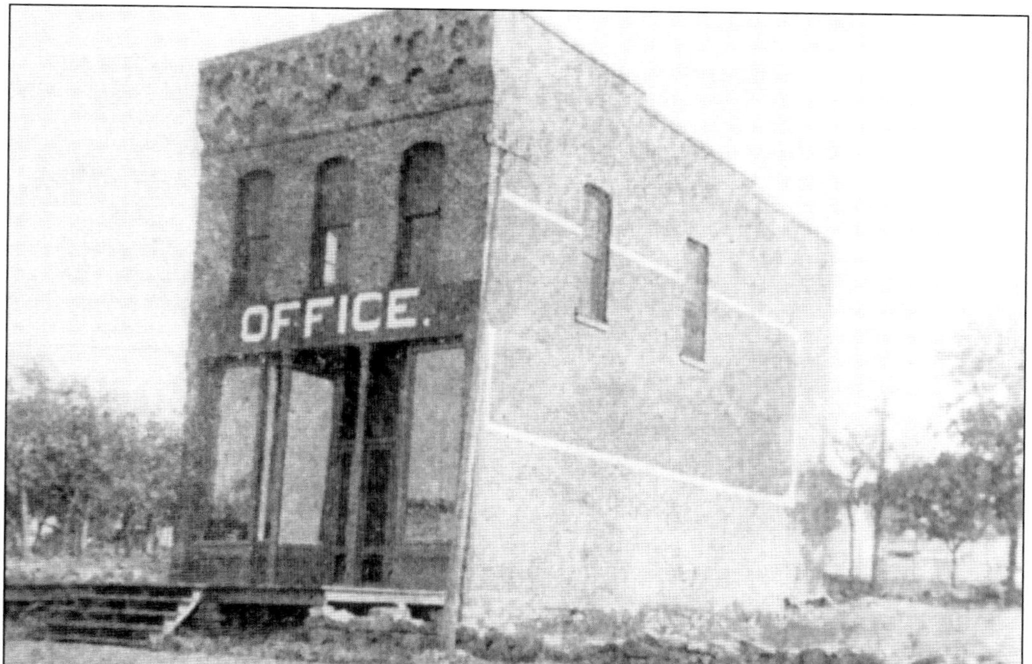

The office of the Kansas & Texas Coal Company, Huntington is shown c. 1900. B.F. Hobart was president and treasurer, and E.V. Loveland vice president. They were miners and dealers in Pittsburgh Coal Mines at Hackett City and Huntington. The capacity of the mines was 200 cars daily. The town of Huntington was laid out in June 1887 by the Missouri, Kansas, and Texas Coal Company. The coal mining works also opened on that date. (Cinda Bell.)

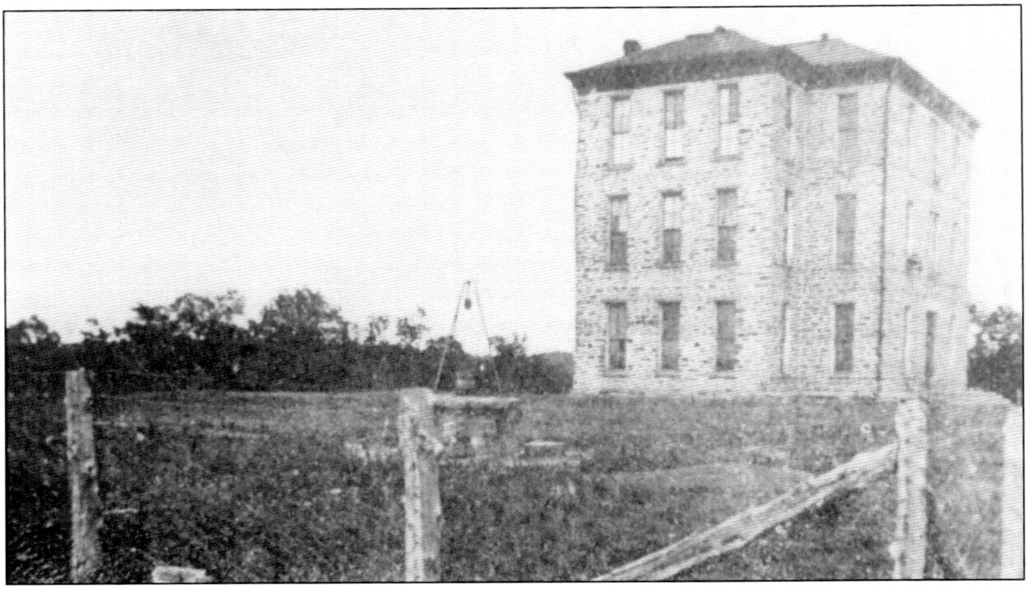

This unique-looking building sitting out on the prairie *c.* 1900 was the Hackett City Public School. It was a grade and high school combined. The upper grades met on the top floors of the school, and the lower grades on the bottom floor. Years later the top floors were removed. The bottom floor is now part of another building. The 4H Club and other such organizations meet in the building now. (Cinda Bell.)

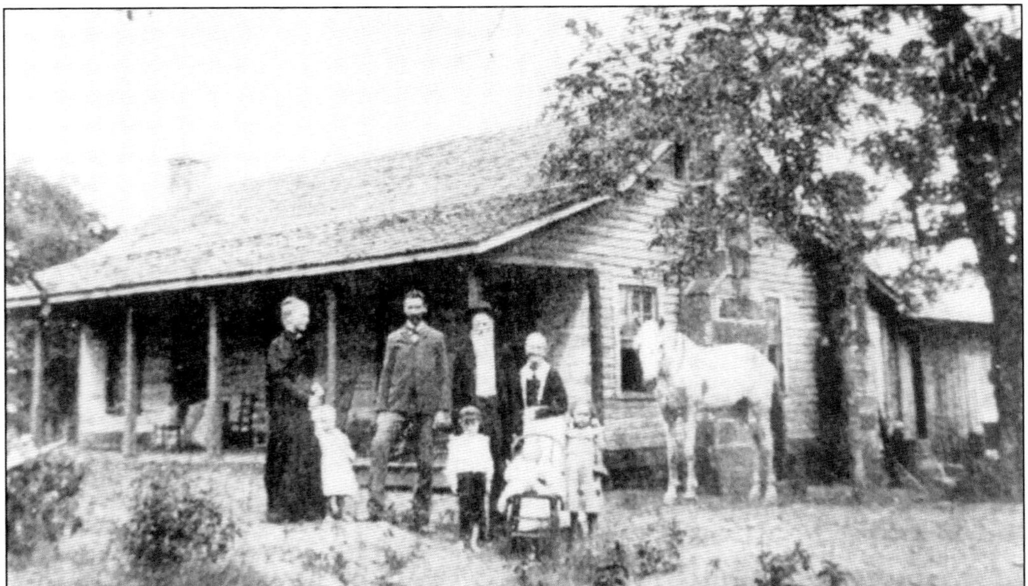

The home of J.W. Bowen is shown here *c.* 1900. Bowen, the elderly man in the center of this image, was born in South Carolina in 1825. When the photo was taken he had been married 52 years and only moved once in his life, when he came to Arkansas in 1878. He was in the Confederate Army during the Civil War and was struck on the side of the head numerous times by minie balls. He was falsely reported as dead during the siege of Vicksburg. (Cinda Bell.)

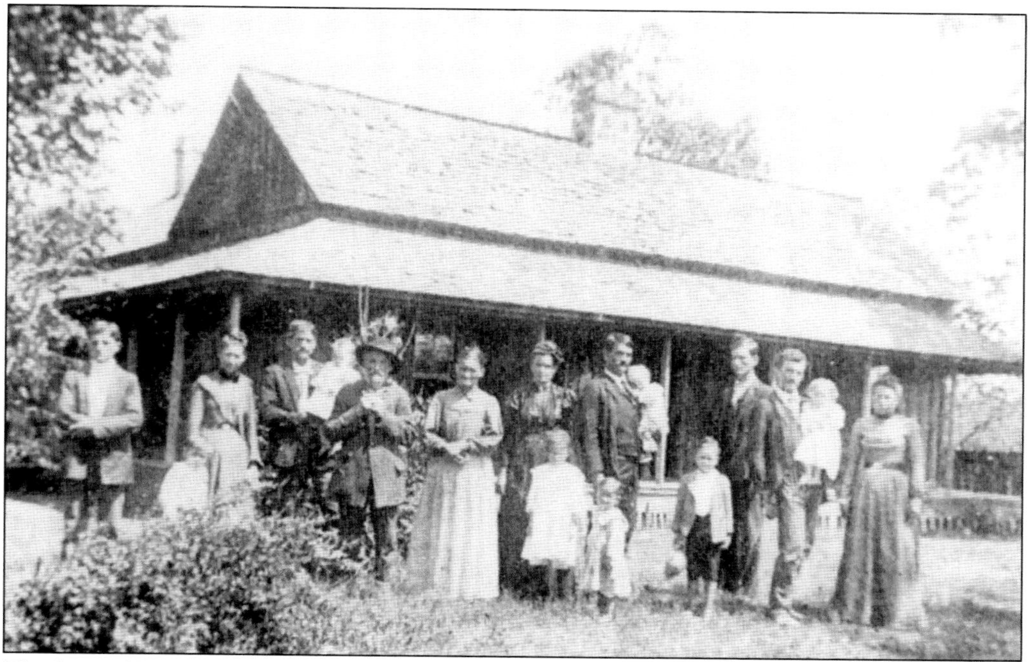

The farm of B.B. Smedley, who was born in Manchester, England, in 1845, contained 600 acres of land. It was underlaid with coal and timbered with oak and pine. Mr. Smedley married Mary Huckaby and they had nine boys and two girls when this photo was taken. B.B. was the great grandson of the historical figure, Reverend Smedley, who was missionary to Fort Smith and Indian Territory in the early years. (Cinda Bell.)

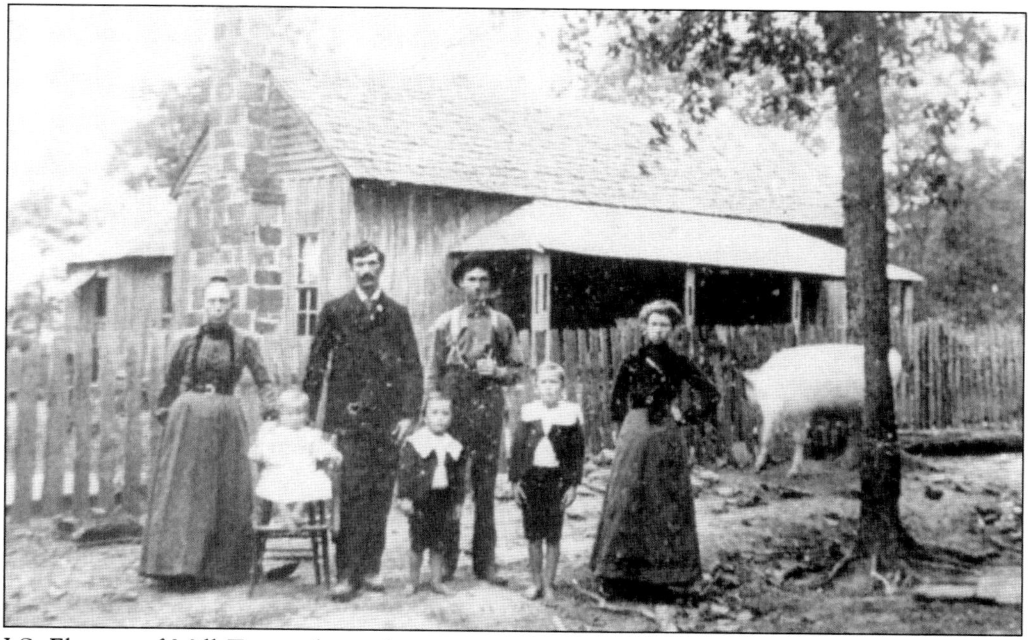

J.S. Elmore, of Mill Town, shown here *c.* 1900, married Alice McBurnett. Both families got all cleaned up in their Sunday best and spruced up the yard to have their picture made. Their large Poland China Hog has wandered off, rather than standing still for the photographer. He is probably looking for food. (Cinda Bell.)

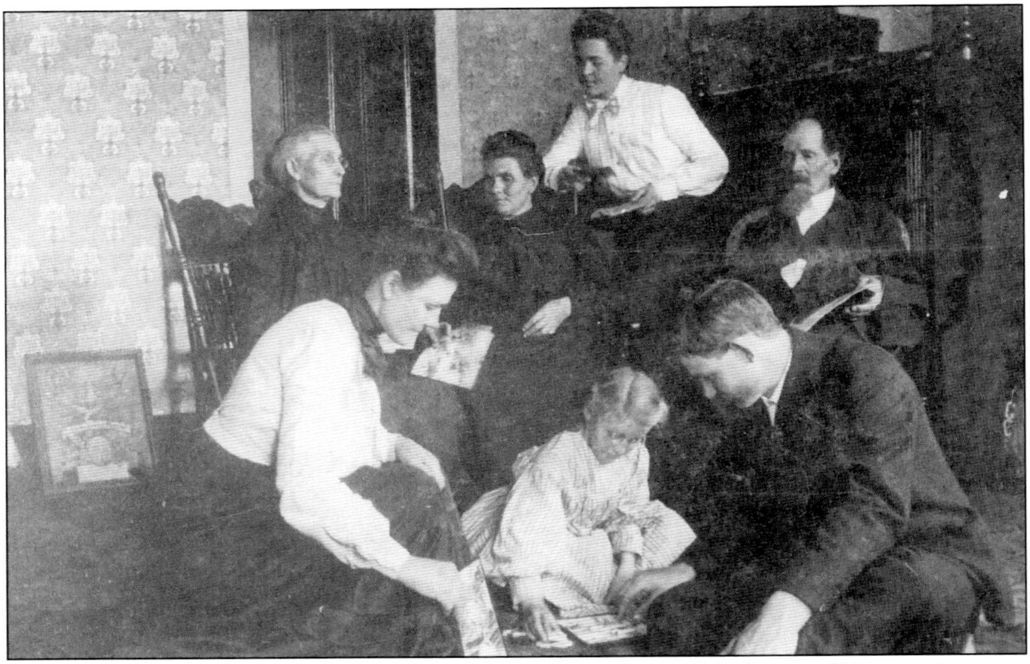

Jewell Osborn Bell is seated in the center of this *c.* 1902 image, at the home of her grandparents, Nathaniel H. and Mary Osborn. Also present are her aunts, Laura and Martha Osborn, and her father, Charles E. Osborn. The home was located east of Greenwood in the Cornish Community, now Fort Chaffee. This was Jewell's first Christmas without her mother, who was recently deceased. The family has gathered around in support of her. This unusual indoor image evokes many emotions. (Cinda Bell.)

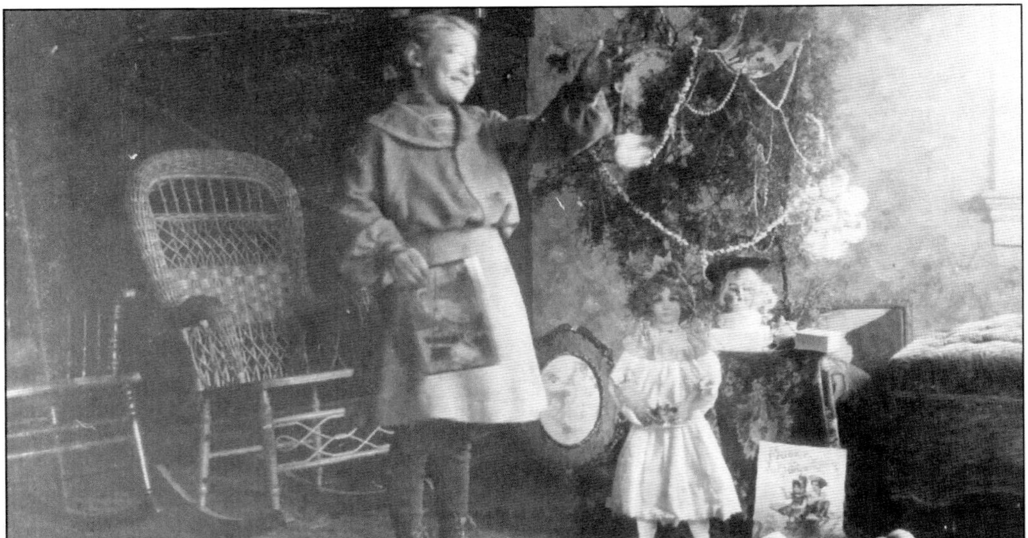

Jewell Osborn Bell is shown Christmas morning *c.* 1902, at her grandparents' home located east of Greenwood in the Cornish Community. Note the life-like doll and the wicker rocking chair. Apparently this image was shot with only the light source from the window. Despite the fact that this was her first Christmas without her mother she appears to have found some measure of joy in the day. (Cinda Bell.)

Eight

Looking to the Future

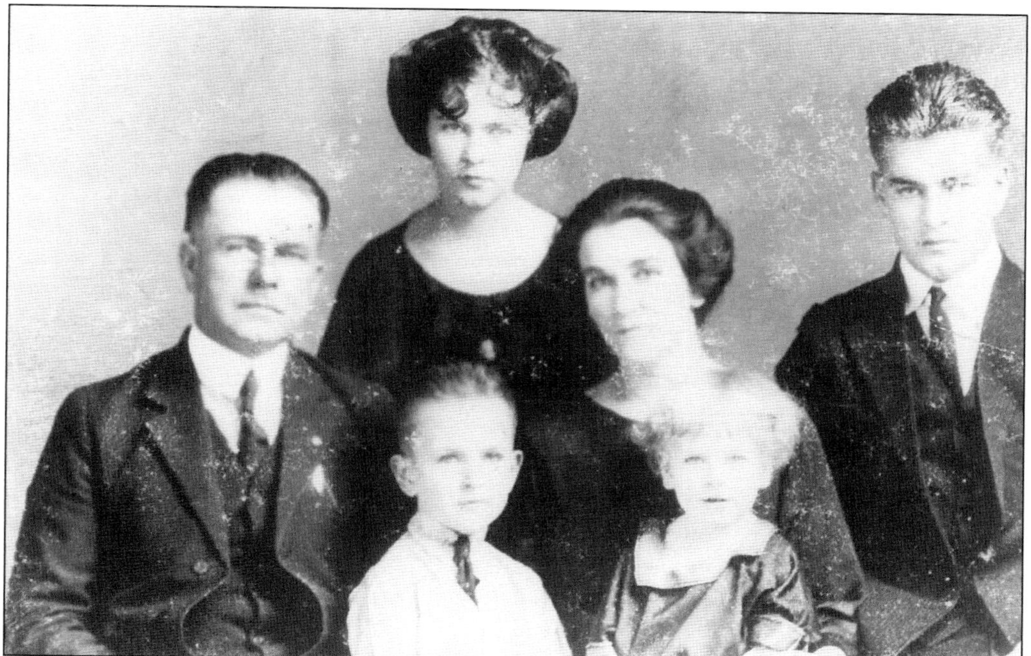

This is the John B. Williams family. From left to right they are: (back row) John B., daughter Marjorie, wife Regina "Jennie," and son Ray. His two children in front are Jimmie and Betty. Williams's beautiful wife, Jennie, was the sister of George Maledon, Judge Parker's executioner. For years John B. numbered among the most popular and successful entrepreneurs in Fort Smith. He hired out wagons, carriages, and horses for many events, such as parades and circus day in Fort Smith. He kept a little zoo, which featured a bear, in his place of business at the Plaza on Texas Corner. He also sold horses and bird dogs. The Williamses are the type of family that has made Fort Smith a successfully enterprising town. (Ruby Yeakley.)

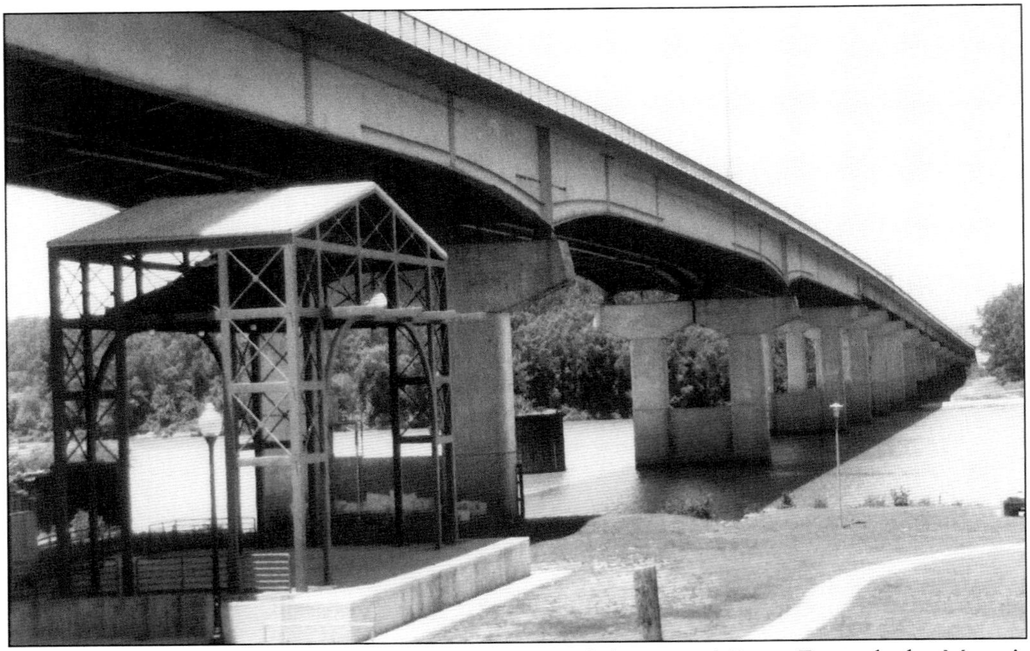

The bandstand at Harry E. Kelley Park is the site of the annual River Festival, the Mayor's Fourth of July fireworks display, and the annual Fort Smith Blues Festival. In this location, by the year 2000, will be an amphitheater which will accommodate 1,126 people. It will feature two gazebos, a 60-foot diameter stage, an arbor at the rear, a river pavilion, an events pavilion, and a park. (Author.)

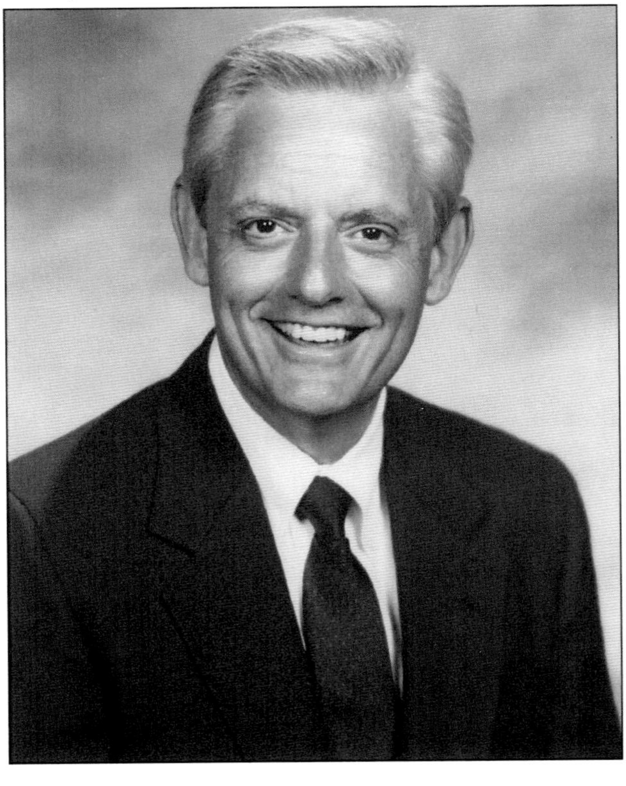

Mayor Ray Baker's enthusiasm for Fort Smith is immediately apparent. He is a full-time mayor in a part-time position. He can be seen at every function, presenting awards and proclamations, making talks and promoting the people of his community. His "Life's worth living in Fort Smith" slogan is as much a part of his persona as his infectious smile. Baker is also a 37-year teacher of civics and history in the Fort Smith Schools. (City of Fort Smith.)

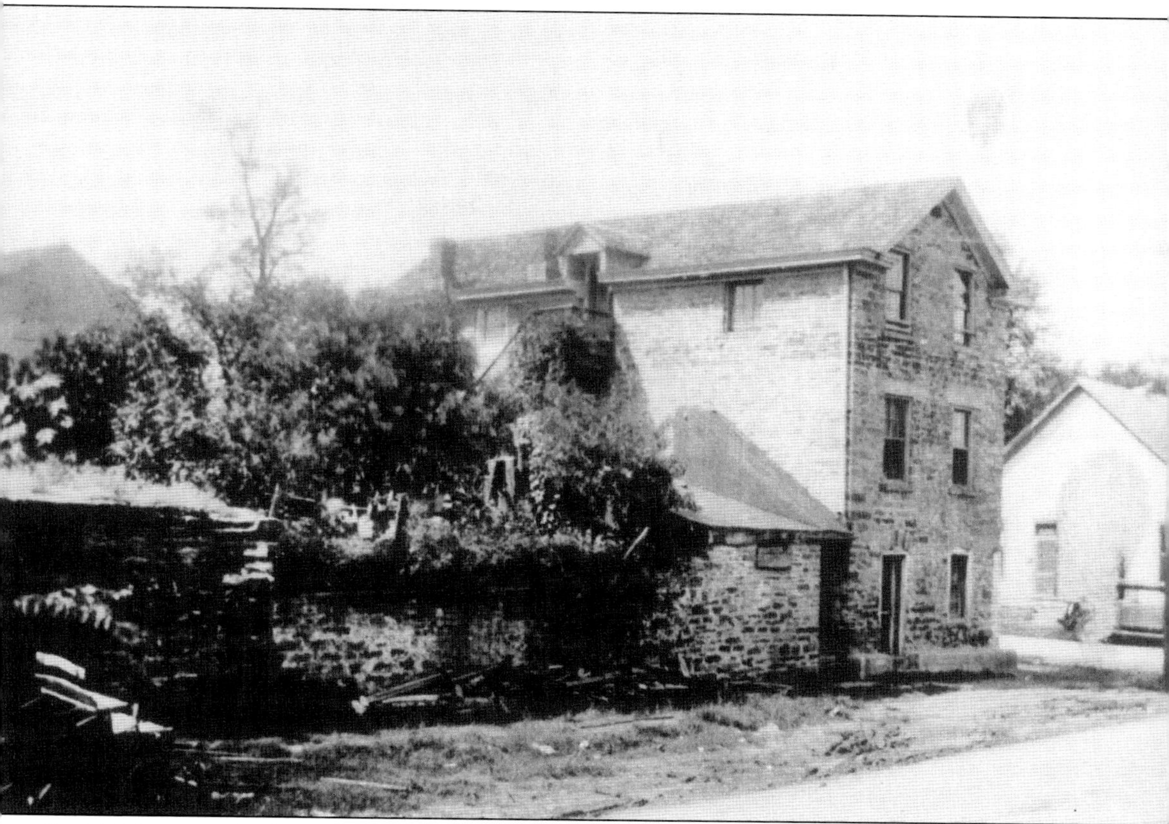

Knoble's Brewery, built in 1848, is an old brewery and beer cellar. It still stands on the corner of North Third and E. Streets. Joseph Knoble, a native of Wittenberg, Germany, constructed the cellar to be approximately 35 feet long, 15 feet wide, and 10 feet from the center of the ceiling to the stone floor. Bill Weidman bought the brewery from Eddell Wortz. The two each did remodeling and restoration of the old building. In the beginning the first floor of the building was a beer hall, the scene of many merry gatherings, especially of the German residents of the city. Joseph Knoble brewed and delivered beer to some 37 businesses along Garrison Avenue. He served 5¢ beer and stick-to-your-ribs vittles. (Fort Smith Public Library.)

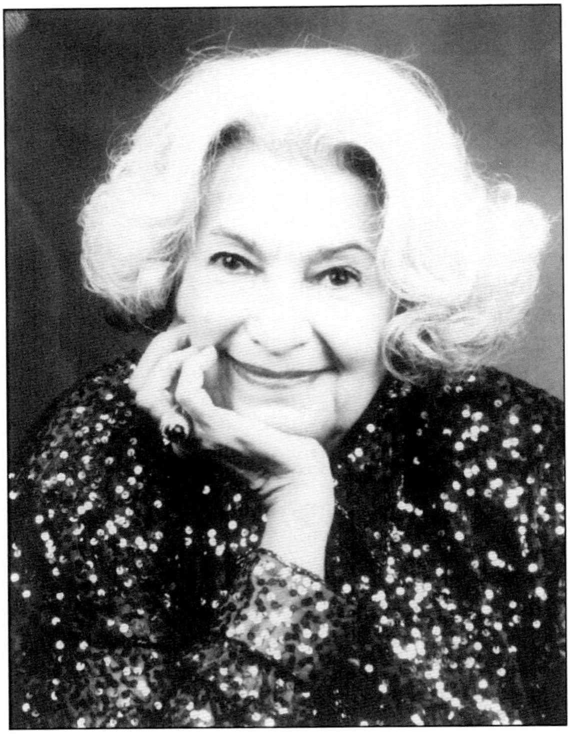

Polly Crews, the perennial talk show host, is an energetic promoter of civic pride and believes the city of Fort Smith has the best people in the world. If she sees an individual with a need or problem, she tries to help them, or does a radio or television show about it so someone else can help them. "The Polly Show" airs Sunday mornings on KPOM, Channel 24, and her radio show airs weekdays on KFSA. One popular feature of her television show is called the "Good Heart Award," where a person is nominated for doing a good deed, or for just being a good person. (Rick Green Photography.)

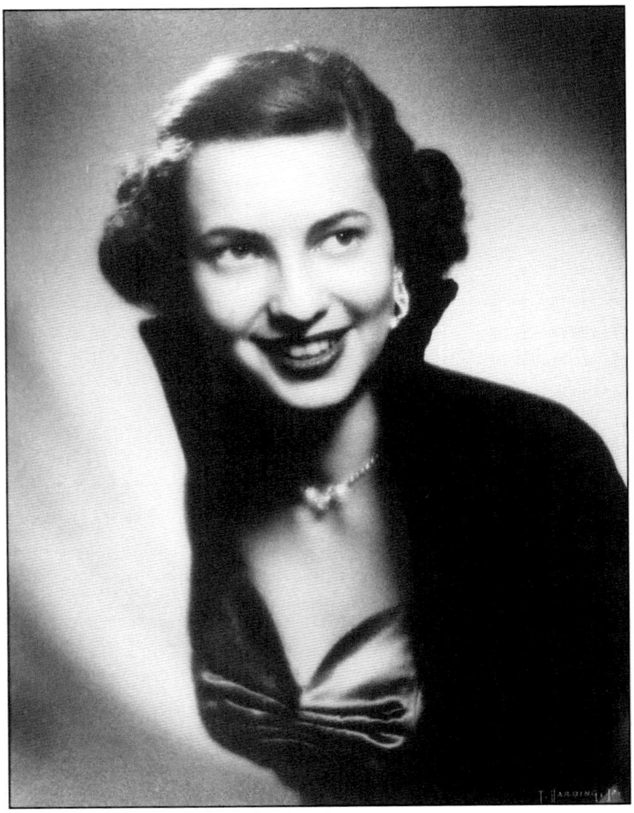

Polly Crews, shown here in an earlier image, has led a successful life, but it has not always been easy. In the late 1960s at age 39 she was the sole support of six children. While working as office manager for a group of psychiatrists she began her television career, on her lunch hour, on KFSM-TV. In 1974 she became director of the Fort Smith Art Center and assisted the Artists Alliance through a successful fund-raising and restoration of the Vaughn/Schaap House. After 20 years she retired to her work in television and radio. (Polly Crews.)

Mr. Peanut, donated to the Fort Smith Art Center by Planters Peanut Company, is pictured in an upstairs hallway, where he commands lots of attention. Mr. Peanut has become one of the world's most familiar trademark characters. He was born in 1916, when Planters offered a prize for the best sketch suitable for adoption as a trademark. A 14-year-old Virginia schoolboy won the prize for his drawing of Mr. Peanut. (Author.)

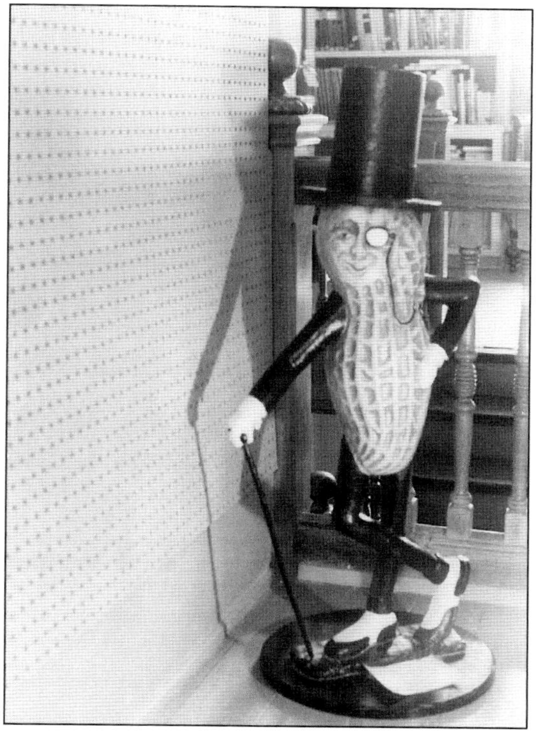

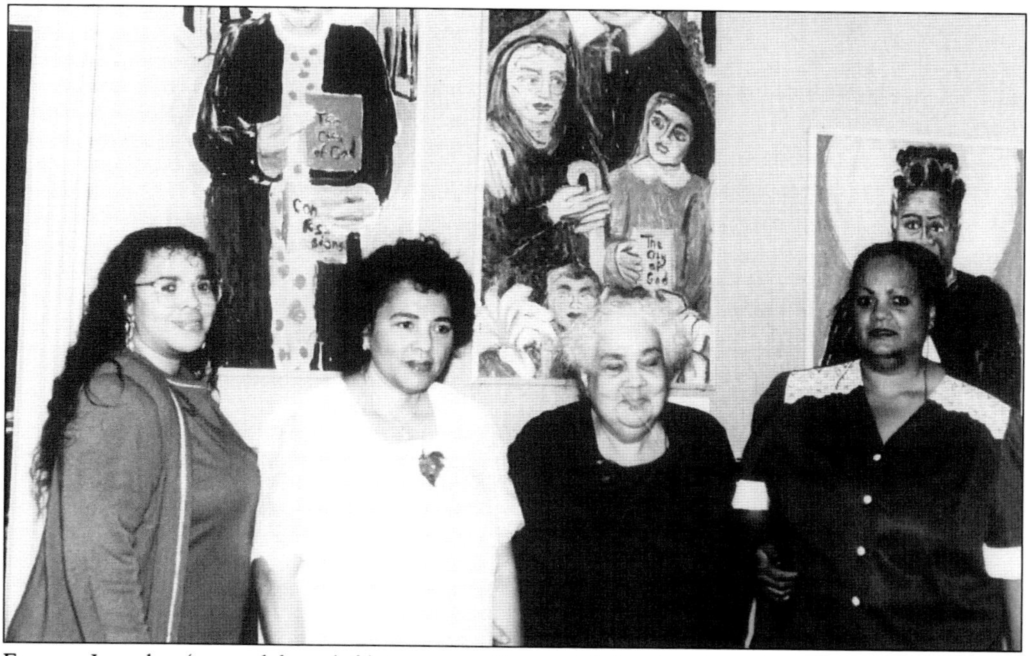

Frances Longley (second from left) is pictured here with her family at the opening reception of her exhibit at the Fort Smith Art Center in February 1998. Longley is a Catholic black artist. Catholicism and deep religious conviction is the creative force behind her artwork. Religious oil panel-paintings are her mode of expression. Through this medium she depicts scenes of Christ, the saints, and the Virgin Mary. Longley has a B.A. in art education, an M.A. in literature, and an M.A. in political science. (Julie Lind Northrip, Fort Smith Art Center.)

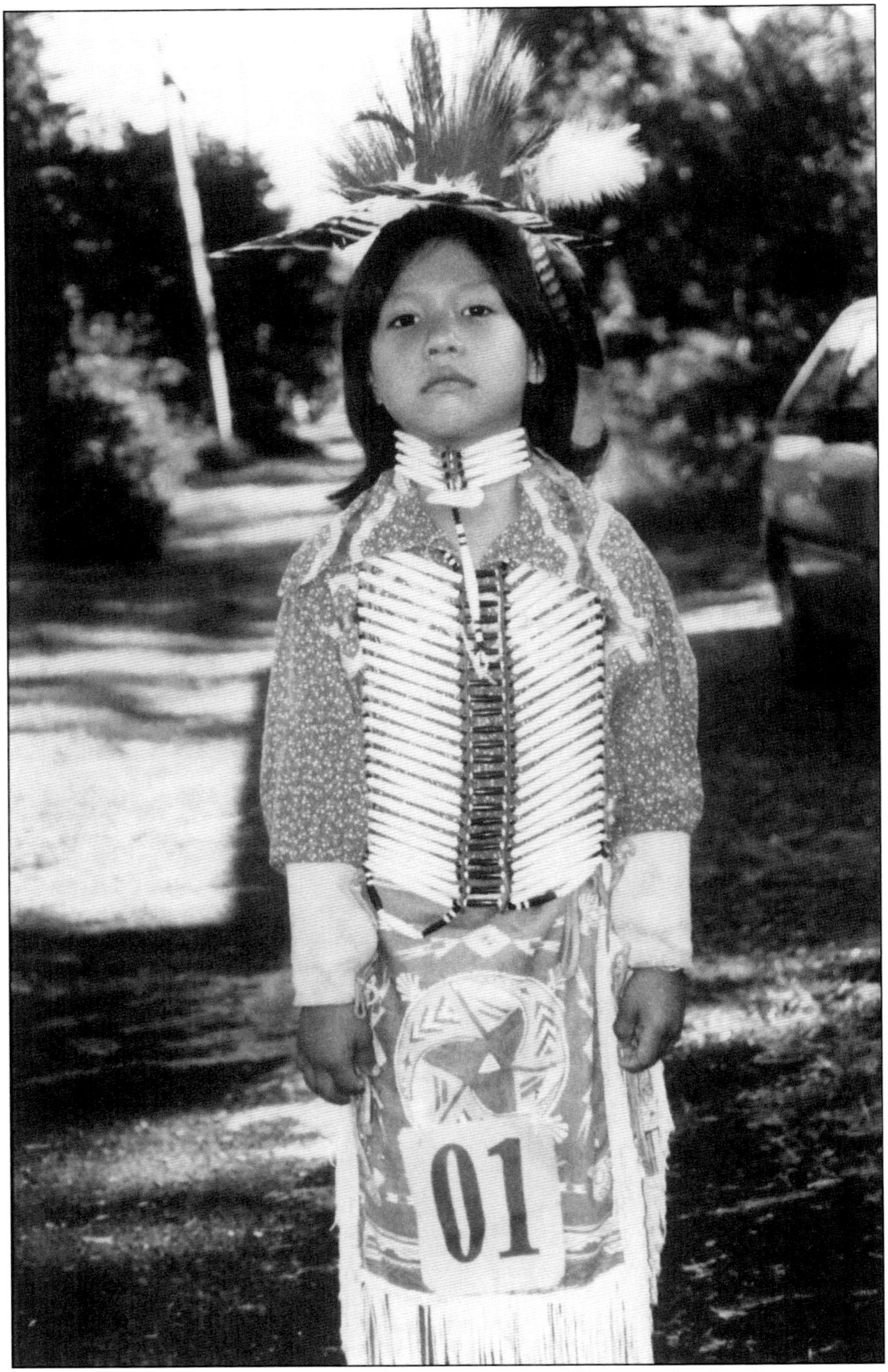

This young Indian dancer is helping to keep the culture of his people alive by participating in the Fort Smith Art Center's annual Native American Festival. A lot of energy is generated by the Native dancers and drummers during this favored portion of the festival. Exhibition dancing is also encouraged, where any tribal member may participate in the dancing. The Indian Pow-Wow is also becoming an annual event at the Northside High School. (Photographic Alliance, Fort Smith Art Center.)

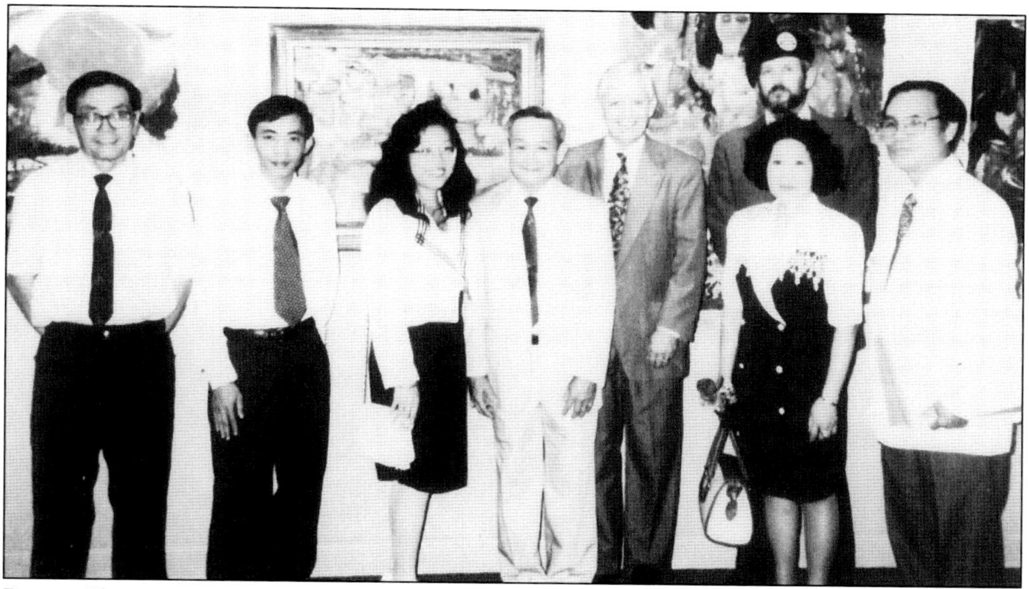

Duong Phuoc Tan, to the far right, and his family are pictured here. Mr. Tan is a member of the Vietnamese Arts and Letters Association. His exhibit of Vietnamese paintings, which opened August 9, 1996, was called "Faded Memories." The longer Mr. Tan resides in America, the more faded are his memories of his native country. Mayor Ray Baker is standing to the rear along with a Green Beret friend of Mr. Tan. (Julie Lind Northrip, Fort Smith Art Center.)

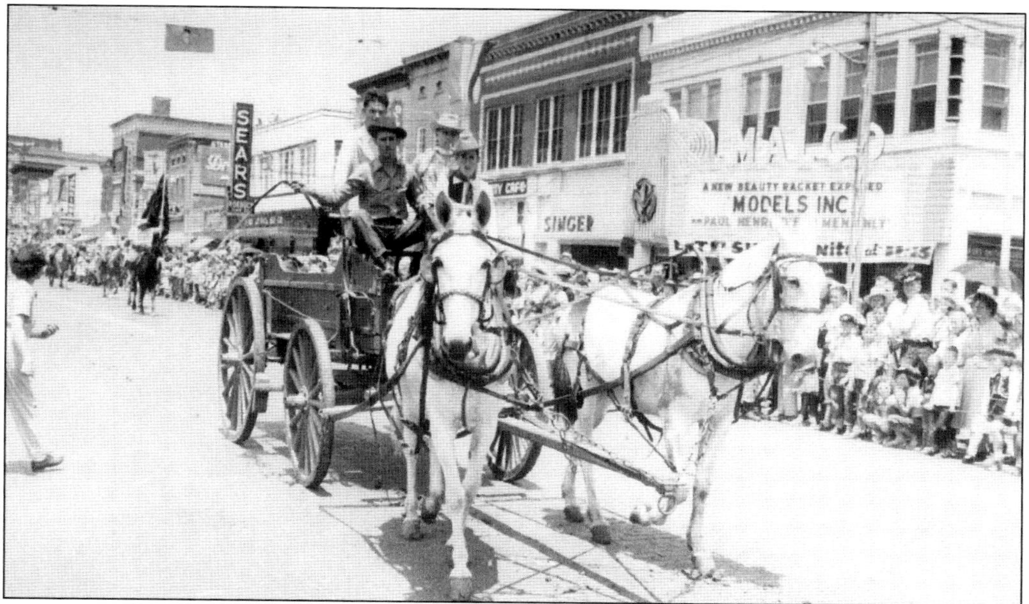

This is an example of early-day transportation, c. 1950, at the Arkansas-Oklahoma Rodeo Parade in downtown Fort Smith. A big sturdy wagon is being drawn by two large, white mules. Note the risqué late movie, *Models, Inc.*, being shown at the Malco Theatre, for men only. Sears, seen down the street, was in that location for years until it moved to Central Mall. Now, the police department's bicycle patrol is located in the Sears building. (Fort Smith Chamber of Commerce.)

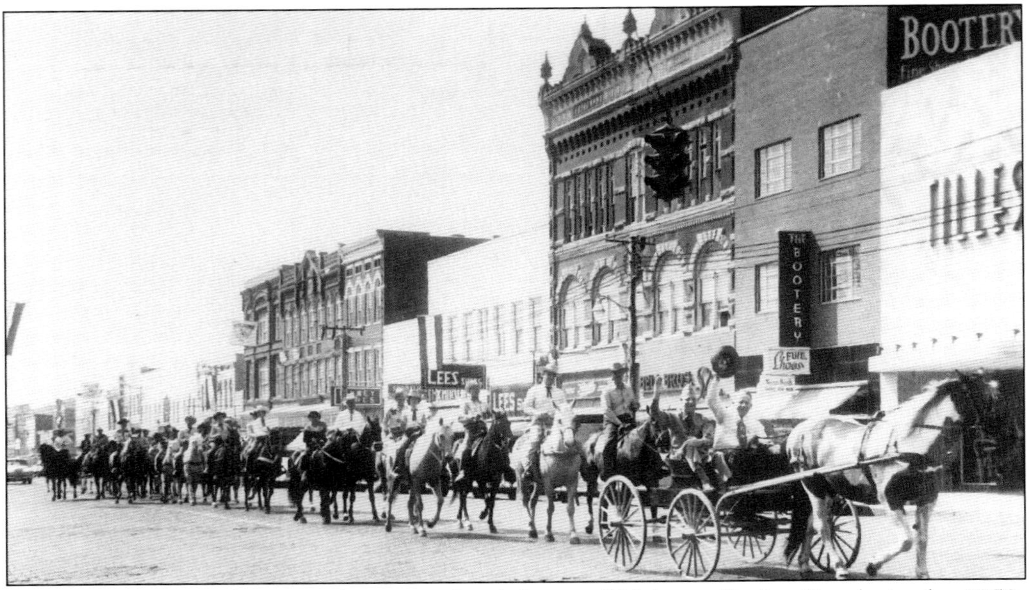

These people are riding two-abreast at the Arkansas-Oklahoma Rodeo Parade in the 1950s in front of the fine old buildings along Garrison Avenue. Tilles was a favorite dress shop of many young women of the era. On Thursdays the stores along the avenue remained open until 9 p.m., so people who worked during the day would have more time to shop. The Boston Store was known for its bargain basement. Note the Army personnel in the carriage. (Fort Smith Chamber of Commerce.)

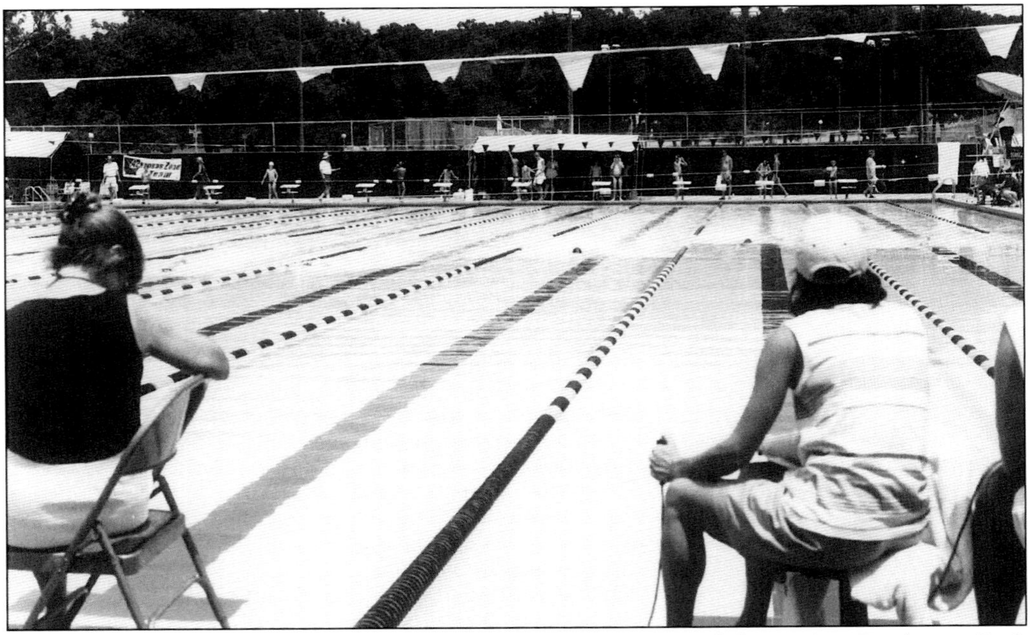

The swimmers at Whittakers Pool of yesteryear would have envied the pool at Creekmore Park today. Twenty-three acres for the park were donated by E.F. Creekmore, 15 acres by Leigh Kelley, and 10 acres were purchased by the citizens of Fort Smith. The land was given with the understanding that it would always be used as a public park and playground and be maintained, policed, and protected from encroachment for now and evermore. (Author.)

Ruth Armstrong, teacher at Darby Junior High School, was a 30-year chairman of the science department. She was founder of the Fort Smith Audubon Society and served as its president for ten years. She was the leading proponent of the creation of the Bird Sanctuary and Nature Trail at Creekmore Park. Her other activities included work with the Committee for Better Schools, which sponsored open meetings for the discussion of school problems and solutions. (Lillian Golden Hissom.)

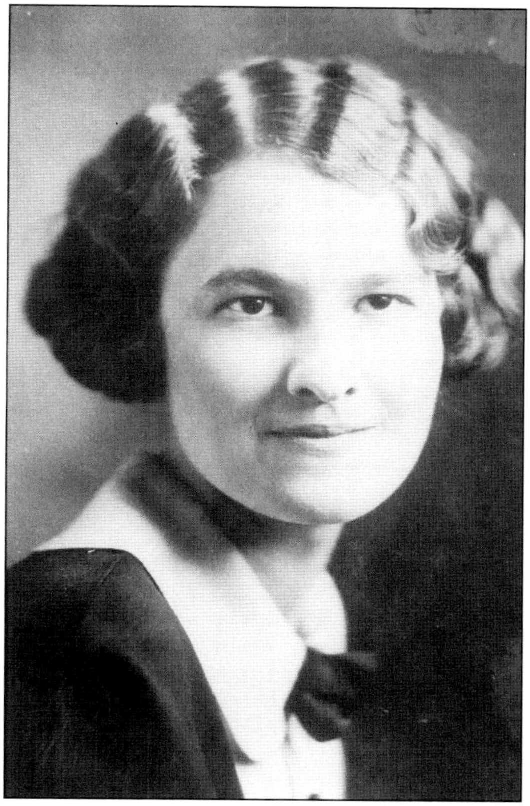

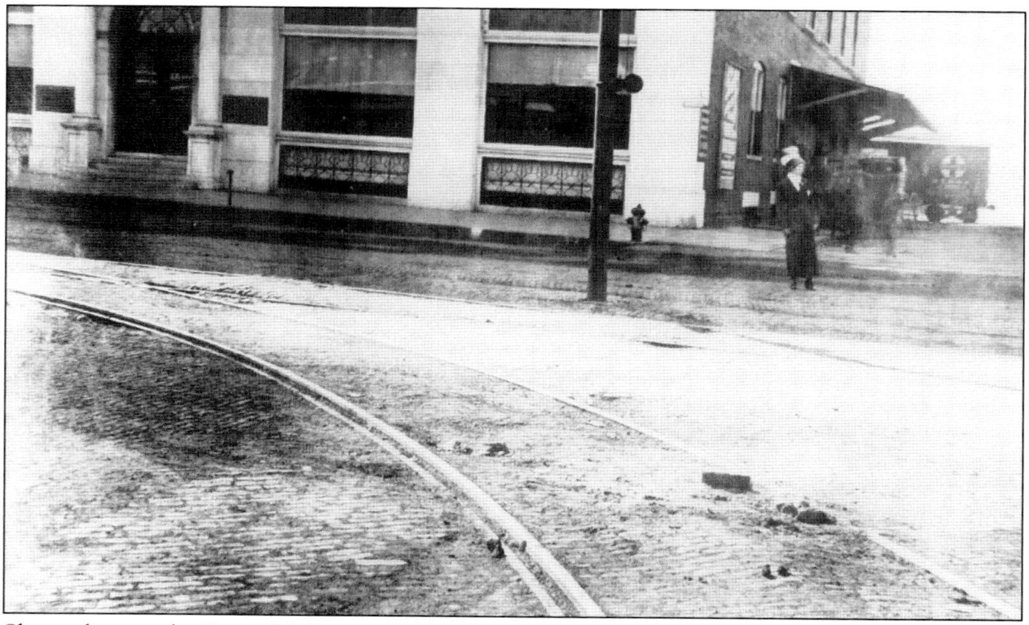

Shown here is the Reynolds/Davis Building, located at the corner of Third Street and Garrison Avenue. The girl in the background and the trolley tracks in the foreground are but memories, and the building will soon be as well. The building was damaged as a result of the 1996 tornado. The space will be used for more parking facilities. (Fort Smith Public Library.)

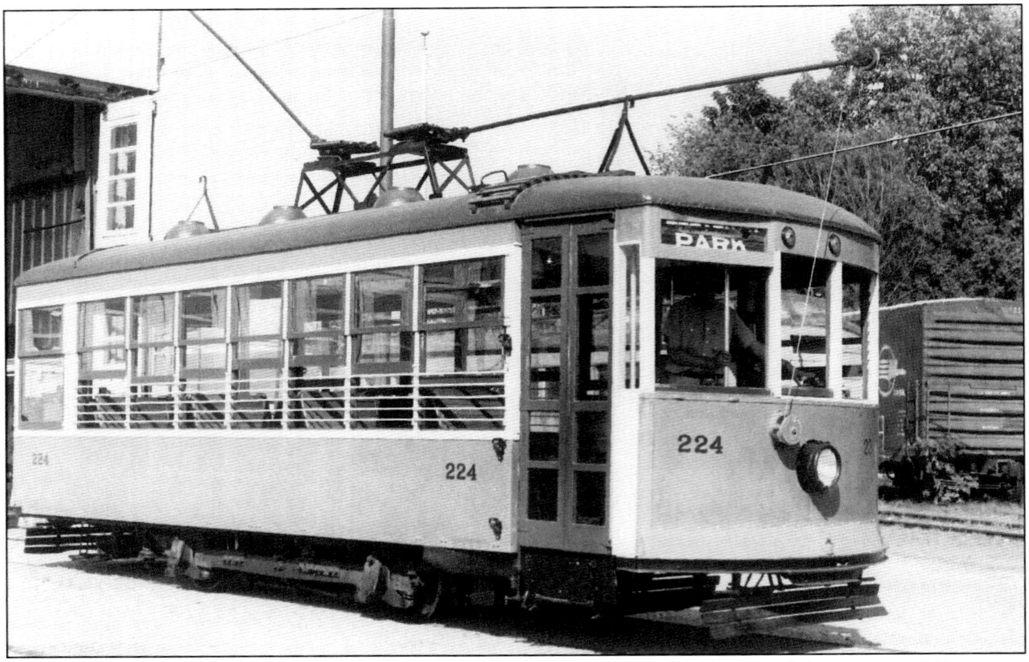

This is a contemporary photo of Birney Safety Car #224 at the Trolley Museum and Barn, in downtown Fort Smith. Dr. Art Martin is the motorman. It has been through the efforts of Dr. Martin and other dedicated streetcar enthusiasts that the Trolley Museum exists today with a working trolley and plans for expansion. (Author.)

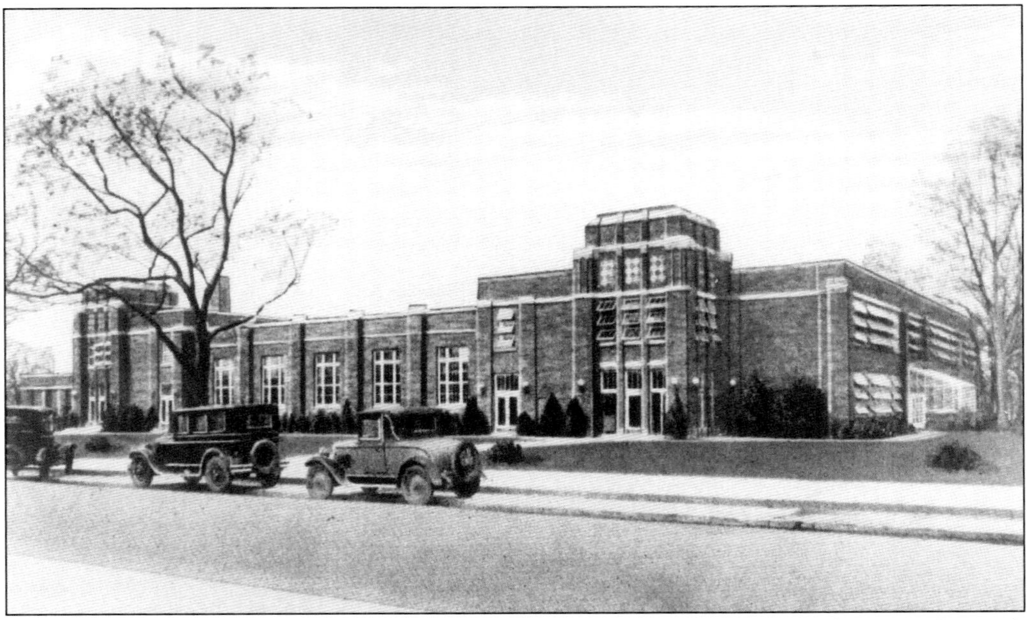

Fort Smith High School and Junior College is shown as it appeared in the early 1930s. Westark College was established in 1928 due to the efforts of G.C. Hardin, a Fort Smith attorney, school board president, and civic leader. For the past 70 years, the college has continued the tradition of excellence and innovation, and today Westark is considered one of the premier higher education institutions of its kind in America. (Fort Smith Public Library.)

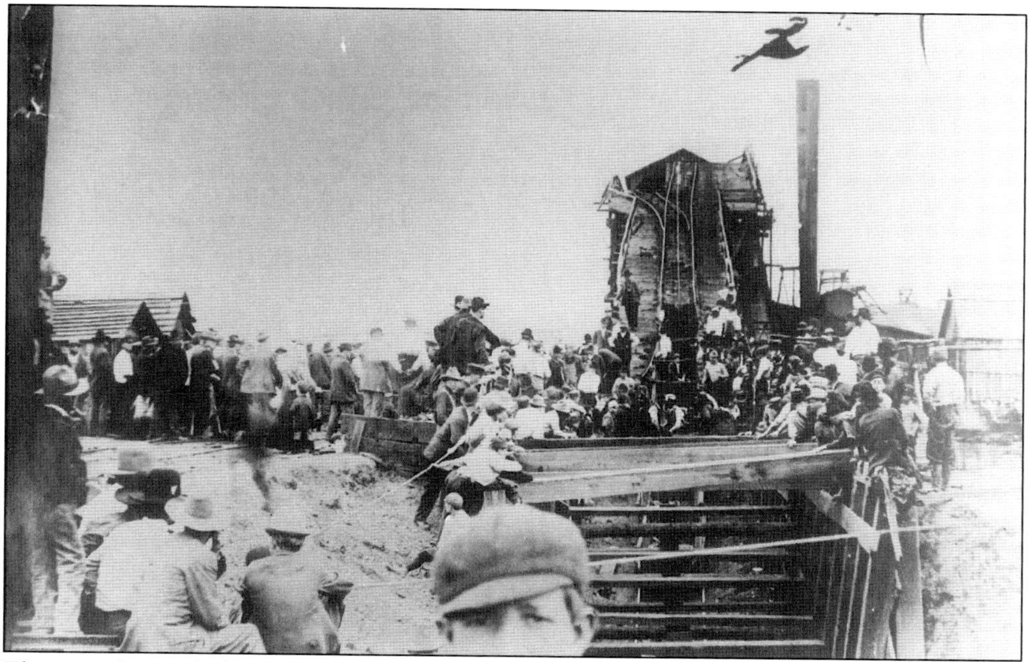

This is a photo of what may have been South Fort Smith Smelter. Folks are gathered around an accident. The rails at the very top of the ramp appear to be damaged. Rails which can barely be seen, travel from underground, beneath the ramp. Note the young face at the bottom of the image. Apparently the photographer did not see him before snapping the photo. (Lillian Golden Hissom.)

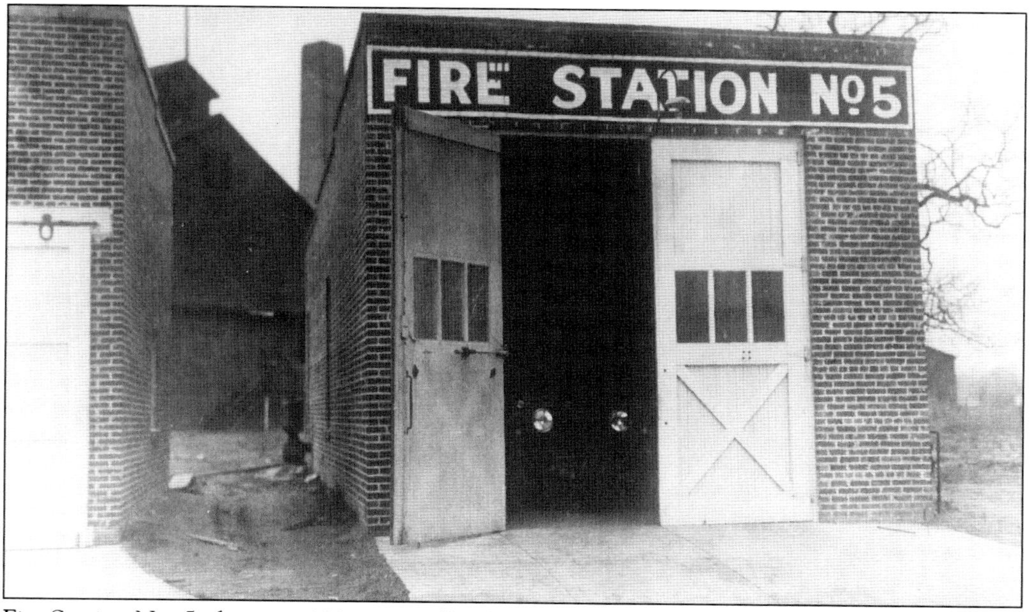

Fire Station No. 5, shown *c.* 1924 on Midland Boulevard and Kelley Highway, was located next door to the Harding Glass Company, which can be seen in the background. A former student of Trusty School, which was located nearby, recalls touring this fire station and sliding down the fire pole. Lillian Golden Hissom lived next door and said it was a very busy fire station, making numerous runs, both night and day. (Anna Golden, Lillian Golden Hissom.)

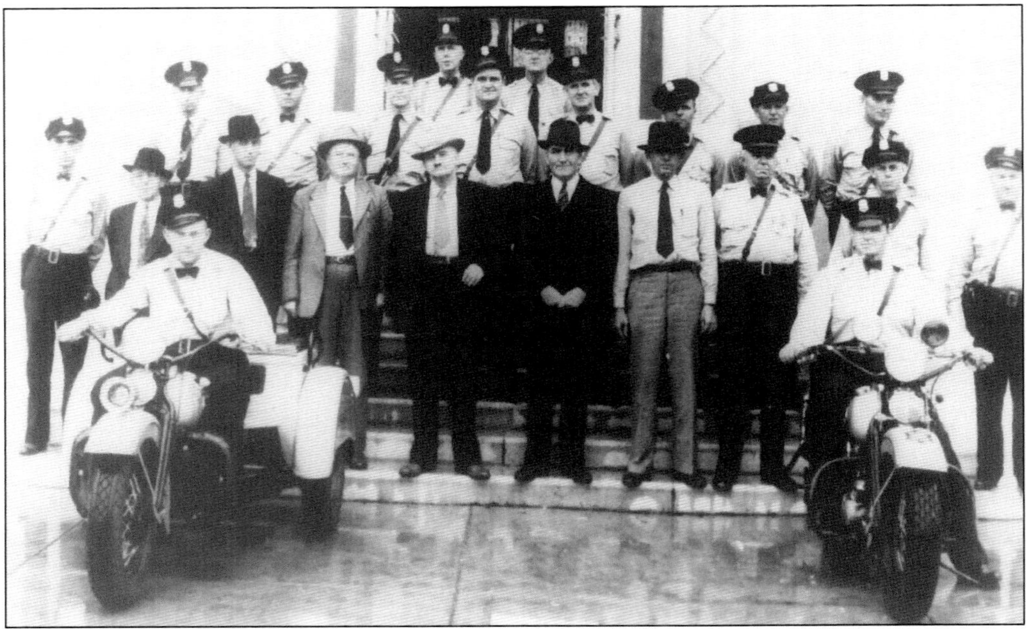

The Fort Smith Police Department, as shown in 1940 after a rain, was proud of its motorcycle patrol. The number of officers and officials of the department standing on the steps of the courthouse is much smaller than the size of the force today. However, those law enforcement people would probably be shocked at what is faced by law enforcement in contemporary times. (Fort Smith Police Department.)

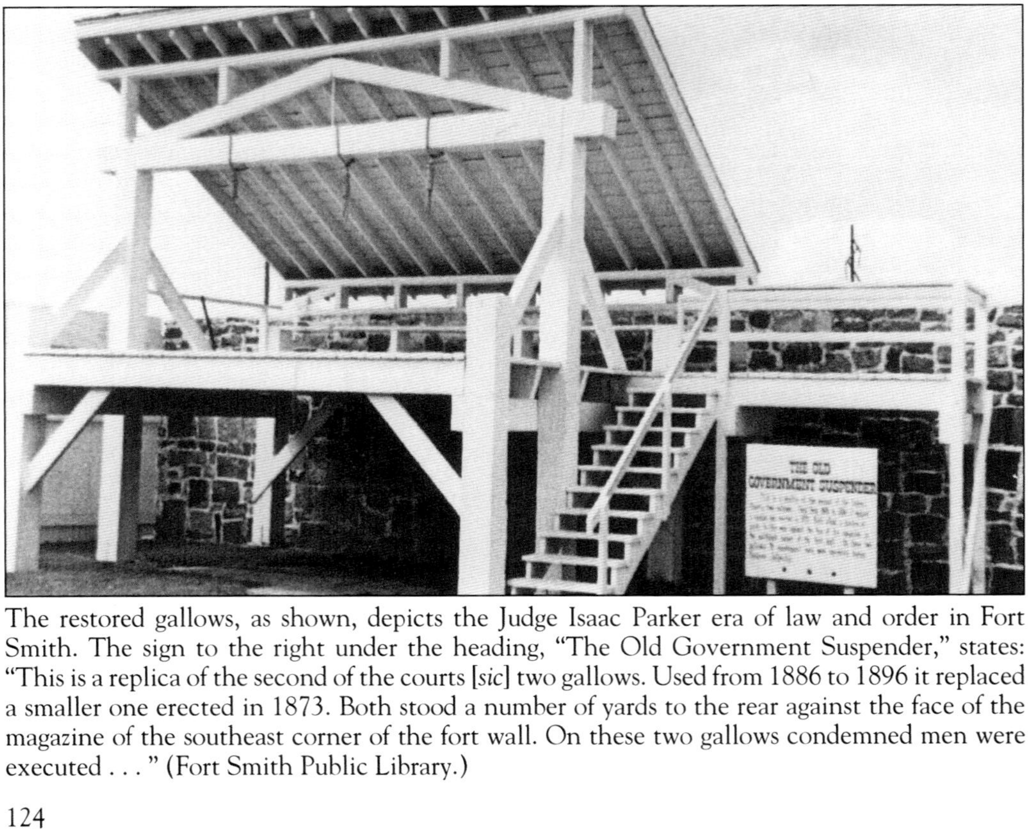

The restored gallows, as shown, depicts the Judge Isaac Parker era of law and order in Fort Smith. The sign to the right under the heading, "The Old Government Suspender," states: "This is a replica of the second of the courts [*sic*] two gallows. Used from 1886 to 1896 it replaced a smaller one erected in 1873. Both stood a number of yards to the rear against the face of the magazine of the southeast corner of the fort wall. On these two gallows condemned men were executed . . . " (Fort Smith Public Library.)

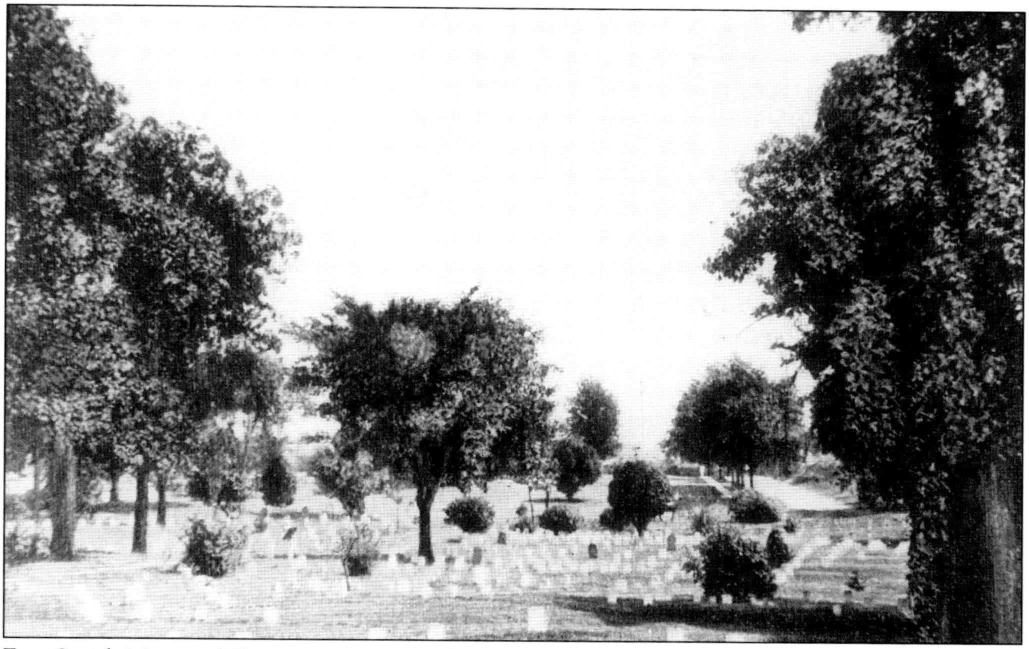

Fort Smith National Cemetery is pictured here when it was not so crowded. Here in this place lies Sarah Perkins Nicks Gibson, who died in 1862. When her husband, John Nicks, died in Fort Gibson in 1832, in an unprecedented move Sarah was appointed sutler and postmaster until a successor could be named. Then she married the new postmaster, Robert Gibson. Sarah was the first woman to hold public office in the present state of Oklahoma. (Fort Smith Public Library.)

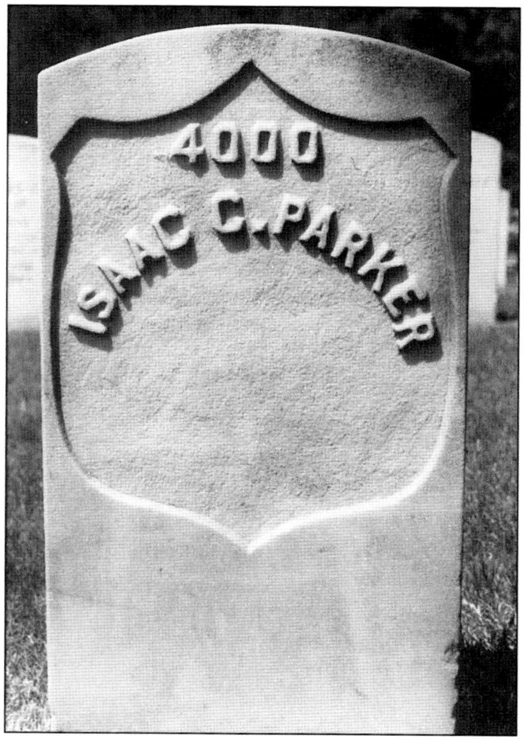

Judge Parker is buried at the Fort Smith National Cemetery. The plain, unadorned stone, as shown, underscores the simplicity of the man. Called the most powerful judge in American judicial history, his authority was tempered with integrity and devotion to duty. His statement to the condemned, "May God, whose laws you have broken and before whose tribunal you must then appear, have mercy upon your soul," reflected a concern for the individual's lost condition. (Author.)

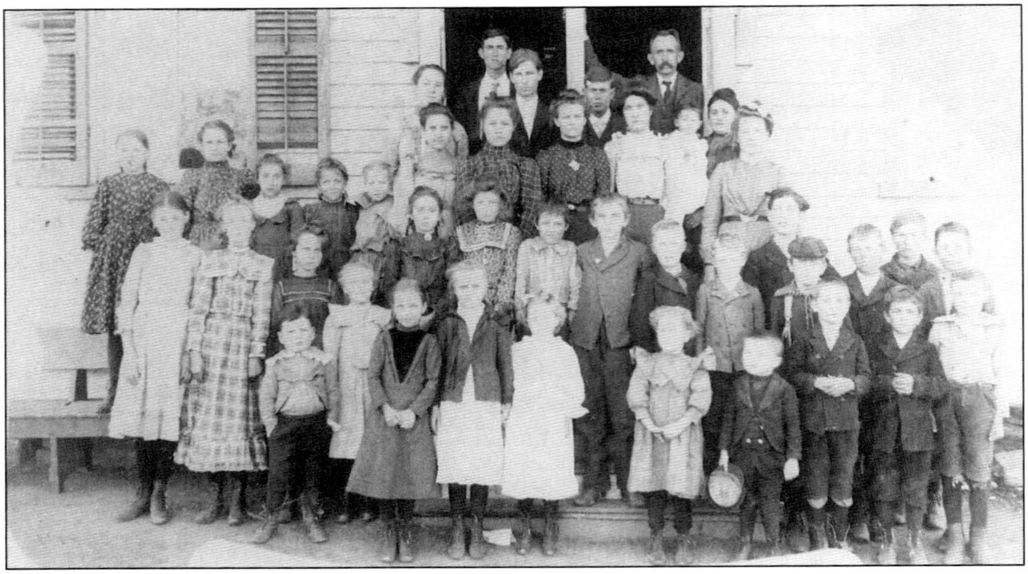

Mill Creek schoolchildren are shown around the turn of the century. In 1904 there was one teacher to instruct grades one through eight. A two-story Mill Creek school was built in 1907. In 1919 Mill Creek Elementary was annexed to Fort Smith. A Mill Creek school was in use until 1969. Note the lady holding the baby. The number of adults present indicates that perhaps it was a special occasion, such as picture-taking day. (Fort Smith Public Library.)

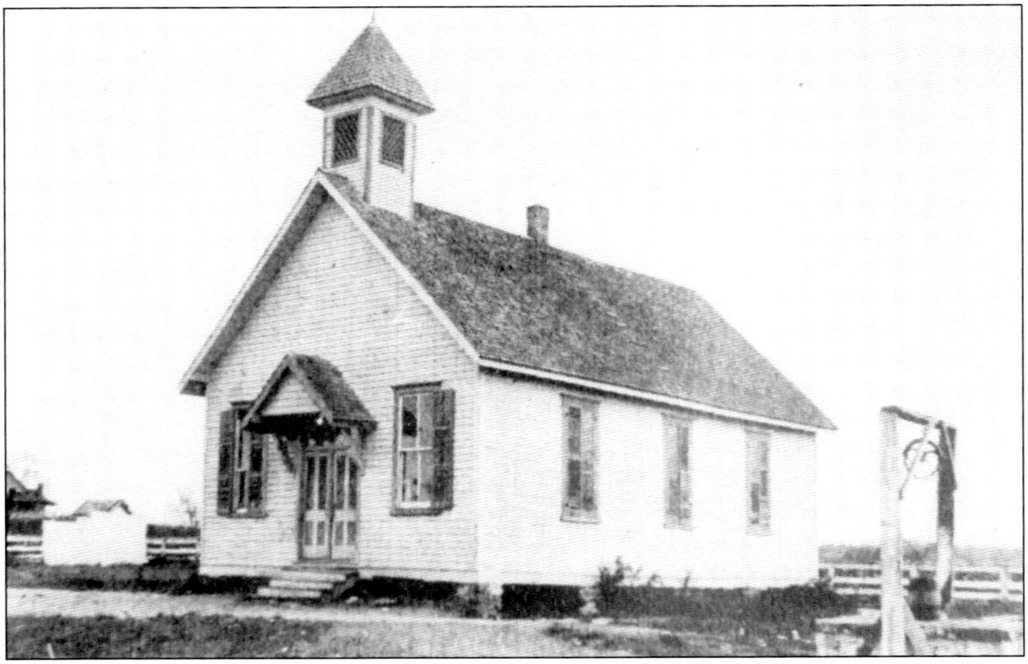

The one-room schoolhouse, such as Mill Creek District #21 school building, shown here c. 1900, has gone the way of the nickel candy bar. Mill Creek was located about where Shoney's Restaurant is today. A small branch called Mill Creek ran through the area. Sometimes the creek would overflow its banks. Manness General Store was located about a block south on Highway 71, where many schoolchildren used to buy spinning tops and marbles. (Cinda Bell.)

Sources

Grateful appreciation to the following: Fort Smith National Historic Site Library and Photo Archives; Fort Smith Public Library and Photo Archives; Fort Smith Chamber of Commerce Photo Archives; Fort Smith Police Department Photo Archives; Coca-Cola Bottling Co. of Fort Smith Photo Archives: *History of Fort Smith 1992* by J. Fred Patton; *Fort Smith, Little Gibraltar on the Arkansas* by Bearss and Gibson; Edmund C. Bearss Notes, Fort Smith National Historic Site; Manuscript of old Fort Smith by J. Frank Weaver; the writings of Mack and Bess Stanley; *Reflections* by Julia Etter Yadon, Sue R. Cross, and Randall R. Viguet; Various Issues of *Fort Smith Historical Society, Inc., The Journal*, Editor Amelia Whitaker Martin; *Law West of Fort Smith*, Glenn Shirley; *Belle Starr and her Pearl*, Edwin P. Hicks; *Starr Tracks Belle and Pearl Starr* by Phillip W. Steele; *History of the Presbyterian Church 1846–1860* by Sydney Yantis Warner and Virginia Louise Foster; *The Arkansas Waterway 1817–1871* by Ruth B. Mapes and the *History of Old Fort Smith* by Ruth B. Mapes; *Twin Territories Newspaper*, Editor Frankie Sue Gilliam; *Marcy's Travels* by Grant Foreman; *Fort Smith, Past and Present a Historical Summary* by William J. Butler; *Fort Smith, An Illustrated History* by Odie Faulk and Billy Mac Jones; Various Fort Smith High School Sounder Annuals; *The Dalton Gang Story* 1992 by Nancy B. Samuelson; *Southwest Times Record* 1998 feature article by Linda Seubold; and various other articles and features of Linda Seubold and of the *Southwest Times Record*.

Consistent with our mission to preserve history on a local level, this book was printed in South Carolina on American-made paper and manufactured entirely in the United States. Products carrying the accredited Forest Stewardship Council (FSC) label are printed on 100 percent FSC-certified paper.

MADE IN THE USA